《金砖国家国别与合作研究》 总主编：李克勇
副总主编：刘玉梅

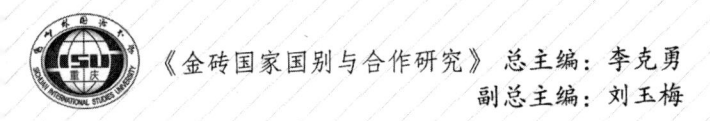

BRICS Studies

金砖国家
国别与合作研究

第一辑

朱天祥·主编

Brazil
Russia
India
China
South Africa

时事出版社
北京

图书在版编目（CIP）数据

金砖国家国别与合作研究. 第一辑/朱天祥主编.
—北京：时事出版社，2019.11
ISBN 978-7-5195-0335-2

Ⅰ.①金⋯　Ⅱ.①朱⋯　Ⅲ.①国际合作—研究
Ⅳ.①D812

中国版本图书馆 CIP 数据核字（2019）第 169904 号

| 出 版 发 行：时事出版社
| 地　　　　址：北京市海淀区万寿寺甲 2 号
| 邮　　　　编：100081
| 发 行 热 线：（010）88547590　88547591
| 读者服务部：（010）88547595
| 传　　　　真：（010）88547592
| 电 子 邮 箱：shishichubanshe@sina.com
| 网　　　　址：www.shishishe.com
| 印　　　　刷：北京旺都印务有限公司

开本：787×1092　1/16　印张：16.5　字数：270 千字
2019 年 11 月第 1 版　2019 年 11 月第 1 次印刷
定价：98.00 元
（如有印装质量问题，请与本社发行部联系调换）

《金砖国家国别与合作研究》编委会

总 主 编：李克勇
副总主编：刘玉梅

编委会委员：（按姓氏拼音为序）
谌华侨　董洪川　郭兵云　李克勇　李小青
刘梦茹　刘玉梅　孟利君　蒲公英　吴　兵
席桂桂　游　涵　严功军　张　庆　朱天祥

学术顾问：（按姓氏拼音为序）
栾建章　　（中共中央对外联络部研究室）
蔡春林　　（广东工业大学）
陈　才　　（西南科技大学）
程　晶　　（湖北大学）
崔　铮　　（辽宁大学）
邓瑞平　　（西南大学）
江时学　　（上海大学）
蓝庆新　　（对外经贸大学）
林跃勤　　（中国社会科学院）
龙兴春　　（西华师范大学）
卢　静　　（外交学院）
王　磊　　（北京师范大学）
徐　薇　　（浙江师范大学）
徐秀军　　（中国社会科学院）
杨　娜　　（南开大学）
张淑兰　　（山东大学）

卷首语

　　四川外国语大学金砖国家研究院成立于2013年5月。经过四年的实践和探索，研究院将人文交流确定为金砖国家研究的主攻方向，这不仅有利于发挥外语学科的传统比较优势，也有助于外语学科与其他人文社会学科的融合发展。因此，研究院借助学校中文、英语、俄语、葡萄牙语、印地语等专业的优势，展开了对金砖五国国别问题尤其是人文交流相关问题的深度研究，如人文交流对政治安全和经贸财金合作的作用与影响等。为了让同仁分享我们的研究成果，也为了给研究该领域的专家学者提供一个专门的发表园地，研究院决定编辑出版《金砖国家国别与合作研究》系列研究成果。

　　本研究成果原则上每年出版一辑，每辑由一名主编署名。《金砖国家国别与合作研究》侧重于展示国内外专家学者关于金砖国家国别与合作研究的最新成果，特别是以金砖国家国别人文状况和金砖国家人文交流合作为重点，力求将本研究成果打造成国内外金砖国家研究，尤其是人文交流研究的重要平台。

　　本研究成果突出三个特点：1. 国内第一本以金砖国家人文交流为研究重心的成果；2. 以中英文双语出版，以便更好地在国内外金砖国家研究领域扩大学术影响；3. 既立足于人文交流，又不局限于人文交流，同样鼓励从人文交流的视角对金砖国家的全方位合作，如政治安全对话与经贸财金合作进行解读，从而更有利于体现跨学科专业的比较优势，进而推出更多跨学科的研究成果。

　　本研究成果设有三个栏目："理论探讨"主要就人文、人文交流，以及人文与政治、经济的互动关系进行学理分析，为金砖国家人文交流构建核心概念，搭建分析框架；"应用研究"主要就金砖国家国别人文状况和人文交流合作中存在的现实问题进行解读，并针对性地提出应对和解决的方案与建议；"学术书评"主要就国内外学者近期发表的学术论文或智库报告进行述评，并就此提出新的观点与看法，激发专家学者的进一步讨论。

　　我们热忱欢迎国内外专家学者不吝赐稿，共同推动金砖国家研究特别是跨学科研究更上一个新台阶。

李克勇

四川外国语大学校长

金砖国家智库合作中方理事会副理事长

四川外国语大学金砖国家研究院院长

《金砖国家国别与合作研究》总主编

2019年10月9日

目　录

理论探讨

推动中外人文交流的重要意义及方式方法 …………………… 江时学 / 003

人文交流何以可能
　　——基于文化"自我"与"他者"身份的
　　探讨 …………………………………… 张　庆　崔亦歌　杨　盛 / 016

"故事外交"：首脑与民众的互动 ……………………………… 谌华侨 / 029

应用研究

金砖国家人文交流机制的经验与完善 ……………… 王　蔚　汪骏良 / 043

金砖国家人文交流质量保障体系构建 ………………………… 孙宜学 / 056

金砖国家高等教育合作问题与前景分析 ……………………… 蒲公英 / 064

中国与金砖国家人文交流 …………………………… 朱天祥　张铭瑶 / 075

学术书评

BRICS：Construir a educação para o futuro-prioridades para o desenvolvimento nacional e a cooperação internacional
书评 ………………………………………………………… 刘梦茹 / 095

CONTENTS

Theoretical Research

How to Promote People-to-people Exchanges between China and
Other Countries ·· Jiang Shixue / 107

How to Make People-to-people Exchanges Possible?
 ——Based on the Discussion of the Cultural "Self"
 and "Other" Identities ············ Zhang Qing　Cui Yige　Yang Sheng / 127

Diplomacy Through Narratives: the Interaction between
 the Head of the State and the Public ····················· Chen Huaqiao / 144

Applied Research

Experience and Improvement of BRICS People-to-people Exchanges
 Mechanism ································ Wang Wei　Wang Junliang / 163

The Establishment of a Quality Assurance System for BRICS People-to-people Exchanges ·· Sun Yixue / 182

Analysis into Problems and Prospects of BRICS Higher Education Cooperation ·· Pu Gongying / 194

China and BRICS People-to-people Exchanges ···························· Zhu Tianxiang　Zhang Mingyao / 210

Book Review

The Book Review of BRICS: Construir a educação para o futuro-prioridades para o desenvolvimento nacional e a cooperação internacional ······················· Liu Mengru / 241

理论探讨

推动中外人文交流的重要意义及方式方法

江时学[*]

摘　要： 国之交在于民相亲。实现民相亲的方式方法多种多样，其中最有效的就是推动人文交流。推动中外人文交流有利于讲好中国故事、传播好中国声音，有利于改善中国的国家形象，有利于提升中国的软实力，有利于推动构建人类命运共同体，有利于消除国与国之间的"信任赤字"，有利于促进对外经贸关系。为了进一步推动中外人文交流，应该采取以下措施：要讲好中国共产党治国理政的故事，要正确理解中外人文交流中的意识形态化问题，要重视话语力的构建，要积极发挥学者的作用，要有力地回击西方的"有色眼镜"，要尽量增加社会色彩。在推动金砖国家的人文交流时，必须遵循以下三个方针：要正确处理人文交流与其他合作领域的主次关系，要突出多边合作的色彩，要恪守开放包容的原则。

关键词： 人文交流；民心相通；措施；方针

中外人文交流是党和国家对外工作的重要组成部分，是夯实中外关系社会民意基础、提高中国对外开放水平的重要途径，也是实施中国特色大

---

[*] 江时学，四川外国语大学特聘教授。

国外交的必要手段。

中外人文交流有利于讲好中国故事和传播好中国声音，有利于改善中国的国家形象，有利于提升中国的软实力，有利于推动构建人类命运共同体，有利于消除国与国之间的"信任赤字"，有利于促进对外经贸关系。

随着金砖国家合作的不断深入，如何强化其人文交流已成为当务之急。毫无疑问，在金砖国家中推动人文交流，同样有利于加强五国的交往和人民之间的了解，有利于增进彼此间感情，也能为推动金砖国家在全球治理等领域的合作奠定基础。

一、推动中外人文交流的必要性与重要性

"国之交在于民相亲。"实现民相亲的手段多种多样，其中最有效的就是推动人文交流。

党的十八大以来，以习近平同志为核心的党中央高度重视人文交流工作，中外人文交流事业蓬勃发展，谱写了新的宏伟篇章，为中国对外开放事业的推进做出了重要贡献，有力推动了全球范围内的人文交流与文明互鉴。[1]

人文交流有狭义和广义之分。狭义的人文交流仅指文化交流，而广义的人文交流则包括文化、旅游业以及教育、体育、科技、媒体、学术、医疗、妇女、工会和宗教等领域的人员交流。就此而言，人文交流囊括了除商品交流以外的国之交往的一切内容。

人文交流的参与者既可以是政党和政府，也可以是民间；既可以是政府组织，也可以是社会组织；既可以是外交部门的"一轨"，也可以是非外交部门的"二轨"；既可以是学术界，也可以是工商界。

与人文交流相提并论的是公共外交。公共外交面向社会各个阶层，包括官方与民间的各种双、多边对话交流，涵盖经济、教育、人文、传媒、

---

[1] 中共中央办公厅、国务院办公厅印发：《关于加强和改进中外人文交流工作的若干意见》，新华网，2017年12月21日，http://www.xinhuanet.com/2017-12/21/c_1122148432.htm.

科技、体育、军事等多个领域。① 由此可见，公共外交不直接从事商品交流，因此它在一定程度上也应该是人文交流的重要组成部分。

中国领导人极为重视中外人文交流，在访问世界各地时，经常会提出一些进一步发展双边关系的建议，其中之一就是推动人文交流。根据国家发展改革委员会、外交部和商务部 2015 年 3 月 28 日联合发布的《推动共建丝绸之路经济带和 21 世纪海上丝绸之路的愿景与行动》，民心相通是"一带一路"建设的社会根基，其宗旨是传承和弘扬丝绸之路友好合作精神，广泛开展文化交流、学术往来、人才交流合作、媒体合作、青年和妇女交往、志愿者服务等，为深化双多边合作奠定坚实的民意基础。2017 年 12 月，中共中央办公厅、国务院办公厅印发了《关于加强和改进中外人文交流工作的若干意见》，对如何加强和改进中外人文交流提出多方面的原则性要求。可见，推动中外人文交流的必要性和重要性是显而易见的。

（一）有利于讲好中国故事，传播好中国声音

2015 年 5 月，中共中央总书记、国家主席、中央军委主席习近平就《人民日报》（海外版）创刊 30 周年做出重要批示，要求"讲述好中国故事，传播好中国声音"。党的十九大报告也指出："推进国际传播能力建设，讲好中国故事，展现真实、立体、全面的中国，提高国家文化软实力。"

讲故事的方式多种多样，其中之一就通过推动人文交流，使中国故事能在世界各地深入人心。

（二）中外人文交流有助于改善中国的国家形象

中国的国际地位与日俱增，国际影响力不断上升。中国的所作所为和一言一语都会在国际上产生或大或小的影响。因此，进一步改善中国的国家形象，有助于强化中国在国际上的影响力。换言之，中国的国家形象与中国的国际影响力是相互影响、相得益彰的。

但是，随着中国的发展，"中国威胁论"在国际上蔓延，有时甚至其

---

① 杨洁篪：《努力开拓中国特色公共外交新局面》，《求是》2011 年第 4 期，http://www.qstheory.cn/zxdk/2011/201104/201102/t20110214_67907.htm。

嚣尘上，对中国的国际形象和国际声望构成严重危害。

"中国威胁论"与历史上的"黄祸论"可谓一丘之貉。① 这种极端民族主义理论认为，黄种人对白种人构成威胁，因此白种人应当联合起来，对付黄种人。

消除"中国威胁论"的有效手段就是开展人文交流，向外界展示中国经济发展的成效及其为捍卫世界和平与发展做出的贡献，消除外界对中国发展的误读、误解和误判。

（三）中外人文交流有助于提升中国的软实力

根据约瑟夫·奈（Joseph S. Nye）的论证，硬实力和软实力的行为方式大相径庭。软实力是一个国家依靠自身的魅力和吸引力，而非通过军事手段或经济制裁等强硬手段来达到目的的能力。② 这意味着，一个国家完全可以通过发挥软实力的优势得到他国的追随和支持，从而在国际事务中实现其追求的目标。中国在壮大硬实力的同时，也应该重视软实力。提升软实力的有效途径之一就是推动中外人文交流，使外部世界能更加容易接受中国的各种理念和言行。

不仅如此，中外人文交流还能为宣传中华文明做出贡献。例如，虽然中国历史上的"四大发明"享誉全球，但是也有少数国家不时挑战这一共识。这些国家的学者利用一些似是而非的考古发现，否认"四大发明"是中国对人类社会发展做出的重大贡献。③ 面对这样的挑战，我们必须加大人文交流的力度，使那些不实之词不攻自破。

---

① 欧洲人曾将13世纪蒙古人西征视为中世纪"最大的黄祸"。俄罗斯人巴枯宁的《国家制度和无政府状态》（1873年）和英国人皮尔逊的《民族生活与民族性》（1893年）使"黄祸论"进一步扩散。（见陈安：《中国特色话语：陈安论国际经济法学》，北京大学出版社2018年版，第163—164页）

② Joseph S. Nye Jr., *Soft Power: The Means to Success in World Politics*, Public Affairs, 2005.

③ 例如，韩国学者以韩国庆州的佛国释迦塔发现的雕版印刷本《无垢净光大陀罗尼经》（1966年10月）为据，认为雕版印刷和金属（铁）活字印刷是韩国人的"发明"，强调韩国是雕版印刷的发源地。他们甚至呼吁召开国际学术会议，邀请联合国教科文组织参加，以便使国际社会承认这一"发明"。（见《北大教授：文化创新是消除"中国威胁论"的必由之路》，中国新闻网，2010年7月29日，http://www.chinanews.com/cul/2010/07-29/2432458.shtml）

(四) 人文交流有利于推动构建人类命运共同体

推动构建人类命运共同体，是习近平新时代中国特色社会主义思想的重要组成部分，是新时代中国外交树立起来的一面旗帜。中共十九大在修改《中国共产党章程》时写入了"推动构建人类命运共同体"，使之成为新时代坚持和发展中国特色社会主义的基本方略之一。2018年3月11日，十三届全国人大一次会议第三次全体会议通过了《中华人民共和国宪法修正案》。宪法序言第十二自然段中将"发展同各国的外交关系和经济、文化的交流"修改为"发展同各国的外交关系和经济、文化交流，推动构建人类命运共同体"。由此可见，构建人类命运共同体已成为中国的国家意志。

但是，外界对于推动构建人类命运共同体的重要性和必要性所知甚少，这就需要我们采取推动人文交流等多种多样的方式宣传中国的外交理念，使这一宏伟的目标早日实现。

(五) 人文交流有利于消除国与国之间的"信任赤字"

孔子曰："人而无信，不知其可也。"信任既是人与人之间和睦相处的前提，也是国与国之间和平共处的基础。在人类历史上，国与国之间因缺乏信任而剑拔弩张、甚至兵戎相见的事例数不胜数。因此，习近平主席将信任视为"国际关系中最好的黏合剂"。确实，以势交者，势倾则绝；以利交者，利穷则散。唯以心相交，方成其久远。

当今世界正面临百年未有之大变局。在这一变局中，虽然和平与发展仍然是时代主题，但不稳定性、不确定性更加突出，全球问题层出不穷、久治不愈，人类面临的共同挑战越来越严峻。因此，2017年，中国国家主席习近平在联合国日内瓦总部演讲时，发出"世界怎么了、我们怎么办"之问。

全球治理的成效是显而易见的。《巴黎气候变化协定》的签署、多哈回合谈判僵局的突破、反恐斗争的方兴未艾、网络犯罪的遏制以及埃博拉疫情的消失，都是有力的证据。但是，与全球问题的严重性尤其是各国人民的期望值相比，全球治理的成效很难说是令人满意的。

全球治理的成效不佳与多方面的因素有关，其中最重要的就是国与国之间的信任不足，中国国家主席习近平称之为"信任赤字"。消弭"信任赤字"的有效手段之一就是扩大人文交流，使本国的外交政策目标能够被外界知晓和理解，从而使世界各国在推动全球治理的过程中能够承担共同而有区别的责任。

（六）中外人文交流有利于促进对外经贸关系

经贸关系不仅是简单化的商品买卖，而是一种蕴含着政治、外交和人文等内容的双边关系。因此，经贸关系的发展提升了人文交流的必要性，人文交流既能促进经贸关系，使贸易伙伴之间的市场信息在更为畅通的渠道内流通，也能增进彼此对对方市场环境和投资气候的认知。很难想象，经贸关系能在缺乏人文交流的国家之间进行。

二、推动中外人文交流的方式方法

在进一步推动中外人文交流的过程中，我们应该采取如下措施：

（一）要讲好中国共产党治国理政的故事

中国共产党是执政党，因此对外讲中国故事时，首先必须讲好中国共产党治国理政的故事。在这方面，习近平主席身体力行，利用一切机会讲故事。他善于把深刻的思想和抽象的理论转化为通俗易懂的故事。因此，在一定意义上，习主席就是一个"故事大王"。

应该指出的是，讲好中国共产党治国理政的故事并不是为了输出所谓的"中国模式"，更不是为了强化子虚乌有的"锐实力"，而是为了让外部世界了解中国共产党如何为中国人民谋幸福，如何为维护世界的和平与发展做贡献。

治国理政是一个宽泛的概念，涵盖面广，内容多。因此，讲好中国共产党治国理政的故事，必须采用多方位、立体的视角。换言之，这一视角既应该有历史的积淀，也应该有今天的现实；既应该注重作为一个整体的中国共产党，也应该着眼于构成这一政党的每一个党员；既应该包含精神文明，也应该囊括物质文明；既应该讲述中国的内政，也应该宣传中国的外交；既应该诠释人类命运共同体理念和"一带一路"倡议，也应该介绍普通中国人的工作和生活。

（二）要正确理解中外人文交流中的意识形态化问题

世界上不同的国家有不同的政治制度、社会制度和文化传统，也有不同的价值观，因此不同国家之间的人文交流不可能去意识形态化。其实，西方发达国家在进行人文交流时，同样没有轻视意识形态的作用，时刻不忘推销其价值观。因此，我们在推动中外人文交流时，同样不必忌讳意识形态。例如，中国的改革开放是中国共产党领导的实现"中国梦"的伟大工程，其成就是有口皆碑的。在推动中外人文交流时，宣传中国改革开放的成就，实际上就是在宣传中国共产党的英明领导。又如，中国的人口超过13亿，这样一个国家的政治制度必然是与众不同的，不能照搬西方的所谓民主政治制度。在推动中外人文交流时，介绍中国人口众多的国情，实际上就是在介绍中国的符合自身国情的政治制度。由此可见，人文交流是难以超越意识形态的。

当然，我们应该抛弃过去那些政治口号式的语言，而是最大限度地使用符合国际风格、易于被接受和理解的文字与表达方式。《开罗宣言》电影海报之类的做法只能适得其反。

还应该指出的是，中外人文交流的目的不应该是在亚非拉等发展中地区实现"去西方化"。这与以下因素有关：第一，"去西方化"与中国坚持的文明多元化和文明大家庭等主张是背道而驰的；第二，中国尚无能力做到"去西方化"；第三，西方文化中的精华为数不少，根本不必"将婴儿与洗澡水一起倒掉"。

（三）要重视话语力的构建

人文交流的重要形式之一是国际传播。令人欣慰的是，中国早已拥有包括电视、广播、书籍、报纸、期刊和因特网等媒介在内的庞大的国际传播体系。

国际传播的支柱是话语体系。话语体系包括话语权和话语力，两者不尽相同。话语权是"发声"的权利和资格，因此世界上任何一个国家都有话语权。话语力是"发声"的穿透力，亦即国际传播的成效。

为了提升话语力，必须做到以下几点：一是要恪守实事求是的原则，避免假话、大话和空话，尽量避免媒体在面向国内受众时经常使用的"报喜不报忧"模式；二是要使用外国受众能够接受的语言，并要提高翻译质量；三是要充分利用现代传媒技术的优势，使我们的宣传在国际上进入更多人的眼睛、耳朵和心灵；四是要尽快消除国际传播专业领域中人才匮乏的不良局面；五是要扩大中国媒介在全球范围内的覆盖面。

《习近平谈治国理政》一书的第一卷和第二卷自2014年9月出版至今已在国际上用20多个语种发行，覆盖160多个国家和地区，在海外的受欢迎程度是前所未有的。该书的国际传播取得巨大成功的原因是多方面的，其中之一就是该书的话语力强。该书不是中国领导人的对外说教，而是用事实说话，介绍中国的发展道路；不是重复已被外人熟知的中国立场，而是提出一系列具有开创性意义的新理念、新思想、新战略；不是使用僵硬、晦涩、难以理解的文字，而是以中国传统文化中的历史典故为基础，用通俗、易懂的语言阐述中共执政方略。

（四）要积极发挥学者的作用

在许多国家，学者因拥有某一专业或某一领域的专业知识而能为其国际话语权的强化做出重要贡献。一方面，国际话语权需要学者提供学术支撑；另一方面，在公众的心目中，政治家的言论完全为政治目的或政府利益服务，而学者的言论则被认为具有较多的公正性和合理性。因此，为了强化中国的国际话语权，有必要采取以下措施：（1）鼓励学者在国际学术刊物或国际媒体上发表其科研成果；（2）减少对退休学者出国参加学术活动的限制；（3）将更多的科研成果翻译成英语或其他主要外语；（4）要求所有学术机构开设外文网站，介绍其学者的主要科研成果；（5）创办更多的外文期刊；（6）为学者在话语权领域的创新提供更大的空间和便利的条件。

随着中国国际地位的上升，越来越多的外国大学开设了与中国政治、经济、外交、文化和社会等领域有关的课程。它们以公开的方式招聘教授，而应聘者主要来自中国以外的国家和地区。这些教授对中国的理解和认知是肤浅的，而且具有很强的片面性。此外，他们很少使用中国出版的教科书。可以想象，这样的课程很难培养出对华友好的学生，也不利于中国话语权的提高。

为了改变这一状况，有关部门应该鼓励中国教授向外国大学提出求职申请，并在人事关系、工资待遇和职称晋升等方面减少其后顾之忧。此外，还应该将中国学者撰写的教材推广到外国大学，以尽快改变外国教授在外国的大学用外国教材开设关于中国的课程这一不利于强化中国话语权的状况。

（五）要有力地回击西方的"有色眼镜"

如前所述，推动中外人文交流的目的之一是消除国外对我的错误认知，以改善中国的国家形象。为了达到这一目的，长期以来，中国已竭尽所能，无所不为，以至于中国学者很难提出更多、更好的政策建议。

毋庸置疑，国际上之所以依然存在对中国的大量偏见和误解，原因之一就是难以消除"有色眼镜"。这意味着，不论中国如何宣传和介绍自己，中国在一些人心目中的形象永远是负面的。

在国际上，透过"有色眼镜"观察中国的人不在少数。在这一偏见的支配下，他们认为，共产党领导下的社会主义制度有着这样那样的"缺点"或者充满了"威胁"。在他们眼中，中国在国际上的所作所为都是为了满足一己之私利。更令人惊讶的是，中国维护国家主权和领土完整的行为被视作"秀肌肉"。

毫无疑问，中外人文交流有助于消除"有色眼镜"，但"有色眼镜"也成为人文交流的巨大障碍。这意味着，一方面，我们要继续持之以恒地做好对外宣传工作，使更多的外国人能听见我们的声音；另一方面，我们也应该继续做好"家庭作业"，使"有色眼镜"不攻自破。

（六）要尽量增加社会色彩

政府拥有足够的经济资源和外交资源，所以应从国家的层面推动人文交流。但是，政府在人文交流中也并非无所不能，而且不少西方人士对中国政府直接参与人文交流颇有微词。例如，美国的智库人口研究所所长斯蒂文·莫什（Steven W. Mosher）在美国国会听证会上别有用心地说，孔子学院是"中国特色的特洛伊木马"，与法国的"法语联盟"和德国的歌德学院相去甚远。他认为，孔子学院受统战部和教育部领导，在海外肩负着政治化的使命（a politicized mission）。[1]

可以说，这样的评论是失之偏颇，甚至是荒唐的。但是，这样恰恰提醒了我们，在推动中外人文交流时，我们必须最大限度发挥社会组织、私人企业和其他一些民间力量的作用。

中国万达集团收购美国好莱坞知名影视制作公司传奇影业以及阿里巴巴集团控股有限公司收购《南华早报》等案例表明，民营企业有能力进入外国的媒体、出版和娱乐业等领域。当然，这一步伐不会一帆风顺。南方报业集团和成都博瑞传播等企业曾试图收购美国《新闻周刊》，但皆因所谓投标人的"国籍"问题而受挫。

三、如何推动金砖国家人文交流

金砖国家加强人文交流的重要意义是不言而喻的。在过去的十年中，金砖国家在加强团结协作、发展经贸关系和参与全球治理等方面取得显著成效，这与金砖国家开展的精彩纷呈的人文交流密不可分。应该指出的是，为了落实五国领导人达成的共识，使金砖国家未来的合作取得更大的成绩，有必要加大人文交流的力度。

2015年7月9日发表的《金砖国家领导人第七次会晤乌法宣言》指出，"考虑到联合国教科文组织1966年国际文化合作原则宣言以及2001年文化多样性宣言，我们承认文化多样性是发展的源泉，相信文化交流与合作将促进相互理解。我们重申金砖国家在文化领域开展合作的重要性。为加强国家及民众间的友好关系，我们将继续通过多种方式鼓励金砖国家

---

[1] Steven W. Mosher, "Confucius Institutes: Trojan Horses with Chinese Characteristics", Testimony Presented to the Subcommittee on Oversight and Investigations House Committee on Foreign Affairs, March 28, 2012. https: //www. pop. org/content/confucius-institutes-trojan-horses-chinese-characteristics.

在文化艺术领域开展直接交流。我们欢迎金砖国家签署政府间文化合作协议，该协议将为扩大和深化文化艺术合作，促进文化对话发挥重要作用，这有助于拉近金砖国家文化和民众的距离"。

2017年9月3日，习近平主席在厦门金砖国家工商论坛开幕式上强调，"我们应该发挥人文交流纽带作用，把各界人士汇聚到金砖合作事业中来，打造更多像文化节、电影节、运动会这样接地气、惠民生的活动，让金砖故事传遍大街小巷，让我们五国人民的交往和情谊汇成滔滔江河，为金砖合作注入绵绵不绝的动力"。[①]

一是要正确处理人文交流与其他合作领域的关系。虽然人文交流是十分重要的，但五个新兴经济体在金砖国家框架内合作的主要目的不应该仅仅是人文交流，而是如何在国际舞台上（尤其是在推动全球治理的过程中）发挥重要作用。换言之，判断金砖国家合作成就的大小，不能局限于举办了多少次文化节、电影节或运动会，而是其在国际舞台上的所作所为。

二是要突出多边合作的色彩。众所周知，中国与其他金砖国家早已开展多种形式的人文交流，而且收效显著。其他金砖国家也与不同的金砖国家进行着不同形式和规模的人文交流。因此，金砖国家的人文交流不是双边交流的简单化叠加，而是在作为一个整体的金砖国家内于多边层面进行的整体性交流。换言之，不能以现有的双边人文交流代替囊括所有金砖国家的多边层面的人文交流。

三是要恪守开放包容的原则。金砖国家开展人文交流的目的不是"去西方化"，而是增进金砖国家的相互了解，夯实民意基础。因此，一些学者提出的所谓"金砖文化"，可能会适得其反，违反开放包容的原则。

事实上，"金砖文化"这一标新立异的概念在理论上和实践中都是欠妥的。金砖国家的文化各有特色，自成一体，难以发展成一种新的文化，更不应该被整合成一种"大杂烩"。为了进一步推动金砖国家的人文交流，有必要采取以下措施：

---

① 习近平：《共同开创金砖合作第二个"金色十年"——在金砖国家工商论坛开幕式上的讲话》，人民网，2017年9月3日，http://cpc.people.com.cn/n1/2017/0904/c64094-29512050.html。

（一）要进一步发挥公共外交的重要作用

公共外交面向社会各个阶层，包括官方与民间的各种双、多边对话交流，涵盖经济、教育、人文、传媒、科技、体育、军事等多个领域。由此可见，虽然公共外交不直接从事商品交流，但它在国际交往中的地位是不容低估的。金砖国家的人文交流应该将公共外交置于至高无上的地位，最大限度地发挥其重要作用。

（二）要建立金砖国家留学基金

目前，每一个金砖国家都有各自不同规模的留学基金，为来自世界各地的留学生提供奖学金。为了在金砖国家层面上扩大留学生交流的规模，有必要设立一个专门面向金砖国家的留学基金。它不是某一个金砖国家单独出资的基金，而是五国共同出资、共同管理的基金。

享受这一奖学金的留学生只能在金砖国家内留学。此外，享受这一奖学金的留学生人数与各国出资的比率配套，即出资的数额与奖学金人数成正比。在最初的几年，可将留学生奖学金总人数控制在每年1000人左右，平均每个金砖国家享受200个名额。

（三）要建立文化产业的合作机制

金砖国家的文化传统博大精深，各有特色，这为它们在文化产业领域开展合作奠定了坚实的基础。五国的政府部门应该顺应"互联网＋"发展趋势，支持商界、学界、媒体、智库、文艺团体等各行各业，以文化旅游、演艺娱乐、工艺美术、动漫游戏、创意设计和数字文化为"突破口"，在文化产业领域建立一种互利共赢的合作机制。

（四）要加大学术研究的力度

顾名思义，人文交流是双向的，不是单向的。这意味着，在推动金砖国家人文交流的过程中，每一个成员国既要让对方了解自己的诉求，也要了解对方的愿望。毫无疑问，只有更好地了解对方，才能有的放矢、事半功倍地推动人文交流。

学术研究在推动人文交流的过程中发挥着举足轻重的作用。中国学者对其他金砖国家的了解越来越深刻，但却很难说业已达到了如指掌的地步，而其他金砖国家对中国的认知也较为肤浅。这样的状况如果不能尽快改变，必将降低中外人文交流的有效性。因此，必须鼓励金砖国家的学者加大对金砖国家合作和基本国情的研究。在条件许可时，可制定金砖国家学者访问计划，加大学者之间的交流。

（五）要大力发挥大使馆和总领事馆的特殊优势

金砖国家的大使馆和总领事馆对驻在国的国情极为了解，而且担负着宣传本国的重任，因此在推动金砖国家人文交流时，必须发挥这些外交机构的特殊优势。

（六）要采用民众喜闻乐见的形式

人文交流是精神层面的交流，因此这种交流必须被物化为民众喜闻乐见的形式，如文化节、电影节、图书展览、文物展览和体育运动会等。此外，金砖国家还应该通过举办旅游年等形式，以及放松签证限制等手段，鼓励本国游客赴其他金砖国家旅游或吸引其他金砖国家的游客来本国旅游。

中外人文交流是党和国家对外工作的重要组成部分，是夯实中外关系社会民意基础、提高中国对外开放水平的重要途径。

2017年元旦，习近平主席就中国正式接任金砖国家主席国致信俄罗斯总统普京、南非总统祖马、巴西总统特梅尔、印度总理莫迪，向四国领导人介绍中方担任主席国期间推进金砖国家合作进程的设想。他希望厦门会晤重点在以下几方面取得进展：一是深化务实合作，促进共同发展；二是加强全球治理，共同应对挑战；三是开展人文交流，夯实民意基础；四是推进机制建设，构建更广泛伙伴关系。由此可见，人文交流已成为金砖国家合作的重要领域之一。

人文交流何以可能

——基于文化"自我"与"他者"身份的探讨

张 庆* 崔亦歌** 杨 盛***

摘 要：把握文化的"自我"与"他者"身份，为深刻认识人文交流的可能性提供了途径。基于人文交流的现代性悖论和"自我"的群体性意识，文化传播主要表现为两种姿态：冲突对抗与和谐平等。体察文化多样性的认识误区有助于认识到文化多样性的统一路径，即可能在文化适应性、思维的共性、人们跨文化交流能力和传媒科技的促进作用等几方面达成。

关键词：人文交流；"自我"；"他者"；身份

随着中国综合国力的增强以及国际地位的提高，人文交流已然成为继政治安全、经济金融之后中外合作的第三支柱。近年来，关于人文交流的讨论不绝于耳，但大多是基于必要性与实现途径的讨论，对其可能与否的本体性思考并不多见。基于文化"自我"与"他者"角度的探讨更有助于

---

* 张庆，四川外国语大学国际关系学院副教授，四川外国语大学金砖国家研究院人文交流研究所所长。
** 崔亦歌，四川外国语大学国际关系学院硕士研究生。
*** 杨盛，四川外国语大学国际关系学院硕士研究生。

认识文化与交流的本质，形成文化主体间性，从而以更加平和的心态去应对文化差异，提升人文交流的效果。

一、人文交流的现代性悖论

从常识判断，只要两个异质的文化族群有彼此交流的意愿以及交流的途径，人文交流就是顺理成章的事情，但现实往往并非如此。近现代工业化与商业化进程为我们提供了较以往更便捷的信息传播渠道，如广播、电影、电视、网络等，但人们似乎并未找到冲破彼此文化藩篱与认识隔阂的有效方法。"我们在走进传播技术所制造的交流神话世界的同时，又掉进了交流的深渊，以致我们用数倍于先前时代的战争、暴力解决着彼此之间的文化冲突。"①

英国作家狄更斯（Charles Dickens）在《双城记》的开篇指出："那是最好的岁月，那是最坏的岁月，那是智慧的时代，那是愚蠢的时代，那是信仰的新纪元，那是怀疑的新纪元，那是光明的季节，那是黑暗的季节，那是希望的春天，那是绝望的冬天。"② 这样的描述对于现代性同样适用。现代性促进了社会的发展与进步，但也催生了一些由工具理性和价值理性的分裂所产生的悖论，如自然的危机、价值的缺失、道德的迷失、世界的抽象化、自由的丧失等。作为分析现代性的经典理论家，德国政治学家马克斯·韦伯（Max Deber）通过"合理化"或"理性化"，思考了现代性的悖论及其产生的根源，提出理性的"吊诡"问题。韦伯认为，现代性就是社会及其文化的"合理化"或"理性化"过程。现代社会的一个核心特征是人们习惯用理性进行思考。正因如此，把握理性成为认识现代社会的关键。"资本主义精神的发展完全可以理解为理性主义整体发展的一部分，而且可以从理性主义对于生活基本问题的根本立场中演绎出来。"③

尽管现代性极大程度地促进了人类的进步、经济的繁荣和社会的发

---

① 单波：《跨文化传播的问题与可能性》，武汉大学出版社2010年版，第2页。
② ［英］查尔斯·狄更斯，石永礼等译：《双城记》，人民文学出版社2004年版，第1页。
③ ［德］马克斯·韦伯，于晓等：《新教伦理与资本主义精神》，三联书店1987年版，第56页。

展,但出乎启蒙思想家的预料,现代性非但未能帮助人类社会跨越历史进程中的种种障碍,走出被奴役的牢笼,得到解放和自由,反而加深了人们的束缚和不自由的状态。正如英国哲学家柏林(Isaiah Berlin)提到的,将理性作为建立社会模式的基础,其"初衷是要将人类从错误中解放出来,从困惑中解放出来,从不可认知但又被人们试图借助某种模式认知的世界中解放出来。但是,毫无例外,这些模式的结果就是重新奴役了被解放过的人类。这些模式不能解释人类全部经验。于是,最初的解放者最终成为另一种意义上的独裁者"。[①]

现代性在满足人们需求的同时催生出人们更多的渴望。美国爱德华大学教授彼得斯(John Durham Peters)认为,"交流(communication)是现代人诸多渴望的记录簿。它召唤的是一个理想的乌托邦。在乌托邦里,没有被误解的东西,人人敞开心扉,说话无拘无束。看不见的东西,渴望愈加迫切"。[②]从另一个角度来说,我们之所以渴望交流,是因为我们痛感社会关系的缺失。彼得斯一方面承认交流的迫切性,"交流是盘根错节的思想文化问题,它把时代的种种自我冲突编进了自己的代码之中。弄清交流具有重大的意义,我们可以得到一个明显的答案,以便解决我与他、私密与公共、内心思想与外在词语的分裂所引起的痛苦"。[③] 另一方面,对于人们之间实现真实的交流缺乏信心,"'交流'的观念说明,我们在历史的此时此刻过着奇怪的生活。它是一个落水洞,我们的希望和畏惧似乎多半流走消失,不见踪影了"。[④]

在彼得斯看来,交流作为沟通的桥梁,是靠符号建构的虚化的尝试,徒有形式的外表,缺乏内容的支撑。交流中没有确定无疑的迹象,只有暗示和猜想。我们的互动不可能是思想的交融,最多不过是思想的舞蹈;在

[①] [英]以赛亚·柏林,吕梁等:《浪漫主义的根源》,译林出版社2008年版,第11页。
[②] [美]约翰·彼得斯,何道宽译:《交流的无奈:传播思想史》,华夏出版社2003年版,第2页。
[③] [美]约翰·彼得斯,何道宽译:《交流的无奈:传播思想史》,华夏出版社2003年版,第2页。
[④] [美]约翰·彼得斯,何道宽译:《交流的无奈:传播思想史》,华夏出版社2003年版,第2页。

这个舞蹈的过程中，我们有时能够触摸对方。① "交流是没有保证的冒险。凭借符号去建立联系的任何尝试，都是一场赌博，无论其发生的规模是大还是小。"② 皮尔斯也对符号意义系统充满不信任，"符号客观上只有一般的意义，其有效解释常常不确定，它把完成确定意义的权利拱手送给解释者自己"。③

此外，交流总是和权力结合在一起，"纯粹的""去权力化的"交流极其困难。"如果我们希望在交流中谋求某种精神圆满或满足，那就是白花精力。既然我们是凡人，交流永远是一个权势、伦理和艺术的问题。"④ 对于这一点，香港城市大学李金铨认为，现代社会交流的障碍在于我们太过重视"跨文化交流"，而对"国际交流"重视不够。要看到，现代世界秩序仍然以民族国家为基本单位。⑤ 国家权力对于跨文化交流的影响不可忽视。但吊诡的是，不同国家、民族间的交往在模糊国家界限的同时需要对国家权力进行必要的维护，因为国家才拥有对抗全球金融和信息风暴的有效手段。⑥

交流的方式直接影响着交流的效果。用对话的碎片思考和说话已经成为我们交流的主要方式。英国思想家威廉姆斯（Raymond Williams）说："我听说，仿佛是第一次听说，按照习惯，仍然叫作所谓戏剧性语言，甚至是叫作对话的东西：首先是听契科夫说的话，我注意到一种习惯性的莫名其妙：人们的声音不再对他人发出，也不再有来有往；人们的交谈，也许是在他人的面前自言自语……没有一个人能够说完他开始说的话；相反，人们互相插话，随意，心不在焉，语词遭到夭折的命运。"⑦ 在现代性

---

① [美]约翰·彼得斯，何道宽译：《交流的无奈：传播思想史》，华夏出版社2003年版，第252页。
② [美]约翰·彼得斯，何道宽译：《交流的无奈：传播思想史》，华夏出版社2003年版，第251页。
③ Buchler, J. Philosophical Writings of Peirce, New York: Dover, 1955: 295.
④ [美]约翰·彼得斯，何道宽译：《交流的无奈：传播思想史》，华夏出版社2003年版，第252页。
⑤ Lee, Chin-Chuan. Internationalizing "International Communication", Ann Arbor: University of Michigan Press, 2015: 1.
⑥ Touraine, A. What is democracy?, Boulder: Westview Press, 1997.
⑦ O'Connor, A. Raymond Williams on Television: Selected Writings, London: Routledge, 1989: 12.

的语境下，交流的实质、内容、途径以及权力色彩都在向我们宣告，"纯粹的""有效的"交流很难发生。"我们不得不承认，作为桥梁的交流是一种真实的幻觉，作为沟壑的交流是一种残酷的现实。"① 异质文化族群之间的交流尤其如此：要么受制于"自我"与"他者"的二元对立意识，难以突破思维定式的藩篱；要么被国家权力所绑架，形成所谓的文化权力支配关系。

鉴于此，彼得斯干脆放弃了对于人们交流可能性的探讨，转而询问"我们能够相互爱护，能够公正而宽厚地彼此相待吗？"②

二、我是谁："自我"的群体性身份

在人际交往中，要科学地判断"自我"的身份特征。从社会学的角度看，社会由不同的"自我"组成，每一个单独的个体在社会大环境下都要放弃一些个性，与群体的公共价值与思维保持一致。此时，特殊的"我"已被共相的"我"、概念的"我"所取代，那个真实的"我"已被"我们"所遮蔽，也就是个体被群体所遮蔽。③ 从心理学的角度看，"自我"的社会性与群体性身份密切相关。人一旦成为社会人，就被赋予了显著的群体性身份。彼此靠社会纽带联系在一起的人具有相似的情感和思维方式，会表现出不同于每个个体的新的特点。随着个性的褪色，一种"集体心理"或"心理群体"逐渐形成。"一个心理群体表现出来的最惊人的特点如下：无论构成这个群体的个人是谁，也无论他们的生活方式、职业、性格或智力相同与否，他们变成一个群体这个事实使他们获得一种集体心理，导致他们的感情、思想和行为变得与他们单独一人时的感情、思想和行为颇为不同。若不是形成一个群体，有些念头或感情在个人身上根本就不会产生，或不可能变成行动。心理群体是一个由异质成分组成的暂时现象，当他们结合在一起时，就像因结合成一种新的存在而构成一个生命体

---

① 单波：《跨文化传播的问题与可能性》，武汉大学出版社2010年版，第3—4页。
② [美]约翰·彼得斯，何道宽译：《交流的无奈：传播思想史》，华夏出版社2003年版，第252页。
③ 单波：《跨文化传播的问题与可能性》，武汉大学出版社2010年版，第9页。

的细胞一样,会表现出一些特点。它们与单个细胞所具有的特点大不相同。"① 在与他人交往的活动中,每个人的言谈举止都会自觉不自觉地带有强烈的群体性色彩,从而有了"自我"与"他者"的区分。"我们是中国人,他们是外国人;我们是公务员,他们是个体户;我们是名门望族,他们是贫寒世家"……我们无时无刻不在用这种"贴标签"的方式强化着群体身份意识。通过表达"我是谁",以区别于那些不具有该群体本质属性的其他人。应该说,这种划分是一把"双刃剑":一方面,有助于简化对于一个人社会地位的认识,从而增进对社会构成的理解;一方面,加速带来了诸如民族和种族主义、政治冲突等群体间偏见。

进一步说,独立的个体在"集体心理"的影响下,其心理会发生本质变化——自我意识的存在空间日益受到压缩,个性发展不断受到打压,久而久之就会把集体心理当成自我心理,突出表现是简单思维与从众心态。② 具体来说,在一种高度社会化的氛围下,个体思维极易受制于社会成员依据身份建构心态对一种身份认同的普遍评价和内在期望。苏联心理学家包达列夫(A. A. Bodalev)曾经做过一个很有趣的实验。他拿了一张照片对一组大学生说:"我给你们看一位大科学家的照片,请你们谈谈对这位科学家面部特征的看法。"大学生们看了照片后的一致看法是:这位科学家那双深邃的眼睛,表明了他思想的深度;他突出的下巴,表明了他在科学研究道路上克服困难的决心。包达列夫随后又拿着这张照片给另一组大学生看,并对他们反复介绍道:"我给你们看一个大罪犯的照片,请你们谈谈对这个罪犯的面部特征有什么看法。"这组大学生看了照片后的一致看法是:这个罪犯双眼深陷,表明了其内心深处的仇恨;他突出的下巴,表明了他死不悔改的决心。两组大学生看的是同一张照片,为什么得出的看法竟然会有如此大的差异呢?原因显然不在于他们各自不同的思维方式、价值观和审美观,而是缘自心理学家包达列夫对照片中人物身份所做的不同介绍。在长期的社会交往中,不同身份所蕴含的基本特征在人们心中有

---

① [法]古斯塔夫·勒庞,冯克利译:《乌合之众:大众心理研究》,中央编译出版社2014年版,第7页。
② 单波:《跨文化传播的问题与可能性》,武汉大学出版社2010年版,第10页。

着固定的意义和模式，人们往往会根据一个人的身份对他的性格特征、行为方式以及行为预期做出基本的判断。①

三、冲突对抗与和谐平等：文化传播的两种姿态

文化之间的冲突和障碍亘古有之，意大利政治学家格拉姆斯（Antonio Gramsci）认为，东方和西方从来没有停止关于"客观上的真实"（objective reality）的讨论，即使在研究中，他们最多只是被作为一种历史的或者传统的建构。"很显然，东方和西方的概念是专断的、传统的建构，因为地球上的每一个地方既是东方，也是西方。对于欧洲人、美国加利福尼亚州人甚至部分日本人来说，日本可能算作远东……"② 尤其同一事件或文字可以表达不同的含义时，极易造成意义建构进程中潜在的抗争。苏联语言学家沃洛希洛夫（V. N. Volosinov）注意到符号的"多音性"（social multiaccentuality of the ideological sign）问题，他指出，一个符号的多重意义可以用不同的发音腔调来呈现，在不同的情况下发挥不同作用，指代不同事物。所以，一个符号常常代表的是"不同社会利益趋向"的聚合点，相当于一个个独立的"抗争场"。③

文化之间的冲突在文化霸权主义和文化帝国主义的思维模式中表现得淋漓尽致。文化霸权主义的"常规"动作就是将符号的意义单一化，将原本意义丰富的各种文化符号通过特定的方式强行统一认识。④ 列宁在《帝国主义是资本主义的最高阶段》一文中解释了何为"帝国主义"，"如果必须给帝国主义下一个尽量简短的定义，那就应当说，帝国主义是资本主义的垄断阶段。这样的定义能包括最主要之点，因为一方面，金融资本就是和工业家垄断同盟的资本融合起来的少数垄断性的银行资本；另一方面，

---

① 夏建平：《认同与国际合作》，世界知识出版社2006年版，第48页。
② Gramsci, A. Prison Notebooks, edited and translated by Joseph A. Buttigieg. New York: Columbia University Press, 1975: 176.
③ Vlolsinov, V N. Marxism and the Philosophy of Language, New York: Seminar Press, 1973: 23.
④ 单波、肖珺、刘学：《全球媒介的跨文化传播幻想》，上海交通大学出版社2015年版，第46页。

瓜分世界，就是由无阻碍地向未被任何一个资本主义大国占据的地区推行的殖民政策，过渡到垄断地占有已经瓜分完了的世界领土的殖民政策。"①据考证，文化帝国主义的概念是由美国传播学研究巨擘、加州大学圣地亚哥分校名誉教授赫伯特·席勒（Herbert Schiller）在1976年出版的《传播与文化支配》一书中首度使用和诠释的。二战后，不少民族国家脱离了西方殖民统治，但其中的绝大多数仍然在经济与文化上严重依赖少数资本主义国家。就传播与文化领域来说，西方几个大型通讯社主导了全球信息的流通与诠释权，国际文化的交流出现严重失衡，新兴国家的文化发展空间受到严重挤压。在他看来，文化信息的呈现"是被那些控制着整个系统的财货与劳务生产的同一些市场动力所决定的"。②

在不同文化群体的交往过程中，冲突对抗只是手段，而并非交流的目的。人们通过文化传播和交流最终要达到和谐相处的状态。在这个意义上讲，冲突不是智慧，因为陷于冲突的各方永远通过划定自我和自我群体的利益边界来固守着各自的文化地盘，从而难以有超越性的表现。在此过程中，我们每个人都有可能变成文化原教旨主义者，不断强化"自我"与"他者"的区别。只有和谐才是智慧，它不仅能在多样性中分辨我是谁、他们是谁，而且能超越性地思考：我们如何恢复跨群体生存的自由？我们之间能合作做成什么？要回答这些问题，就要处理好"我、我们和他们"的关系。第一，在认识到文化差别的同时，承认每个人都有选择和认同不同文化的自由；第二，建构不同文化群体在交往过程中的平等地位；第三，尽量缓解交往中存在的紧张感以及由文化差异性带来的负面后果；第四，在制度层面弱化群体间交往的权力支配体系，从而保障文化群体的自由生存空间。③

---

① 孙晶：《哲学系列：文化霸权理论研究》，社会科学文献出版社2004年版，第61页。
② Schiller, H I. Communication and Cultural Domination, New York: International Arts and Sciences Press, 1976: 6.
③ 单波：《跨文化传播的问题与可能性》，武汉大学出版社2010年版，第14—15页。

四、文化多样性的认识误区

早在几千年前，人们就用"巴别塔"一词来指称交流的困难。据《旧约·创世纪》记载，大洪水之后，走出方舟的诺亚子孙们说着共同的语言，建立了许多国家。这些生活在两河流域的人们为了传扬自己的名声，决定建造一座通天高塔。这些人相互合作，真的在肥沃的平原上建造起一座高耸入云的巨塔。上帝看到人们团结起来的巨大力量，震惊了，于是打乱了人类的语言，使其无法交流，从而再也不能齐心合力建塔。"巴别塔"的故事一方面说明了人们对于语言"同一性"的向往；另一方面，上帝变乱人类语言，不只是对人类妄想、妄语的惩罚，也可看作是对人类语言多样性的一种恢复，即多样性的语言对应于多样性的人类种属。[1]

经过不断探索，人们逐渐形成文化多样性的共识。19世纪，工业化和殖民化的甚嚣尘上使得社会学家开始认识到不同群体之间文化平等性的问题。20世纪下半叶，随着对现代性的批判不断加深，那些少数族群尤其是民族性少数族群（national minorities）和移民的种族性群体（ethnic groups），越来越多地要求保留其独特的社会形态，通过各种形式的自主或自治确保其作为独特文化载体的存续。[2] 20世纪90年代以来，联合国教科文组织将文化多样性融入其组织原则中。1995年，联合国教科文组织出版的《我们的文化多样性》报告指出："文化多样性如生态多样性客观存在，表明人类创造力的无限延展，它的美学价值通过多种途径得以体现，并不断激发新的创造。"2001年，联合国教科文组织通过了《文化多样性宣言》，强调在经济全球化的过程中，尊重、维持文化多样性对全人类生存与发展的重要意义。[3]

应该说，将文化多样性类比为生态多样性具有积极意义。正如19世

---

[1] 高文平：《语言之界》，重庆大学出版社2015年版，第58页。
[2] [加] 威尔·金里卡，杨立峰译：《多元文化公民权：一种有关少数民族群权利的自由主义理论》，上海译文出版社2009年版，第12—13页。
[3] 郑育林：《唤醒遗迹：城市化背景下的大遗址保护与利用问题》，文物出版社2014年版，第209页。

纪德国动物学家恩斯特·海克尔（Ernst Haeckel）所言，多样性意味着"自然环境中各要素的互动以及此种互动如何导致了平衡健康的环境"。[1]与此同时，我们更应该注意的是这种生态学类比的思维陷阱。在生态系统中，各种生物在生物链（biological chain）和食物链（food chain）中占据着不同的位置，呈现出不同的力量，发挥着不同的影响。物竞天择、适者生存是它们基于权力支配体系的唯一生存法则。而一旦将权力支配体系导入文化多样性的范畴，我们就有寻求一种支配性的文化力量的冲动。"我们会错把谋求同化的美国文化大熔炉（the melting pot）当作多样性，错把基于种族与文化差异的绝对性而实行的种族隔离（segregation）当作多样性，错把文化的主流与边缘的架构当作多样性。"[2] 认识文化多样性面临的另一个难题是如何统一的问题。联合国教科文组织对此的判断是"发展有一个特征对于人类的未来至关重要，那就是统一性与多样性之间的平衡。这种平衡对于所有的发展和进化形式来说都是基本的，在自然界和历史中也是如此。一旦离开了一定程度的统一性或者多样性，任何事物都不能成长和发展……没有多样性，各个部分便不能形成一个能够生长、发展、繁殖和创造的实体。没有整合，各种不同的成分便不能结合成一个单一的能动的结构"。[3] 这段话向我们描述了一种文化多样性的完美状态，即二者的和谐与平衡。现实的问题是：通向此种和谐平衡的路径在哪里？换句话说，基于权力话语的逻辑，文化多样性的统一应该由谁来支配，谁来主宰？在经济全球化的浪潮中，资本的力量在各国文化传播过程中的影响力仍不可忽视。在当代社会，一个贫穷落后的民族是难以在平等的文化对话中赢得先机，去影响或同化另外一个经济科技发达、文化均衡发展的民族的。[4] 另外，资本的全球扩张也在侵蚀着民族文化的基础。现代化进程或明或暗让不符合现代性的民族文化消亡，从而走向全球文化同质化。这种

---

[1] Postman, N. The Humanism of Media Ecology, Proceedings of the Media Ecology Association, 2000 (1): 10-16.

[2] 单波：《跨文化传播的问题与可能性》，武汉大学出版社2010年版，第16页。

[3] [意]欧文·拉兹洛，戴侃等译：《多种文化的星球：联合国教科文组织国际专家小组的报告》，社会科学文献出版社2001年版，第11页。

[4] 李炎：《西部文化产业理论与实践》，云南大学出版社2015年版，第3—4页。

现代化模式与其说是促进民族发展的路径，不如说是强制实行民族同化的"温柔方式"。① 更有甚者，按照权力支配体系的逻辑，多种文化的统一进程排除了跨文化交流的必要性。"如果人们只是思想的囚徒，遵照意识形态进行交流、理解或者语言的实践，那么作为意识形态傀儡的主体是根本不需要进行跨文化传播的，只需要被某种意识形态征服而服从罢了，或者跨文化传播因意识形态霸权而变得完全不可能实现，最终成为一个伪命题。"②

五、文化多样性的统一路径

依据前文所述，文化多样性似乎是摆在面前的铁定事实，而文化统一性则是无源之水、无本之木。我们也不可断然做出此种判断，毕竟多元文化有其自身的生长逻辑，不可能完全受制于权力支配体系。据此，英国文化批评理论家斯图尔特·霍尔（Stuart Hall）提出著名的"联结"理论（articulation），认为联结可以在特定的条件下将不同要素统一起来，这种关联并非在任何时候都是必要的、确定的、绝对的和本质的。所谓的"统一"，实质上就是不同要素的联结。需要注意的是，这些要素没有必然的"归属"，所以它们可以通过不同的方式再次联结。③ 在人际交流中，彼此交流的信息在不同的语境下传递出迥然相异的意义。霍尔认为意义通过文化和政治实践，在其可能的范围之内进行运转和操作，联结到不同社会位置，又在可能的范围内构造和再造了社会主体。④ 也就是说，现实生活中只有"信息"的存在，意义是建构起来的、多义性的、语境化的。意义更强调的是过程而非结果。事物之间若即若离的"联结"为多样文化的交流与统一提供了如下可能性。

---

① 金星华、张晓明、兰智奇：《中国少数民族文化发展报告（2008）》，民族出版社2009年版，第168页。
② 单波：《跨文化传播的问题与可能性》，武汉大学出版社2010年版，第18页。
③ Morley, D., Chen, K. Stuart Hall: Critical Dialogues in Cultural Studies, London: Routledge, 1996: 141.
④ Dervin, B., Grossberg, L., O'Keefe, B J., and Wartella, E. Rethinking Communication, California: Sage Publications, 1989: 45.

首先，文化的适应性为文化交流提供了前提和基础。社会的形构、阶级、文化之间的关系，既不是一对一的对应关系，也不是不一致的关系，而是建构出来的，既不是一定有，也不是一定不存在，它是社会群体间不断斗争与相互碰撞而产生的。① 在"自我"与"他者"的互动过程中，"自我"既影响着"他者"，同时又被"他者"所塑造。双方需要在持续接触与碰撞中表达观点、了解对方、修正策略，最终达到交流的目的。

其次，通过反思语言的差异性来建构思维的共性。虽然不同族群文化形态各异、内容多样、表现多元，但其具有人类所共有的价值取向——寻真、向善、求美。不同文化本身存在着价值趋同性，这也是异质文化之间的"最大公约数"。② 作为文化的代码与载体，语言的差异性更多是形式上的表现。有着不同语言背景的族群可以通过翻译在各领域进行相互了解与沟通。③ 人们研究语言背后的哲学和语言形成的逻辑，力图跨越种种语言障碍，寻求思维的共性，以续写"巴别塔"的奇迹。

第三，重视文化交流的主体因素，提升人们的跨文化交流能力。一方面，要不断修正"自我"主体的文化观念和认知能力；另一方面，提高移情意识，即站在"他者"的角度和立场，使"自我"的语言与行为符合"他者"的文化习惯和心智模式。

第四，探索现代传媒科技对于人文交流的促进作用。现代传媒技术的迅猛发展不仅有效克服了文化交流的空间障碍，也有利于扩大各种文化的影响范围，提高传播速度，改善文化认知。这一场波澜壮阔的技术革命重构了文化民族性和世界性的关系，也改变了文化自身具有的稳定性、保守性、排他性与渐变性。④ 在此背景下，我们要在探寻现代传媒技术本质的基础上思考其对于文化交流的全面影响，例如如何克服它不断彰显的技术理性问题；如何将现代传媒技术与优秀的叙事方式相结合，以增强文化传

---

① 林立树：《现代思潮：西方文化研究之通路》，中央编译出版社2014年版，第161页。
② 胡惠林、陈昕：《中国文化产业评论（第24卷）》，上海人民出版社2017年版，第253页。
③ 单波：《跨文化传播的问题与可能性》，武汉大学出版社2010年版，第20页。
④ 李炎：《西部文化产业理论与实践》，云南大学出版社2015年版，第4页。

播的表现力等等。①

  总体来说，人文交流并非旨在消除不同文化族群的差异性，也并非为了强化"自我"身份的独特性，而是努力达成人们之间互相倾听、理解与包容的文化心态与意识。要做到这一点，需要站在"他者"的角度，形成彼此尊重的文化主体间性。在此关照下，人文交流的最终表现形式为文化融合。同自然万物一样，文化并非一成不变的静态表现，而表现为发展与衰亡的动态过程。人文交流通过人们之间平等的对话为各自传统文化的母体注入了新思想的基因，促进了一种新文化的孕育与生长，从而将人类文化的整体发展提升到更高阶段。

---

① 胡惠林、陈昕：《中国文化产业评论（第24卷）》，上海人民出版社2017年版，第255页。

"故事外交"：首脑与民众的互动

谌华侨[*]

摘　要：国家间人文交流尚存在不同国家大众之间的信息差异和认知差异，应该及时化解打破信息封闭问题。不同国家间可以通过"故事外交"的形式推动人文交流，即将百姓亲历的故事，经过媒体的挖掘，使之成为领导人外事访问中公共演讲的素材，再通过领导人讲故事的方式及媒体的报道，强化故事在民众中的传播效果。重庆万州母子为苏联红军守库里申科墓半个多世纪的故事，经过媒体广泛报道，成为中国国家领导人首次国事访问时在莫斯科国际关系学院演讲的素材。经过领导人的故事分享，新闻媒体又进行了系列跟踪报道，相关单位随后还拍摄了电影，该故事由此在两国之间得以进一步传播，拉近了中俄两国民众的距离。

关键词：故事；外交；民心相通

在外交话语中，一些生动的故事有助于唤起大家的感性认知，形成积极认同。作为具有强烈个人特质的外交形式，首脑外交因最高领导的亲自参与而具有了显著于其他外交形式的特质。国家领导人在外事访问过程中

---

[*] 谌华侨，四川外国语大学重庆非通用语学院副教授。

的讲话容易引起国内外民众的广泛关注，讲话中涉及的故事有可能产生深远影响。本文聚焦首脑外交中的公共演讲部分所讲述的故事，在初步界定"故事外交"的概念后，尝试着从中提炼出"故事外交"的一般生成逻辑，并通过典型案例来验证这样的逻辑存在，进而有针对性地提出促进"故事外交"的有益举措。

一、"故事外交"的概念界定

首先，通过中外经典词源检索，逐步确定故事的概念及其内涵。随后，通过外交学研究成果，确定首脑外交的概念和功能。最后，通过既有的概念，运用逻辑学属性与种差的关系，建构"故事外交"的概念，并明确其内涵与特性，为后续研究奠定学理讨论基础。

（一）故事的界定

在《辞海》中，作为名词时，故事被界定为"旧事"；作为手段时，故事被界定为"文学体裁的一种，侧重于事件过程的描述，强调事件的生动性和连贯性，较适用于口头讲述，通俗易懂"。[①]

在《现代汉语词典》中，故事是名词，表示"真实或虚构的用作讲述对象的事情，有连贯性，富吸引力"。[②]《柯林斯高阶英汉双解词典》将故事（story）界定为"对已经发生过的事情的叙述或讲述，尤其是口述"。同时，故事也可以理解为"报纸或新闻节目中的新闻报道"。[③] 在《朗文当代高级英语辞典》中，作为名词时，故事（story）被界定为"真实或虚构的事件"，或者是"新闻或杂志等媒体中的文章"。[④]

从上述中英文的词源来看，故事至少有如下几层意思：作为名词时，

---

① 辞海编辑委员会：《辞海》，上海辞书出版社1999年版，第4172—4173页。
② 中国社会科学院语言研究所词典编辑室编：《现代汉语词典（第5版）》，商务印书馆2005年版，第493页。
③ 英国柯林斯公司编，姚乃强等审译：《柯林斯高阶英汉双解词典》，商务印书馆2008年版，第1575页。
④ 朱原等译：《朗文当代高级英语辞典》，商务印书馆1998年版，第1522页。

故事是真实或虚构的用口头讲述的事情；同样作为名词时，故事也是报纸或新闻节目中的新闻报道；作为一种表达手段时，故事是对事件过程的口头描述。概而言之，作为一种客观存在时，故事是口头讲述的事情；作为与媒体的关系存在时，故事是报纸、新闻等媒体中的报道；作为表达客体存在时，故事是表达主体对事件过程的口头描述。

（二）首脑外交的界定

一般而言，外交是"主权国家（以及国家联合体）为了实现其对外政策目标，以国际法和有关惯例为基础，通过正式代表本国的最高领导人和以专职外交部门为核心的中央政府部门，以及在他们的领导下通过其他半官方和非官方的机构、社会团体以至个人，以通信、访问、会谈、谈判、签订协议等和平方式处理国际关系和国际事务的行动和过程"。首脑外交是"国家和国际组织的最高领导人为了实现本国的外交政策亲自从事的外交活动"。[1]

相比一般的外交形式，首脑外交是外交主体和外交执行者高度统一的外交活动，其显著特性在于最高领导人亲自参与其中，外交主体级别高，引领示范性强。二战以来，随着技术革命带来的新媒介的不断涌现，首脑外交大放异彩。国家最高领导人亲自参与的外交活动通过媒体的报道，让更多民众及时知晓高层的外交活动内容。首脑外交也因此具有沟通功能，成为国家最高领导人与普通民众之间进行沟通的有效方式之一。

（三）"故事外交"的界定

首脑外交主要包括首脑通信与通话、首脑特使外交、首脑宣言与申明、首脑访问、首脑会晤等形式。依据首脑访问重要程度的不同，又可分为国事访问、正式访问、非正式访问、友好访问、礼节性访问和"国事停留"等。国事访问是首脑访问的最高形式，一般是指一国元首应他国元首正式邀请进行的访问，包括正式欢迎仪式、检阅仪仗队、鸣放礼炮、公众

---

[1] 陈志敏、肖佳灵、赵可金著：《当代外交学》，北京大学出版社2008年版，第5—6，195页。

演讲、议会演讲、新闻记者招待会等。[1] 一般而言，国事访问的主要活动皆通过多种媒体进行现场直播，并在黄金时间再次播放，往往成为访问期间有关国家媒体报道的热点，引起普通民众的广泛关注。

据逻辑学的研究显示，用"属加种差定义"来解释一个词项的规约内涵比任何其他方法都有更广泛的可应用性。被分为子类的类为"属"，而各种各样的子类都是"种"。一个属可以分为多个种，用来区分一个属内不同种的性质即为"种差"。[2]

根据逻辑学研究成果的一般适用性原则，我们将"故事外交"界定为首脑外交访问中公共演讲的一种重要形式。根据"属加种差定义"方法，"故事外交"具有首脑外交的属，兼具公共演讲的种差。为此，本文将"故事外交"定义为一国元首在国事访问过程中，在公共演讲时讲述反映不同国家普通民众之间的真实感人事情，从而拉近两国人民的距离。

"故事外交"因为具有首脑外交的属，因而被赋予首脑外交的沟通功能。首脑本人来讲述真实故事，可实现一国领导人与东道国民众的直接交流，拉近了首脑与普通民众的距离。如果这一公共演讲过程被媒体现场直播，并再次播放，有利于强化真实故事在普通民众中的传播范围。

二、"故事外交"的生成逻辑

根据定义可以看出，"故事外交"的全过程涉及三方面的行为主体，即民众、媒体和首脑。根据事件发展的时间顺序，"故事外交"需要依次经历民众亲历事件、媒体挖掘案例、首脑讲述故事三个阶段，每个阶段的主要行为主体都要采取明确的行动，并指向明确的施动对象，进而产生一定的结果。这样的行为主体，在不同阶段采取的不同行动，根据一定的时间序列，产生了一个特定结果，并最终产生一个较为稳定的机制，[3] 即

---

[1] 陈志敏、肖佳灵、赵可金著：《当代外交学》，北京大学出版社2008年版，第205页。
[2] ［美］欧文·M.柯匹、卡尔·科恩著，张建军等译：《逻辑学导论（第11版）》，中国人民大学出版社2007年版，第142—143页。
[3] 关于机制的一般性解释，参见 Mario Bunge, "Mechanism and Explanation," *Philosophy of the Social Sciences*, Vol. 27, No. 4, 1997, pp. 410-465。

"故事外交"的生成逻辑。

（一）民众亲历事件

随着科学技术的进一步发展，交通工具的日益改进，远距离通勤的时间不断压缩，普通民众的活动范围逐步突破一国边界的传统范畴，在世界范围呈现更加频繁的自由移动。仅仅根据国际民航组织部分年度的统计数据可知，乘坐国际航班的乘客由2006年的8.08亿人次增长到2015年的14.36亿人次，航空里程分别从2.5万亿公里增加到4.1万亿公里。[①]

随着全球范围内人口跨界流动的增强，一国居民与外国居民的互动越发频繁，不同国家间普通民众之间的交流日益密切，亲历的各类事件极有可能大幅增加。这些亲历事件中，部分典型事件有可能通过多种方式得以记录并保存下来，成为国家间关系的重要历史见证。更多的亲历事件可能以轶事（anecdote）的方式留存于普通民众之间。

民众亲历事件增加是人口进行跨国流动之后产生的必然结果。随着科技的发展，全球一体化的进程进一步加快，人口的跨国流动必然加速。可以期待的是，人口跨界流动导致的亲历事件会大概率地发生。

（二）媒体挖掘案例

普通民众在对外交往中所经历的事件极有可能是无意识事件，并且随着时间的流逝，这些对外交往亲历事件有可能消失在公众视野中，成为尘封的历史。新闻媒体从业人员基于自身敏锐的职业嗅觉，在日常的生活或工作中，很容易发现这样的报道题材。随着媒体行业的不断发展，新闻媒体从业人员之间的竞争日益激烈，新闻媒体从业人员需要掌握能够深度挖掘新闻报道背后故事的能力，将这些尘封的事件进行再报道，让公众得以知晓。

媒体深度挖掘新闻背后的案例，这不仅是在全媒体时代媒体生存的必然要求，也是新闻媒体从业人员基本的能力要求。在行业环境和个人素质

[①] 详细数据参见国际民航组织官方网站年度报告，https://www.icao.int/sustainability/Pages/FactsFigures.aspx，2019年5月6日登陆。

的内外双重驱动下,媒体及其从业人员极有可能从一般事件中挖掘出更多的典型案例。

(三) 首脑讲述故事

在首脑的外事活动尤其是国事访问中,首脑往往会在出访前接受媒体的联合采访,首脑也常常选择在东道国主要媒体发表署名文章,在访问时会在欢迎宴会或国会演讲过程中发表重要演讲。在这些面向本国和东道国普通民众的署名文章和重要演讲中,首脑的文章或讲话往往会涉及媒体报道过的关于两国民众交往的感人故事。

这样的故事,经过首脑在外事访问过程中的亲自阐述,并通过媒体报道得以在更大范围内扩散,实现了首脑与更多普通民众之间的沟通,引起了普通民众的共鸣。不仅如此,这样的故事通过两国媒体的广泛报道,还可实现在两国普通民众中的广泛扩散。

综上所述,"故事外交"历经民众亲历故事、媒体挖掘案例和首脑讲述故事这三个阶段,逐步由普通民众之间的事件,经过媒体的挖掘和报道,由首脑在国事访问过程中进行讲述,上升为首脑外交的一部分,成为国际关系的构成内容。

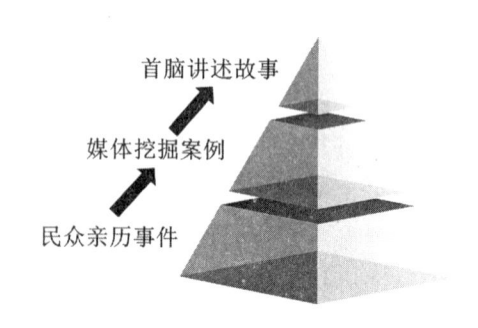

图3—1 "故事外交"的生成逻辑

资料来源:笔者自制。

从"故事外交"的生成逻辑来看,基于大量民众对外交往的频次,民众亲历事件极有可能存在一个相当大的数量。由于工作性质的差异,媒体关注的焦点较为有限，能够深入挖掘的案例相对于大量的民众亲历事件而言，仅仅是其中较为典型的一部分。首脑在国事访问过程中所讲述的民众交往的故事，极有可能是此前媒体挖掘并报道的案例中最能体现两国普通民众交往的故事。不同行为体关注的焦点不同，"故事外交"的生成过程也是对民众亲历事件的一个再次筛选过程，在数量上存在一个由多到少的过程。

三、"故事外交"的典型案例

根据笔者的不完全统计，中国国家主席习近平在国事访问过程中发表的重要演讲皆涉及两国民众交往过程中的真实故事。[①] 在典型案例部分，我们选择习近平主席首次国事访问过程中的"故事外交"，期待通过这一典型案例来窥见"故事外交"的生成逻辑。

（一）库里申科事件原型

乌克兰人格里戈里·库里申科原为苏联飞行大队长，世界反法西斯战争爆发后，他和考兹洛夫受苏联政府派遣，于1939年率两个"达莎式"轰炸机大队来中国援助抗日，进驻成都南郊太平寺机场。1939年10月14日，库里申科接到作战任务，率队出击日本军事基地。机群飞临武汉上空时，遭到日本敌机的拦截。激战中，库里申科率领的飞行大队炸毁敌机103架，击落6架。但他所驾驶的飞机遭到日本飞机重创，仅靠着一个发动机沿长江向上游驻地返航。当飞机到达万县（现重庆市万州区）上空时，机身失去平衡，为了避开陆地上的建筑，飞机最后迫降到万县城区的长江江面上。机上的轰炸员和射击员纷纷跳水游到岸上，而他却因长时间激战，体力透支，无力跳出机舱，被无情的江水吞没。

库里申科牺牲后，其遗体安葬在万县，万县政府和人民为他举行了隆重的追悼大会。中华人民共和国成立后，万县市人民政府于1958年7月在长江边上风景秀丽的西山公园为库里申科修建了烈士陵园，并举行了隆

---

① 统计的范围主要是以国事访问过程中《人民日报》和新华社的文字稿为准。

重的迁葬仪式。此后，英雄长眠于长江畔的重庆万州区西山公园。① 谭忠惠也从1958年开始为库里申科守墓，她年事已高后，她的儿子魏映祥又从她手中接棒守墓事宜。母子两代人绵延半个多世纪的守护，感动了成千上万的人，也成为两国深厚友谊的见证。

（二）中俄媒体联合报道案例

库里申科牺牲后，他的事迹在中国被媒体广为报道，在当时引起巨大的社会反响，然而在他的祖国苏联却毫无动静，这是因为当时援华志愿人员的去向是保密的。库里申科在给妻子的家书中也只是写到他调到东方的一个地区工作，这里的人对他很好，他就像生活在家乡一样。当时库里申科的家人不知道他牺牲的经过，也不知道其葬身之地。正式通知上只写着他在执行政府任务时牺牲，家人很想知道他献身的地点、时间和原因。②

直到1954年，到苏联留学的中国留学生朱育理发现入学班级的班长名字叫依娜·库里申科，不由得想起自己九岁那年崇拜的苏联英雄——格里戈里·库里申科，于是询问班长是否认识这位英雄，而这位同学正是英雄库里申科的女儿，由此揭开了这段尘封的往事。家人得知库里申科牺牲在万州后，终于找到了亲人的埋葬地，并多次前往祭拜。1958年国庆节前夕，依娜·库里申科和母亲访问中国时，受到周恩来总理的亲切接见。

2010年12月18日，中央电视台联合俄罗斯国家电视台录制并播出中俄大型跨国公益寻亲节目《等着我》。该节目第一期就讲述了朱育理与苏联同学依娜·库里申科交往，并找到英雄家人的故事，后来这段感人至深的故事又被搬上了银幕。

（三）习主席讲述守墓故事

2013年3月23日，习近平主席在对俄罗斯的首次国事访问中，就在莫斯科国际关系学院发表了《顺应时代前进潮流，促进世界和平发展》的

---

① 库里申科牺牲过程的详细记录参见魏拥锋：《一曲中苏友谊之歌：纪念库里申科诞辰110周年》，《中国档案》2013年第6期，第78—79页。

② 魏拥锋：《一曲中苏友谊之歌：纪念库里申科诞辰110周年》，《中国档案》2013年第6期，第79页。

主题演讲。在演讲过程中，习主席在谈到坚定不移发展两国人民友好关系时，提到了两国人民相互支持和帮助的三个典型事例。其中第一个事例便是重庆万州母子为苏联空军守墓半个世纪的感人故事："抗日战争时期，苏联飞行大队长库里申科来华同中国人民并肩作战，他动情地说，'我像体验我的祖国的灾难一样，体验着中国劳动人民正在遭受的灾难。'他英勇牺牲在中国大地上。中国人民没有忘记这位英雄，一对普通的中国母子已为他守陵半个多世纪。"①

不仅如此，习主席在此次演讲过程中，还讲述了中俄民众所亲历的另外两个故事，即别斯兰人质事件和汶川大地震后，中俄两国对受害儿童的康复治疗。

"2004年俄罗斯发生别斯兰人质事件后，中国邀请部分受伤儿童赴华接受康复治疗，这些孩子在中国受到精心照料，俄方带队医生阿兰表示：'你们的医生给孩子们这么大的帮助，我们的孩子会永远记住你们的。'"

"2008年中国汶川特大地震发生后，俄罗斯在第一时间向中国伸出援手，并邀请灾区孩子到俄罗斯远东等地疗养。三年前，我在符拉迪沃斯托克'海洋'全俄儿童中心，亲眼目睹了俄罗斯老师给予中国儿童的悉心照料和温馨关怀。中国孩子亲身体会到俄罗斯人民的友爱和善良，这应验了大爱无疆这句中国人常说的话。"②

（四）"故事外交"的后续进展

习近平主席在莫斯科国际关系学院发表演讲后，多个方面又有持续跟进。发表演讲的第二天，即2013年3月24日，中央电视台《新闻直播间》栏目通过《库里申科烈士陵园：友谊的见证》《库里申科：为中国抗日牺牲的苏联英雄》《库里申科墓园：鲜花献烈士 友谊存心间》《库里申科：为中国抗日牺牲的苏联英雄》《库里申科墓园，两代人的守护》《中俄大型跨国公益寻亲节目〈等着我〉》等多个短片对库里申科的英雄事迹和

---

① 习近平：《顺应时代前进潮流，促进世界和平发展》，中国共产党新闻网，http://theory.people.com.cn/n/2013/0323/c49150-20892222.html，2019年5月12日登陆。

② 习近平：《顺应时代前进潮流，促进世界和平发展》，中国共产党新闻网，http://theory.people.com.cn/n/2013/0323/c49150-20892222.html，2019年5月12日登陆。

魏映祥母子守墓事件进行了密集的专题报道。2014年前夕，中央电视台新闻频道的三名记者前往万州区档案局进行采访，调研库里申科英雄的事迹。2015年9月4日，中央电视台前往莫斯科专门采访依娜·库里申科，并在《朝闻天下》栏目通过《女儿眼中的库里申科》这一短片予以播放。在纪念世界反法西斯战争胜利70周年前夕，即2015年5月10日，中央电视台《朝闻天下》栏目以《库里申科：用生命保卫中国人民》为名，对他的事迹进行了再次报道。

近年来，万州区档案局高度重视对库里申科珍贵档案的抢救保护与利用工作。一方面，加强对库里申科珍贵档案的日常管护工作；另一方面，与区博物馆合作，联合开展纪念库里申科烈士诞辰110周年《深切缅怀·世纪守护》专题图片展览活动。

2014年12月24日，以库里申科真实故事为蓝本，由八一电影制片厂和中共重庆市委宣传部等单位联合摄制的电影《相伴库里申科》在重庆市万州区库里申科纪念园举行开机仪式，该电影后于2015年在纪念世界反法西斯战争胜利70周年之际正式上映。

四、"故事外交"的促进举措

从上述"故事外交"的典型案例可以看出，大量普通民众所经历的事件可能会随着时光的流逝而不被大众所铭记。若想让感人至深的事件历久弥新，成为媒体报道的焦点，成为外事访问过程中国家最高领导人向公众讲述的典型故事，可以从以下几个方面来促进"故事外交"的生成，使之发挥更大的民心沟通的功能。

（一）运用互联网平台建立人文交流故事库

随着普通民众的活动突破一国边界，在对外交往日益频繁的情况下，各国民众间的人文交流故事数量越来越多，并且因时间的推移而有望形成海量信息。因此，有必要借用现代信息技术，建立在线故事征集平台，并逐步建成人文交流故事库，为"故事外交"提供数量充足、类型多样的大数据平台。

（二）各类媒体要善于发掘具有国际关系寓意的人文交流故事

各国民众间的人文交流故事因为类型属性的差异，尚留存在各类特定的时空之中，大量感人的故事尚不被世人所知。各类媒体因为其职业属性，容易发现这样的故事，并通过不同的媒体渠道向外界进行报道，让世人知晓被历史尘封的感人故事。为此，相关媒体应该强化案例意识，深挖新闻背后的故事，丰富国家间人文交流的故事维度。

（三）充分发挥首脑外交的示范作用，提升人文交流故事的感染力

首脑外交因为国家最高领导人的亲自参与，对国际关系的发展往往起到引领示范的作用。各国媒体在首脑外事访问过程中一般会对相关活动进行多类型的广泛跟踪报道，民众容易知晓首脑讲话的内容。人文交流故事容易在这样的特殊时刻通过多类型的媒介向外界传播，从而在更大范围内扩散开来。

五、启示

近年来，用"故事"替代"口号"，尝试以生动立体的叙述形式消解文化间的疏离，"讲好中国故事"已成为中国跨文化传播的创新转向，[①] 中国的对外传播正呈现出新的态势。中国越发从更贴近自然人际交往的话语出发，用更接地气的话语风格向国外民众讲述中国与东道国之间的人际交往故事。

因此，承载着两国人民交往历史的轶事在外交中的重要性逐步凸显，作为轶事主角的人逐步回归到外交实践中。人际交往中的轶事，通过媒体报道及领导人在国事访问中的亲述，成为国际关系的重要见证，实现了从人际关系到国际关系的蜕变，从而形成一条国际关系的人本主义回归路径。

[①] 徐明华、李丹妮：《情感畛域的消解与融通："中国故事"跨文化传播的沟通介质和认同路径》，《现代传播》2019年第3期，第38—42页。

不同国家民众间的轶事是当事人所在国家之间的宝贵历史遗产，是一种饱含精神价值的国际社会资本。不同国家之间的人员往来轶事因为时间的积累，将不断聚集增多，再经由媒体和政府这样的个体与集体行动者的开发，会逐步显现出当代价值。由轶事而生成的国际社会在首脑外交的作用下合流，资本将实现最优化配置，并实现价值最大化。

　　我们清醒地认识到，本文的研究还有待进一步拓展。本文所研究的民众亲历事件还有所限定，应该包括更大范围内的轶事。不仅如此，还需要进一步挖掘"故事外交"的主体和客体内容，从体系的角度去探讨"故事外交"的作用机制，分析轶事通过何种途径，经过哪些步骤，逐步由非物质性转化为物质性国际社会资本，并通过何种方式实现资源配置最优化，实现其最大价值。这样的探索有利于进一步丰富人文交流对国际关系的作用机理，厘清人文交流在国际关系中的理论和现实价值。

应用研究

金砖国家人文交流机制的经验与完善

王　蔚[*]　汪骏良[**]

摘　要：2018年7月25—27日，金砖国家领导人第十次会晤在南非约翰内斯堡成功举行，并发布《约翰内斯堡宣言》。金砖国家领导人峰会已经走过十年的历程，开始迈入新的金色十年。在目前复杂多变的国际环境中，作为新兴市场国家代表的金砖五国能够维持并不断加强这一多边合作机制，对于维护世界的多极化和多边主义是非常重要的。经过十年的发展，金砖国家合作已经由最初的经济领域逐步扩展和深入，形成政治安全、经济金融和人文交流三大支柱。其中，人文交流虽然起步较晚，但发展迅速，领导人峰会宣言中人文交流内容的比重不断增加，而且相关领域部长级会议的召开已成惯例。金砖国家人文交流的特点也日益明晰：基本价值认同是人文交流的基础；人文交流的覆盖领域不断扩大；交流形式逐渐成建制。在取得发展成果的同时，我们也应当看到金砖国家在人文交流方面尚有短板：成员国参与人文交流的程度还不够均衡；民间力量在人文

---

[*] 王蔚，教授，博士生导师，国际关系法学博士，中国—上海合作组织国际司法交流合作培训基地管委会副主任，上海政法学院"一带一路"安全研究院院长。
[**] 汪骏良，法学硕士，上海工商外国语职业学院教师。

交流中的作用尚不突出等。为此，要继续重视和发挥人文交流的纽带作用；突出人文交流的重点并形成品牌；利用互联网技术的优势，丰富人文交流的形式；继续夯实人文交流的语言和国情认知基础，完善人文交流的保障机制，使得人文交流在金砖国家合作的下一个金色十年发挥更加重要的作用。

关键词： 金砖国家；人文交流机制；经验

一、人文交流已经成为金砖国家合作的支柱之一

2018年7月25—27日，金砖国家领导人第十次会晤在南非举行，开启了新的金色十年。"金砖国家"这一最早用于特指世界新兴市场的概念，经过十年的发展，已经成为新兴市场国家相互沟通、交流与合作的重要国际机制。合作各方由最初的四国增加到五国；各国之间沟通、交流与合作的领域也从经济、贸易领域逐步拓展到政治安全、人文交流等领域，使得金砖国家之间合作交流的议题不断增多，合作交流的范围日益广泛，合作交流的程度越发深入。在不断的发展与实践中，金砖国家之间已经形成政治安全、经济金融和人文交流三大合作支柱。

相较于政治安全和经济金融领域的合作交流，人文交流领域的合作在金砖国家合作交流机制中处于后发的位置。一方面，后发就意味着存在短板，需要五国共同努力来补齐。学者总结了短板的两大表现形式：一是各国民众对其他国家文化在认识和了解上存在"赤字"；二是五国文化"软实力"在国际范围内并不强，与经济等"硬实力"在世界范围所处的位置不匹配。另一方面，后发更意味着具备实现加速发展和"弯道超车"的条件与可能。应该清楚地认识到，金砖国家人文交流的后发位置是具有一定合理性的：第一，与该机制建立伊始的目的和当时主要解决的问题有关。如前文所述，金砖国家最早是一个经济学概念，后发展为国际合作的平台也主要是为了解决逐步崛起的新兴市场国家共同面临的经济、金融、安全等问题，加之2009年的首次领导人会晤是在国际金融危机的大背景下举行的，经济领域的交流合作也就不可避免地成为主要议题。第二，符合国际合作中经济交流与人文交流的互动关系：经济贸易的交流合作成果是人

文交流合作的基础与基石，人文交流合作可以更加深化经济贸易交流合作的成果。

其实，中国早在2009年参加首次金砖国家领导人叶卡捷琳堡会晤时就明确提出把推进人文交流作为金砖国家下一步合作的重要议题。时任国家主席胡锦涛在会晤时的讲话中指出："我们四国历史文化悠久，人文底蕴深厚，人民友谊源远流长。我们应该积极拓展文化、教育、卫生、旅游、体育等领域交流合作，促进人民相互了解，推动各界成为好朋友、好伙伴，为深化全方位合作打下坚实社会基础。"[①] 随着金砖国家合作的全面铺开和深入，以及经济、政治、社会和文化领域的相互交织，各种关于人文交流的倡议和计划频频成为金砖国家合作的重要组成部分并取得丰硕的成果，这些均从金砖国家历次领导人会晤后的宣言文件以及金砖国家人文交流涉及领域部长级会议的召开情况中得到体现（详见表4—1和表4—2）。

表4—1 历次金砖国家领导人会晤后宣言文件中涉及的人文交流领域

年份	宣言文件名称	涉及人文交流领域 （括号内为宣言文件中的序号）
2009年	《"金砖四国"领导人俄罗斯叶卡捷琳堡会晤联合声明》	科技与教育（11）
2010年	《2010年金砖国家领导人第二次会晤联合声明》	智库、科技、文化、体育（25、27、28、29）
2011年	《三亚宣言》	青年、公共卫生、科技和创新（24、28）
2012年	《德里宣言》	公共卫生、科技、青年、教育、文化、旅游、体育（42、43、48）
2013年	《德班宣言》	互联网、卫生、智库（34、41、42）
2014年	《福塔莱萨宣言》	教育、智库、科技创新（56、59、66、67）
2015年	《乌法宣言》	旅游、卫生健康、科技创新、教育、智库与学术、青年（56、60、62、63、64、73、74）

---

① 胡锦涛：《在"金砖四国"领导人会晤时的讲话（2009年6月16日，俄罗斯叶卡捷琳堡）》，中国新闻网，http://www.chinanews.com/gn/news/2009/06-17/1736908.shtml，2018年8月4日最后访问。

续表

年份	宣言文件名称	涉及人文交流领域（括号内为宣言文件中的序号）
2016年	《果阿宣言》	智库、卫生健康、教育、妇女、科技、青年、旅游、电影、体育（45、71、72、73、74、77、78、79、80、94、95、99、103）
2017年	《厦门宣言》	教育、科技、体育、卫生、媒体机构、图书馆、博物馆、美术馆、戏剧、智库、青年、民间社会组织（6、60、61、62、63、64、65、66）
2018年	《约翰内斯堡宣言》	体育、青年、电影、文化、教育和旅游、卫生、智库与学术、社会组织（5、86、87、90、91、92、93、94、95、96、97、98）

资料来源：http://www.Xinhuanet.com/world/2016-10/17/c-111877552.htm；http://www.mod.gov.cn/topnews/2017-09/04/contert/4790820.htm；http://www.Xinhuanet.com/2018-07/27/c-1123182948.htm。

表4—2 金砖国家人文交流涉及领域部长级会议召开情况统计

会议名称	召开时间	召开地点	主要成果
文化部长会议	2015年	俄罗斯莫斯科	磋商《金砖国家政府文化合作协定》
	2017年	中国天津	签署《落实〈金砖国家政府间文化合作协定〉行动计划（2017—2021年）》
教育部长会议	2013年	法国巴黎	建立金砖国家—联合国教科文组织工作组；建议建立五国间长效合作机制；推动学历互认，共享教育信息，加强各层次教育交流，重点加强高等教育和职业教育的合作；将双边务实合作扩展到五国；建立五国与教科文合作机制，共同推动全球教育议程，开发教育质量标准和评价工具等
	2014年	巴西巴西利亚	
	2015年	俄罗斯莫斯科	签署《第三届金砖国家教育部长会议莫斯科宣言》和《关于建立金砖国家网络大学的谅解备忘录》
	2016年	印度新德里	发表《新德里教育宣言》
	2017年	中国北京	以"金砖国家教育合作：促进卓越和公平"为会议主题；通过《第五届金砖国家教育部长会议北京教育宣言》等成果文件

续表

会议名称	召开时间	召开地点	主要成果
卫生部长会议	2011 年	中国北京	《首次金砖国家卫生部长会议北京宣言》发表
	2013 年 1 月	印度新德里	发表《德里公报》
	2013 年 11 月	南非开普敦	发表《开普敦公报》
	2014 年	巴西巴西利亚	发表"联合公报"
	2015 年	俄罗斯莫斯科	发表《俄罗斯宣言》
	2016 年	印度新德里	发表《德里宣言》
	2017 年	中国天津	发表《天津公报》
科技创新部长会议	2014 年	南非开普敦	会议主题：通过科技创新领域的战略伙伴关系推动公平增长和可持续发展； 发表《德班宣言》
	2015 年 3 月	巴西巴西利亚	发表《巴西利亚宣言》； 签署《金砖国家政府间科技创新合作谅解备忘录》
	2015 年 10 月	俄罗斯莫斯科	主要议题：制定金砖国家研究和创新倡议及金砖国家科技创新工作计划等； 发表《莫斯科宣言》； 通过了《金砖国家 2015—2018 工作计划》
	2016 年	印度斋普尔	发表《斋普尔宣言》
	2017 年	中国杭州	会议主题：创新引领，深化合作； 发表《杭州宣言》《金砖国家创新合作行动计划》和《金砖国家 2017—2018 年科技创新工作计划》
旅游部长会议	2016 年	印度卡久拉霍	

资料来源：www.brics.utoronto.ca。

除了在领导人会晤和部长级会议中讨论并确定有关人文交流的内容和计划外，更重要的是要充分落实与执行这些会议决定和计划。因此，金砖国家电影节、国家文化节、国家青年论坛、国家工会论坛、青年科学家论坛、青年论坛、青年外交官论坛、国家展览组织研讨会、政党智库和民间社会组织"三合一"论坛、国家运动会、图书馆联盟、博物馆联盟、美术馆联盟、青少年儿童戏剧联盟、大学联盟等接地气、惠民生的实践活动纷纷落地,让金砖国家的人民切实感受到金砖国家人文交流的成果,进一步拉近了各国之间的距离。

二、金砖国家人文交流的特点与经验

金砖国家之间人文交流在取得丰硕成果的同时,也形成自己的特点,可以总结为以下三个方面:[①]

(一)基本价值认同是人文交流的基础

金砖五国遍布亚洲、南美洲、欧洲和非洲,各国都拥有自己的历史文化传统,彼此之间存在着差异:"中国,就像其他东亚国家一样,近似于明确的集体主义倾向的道路是其主要特点。印度和俄罗斯文明的特点是一种中间道路——粗放式发展,但是远非纯粹的集体主义或个人主义倾向。因此,如果说印度的道路已相当明确的话,那么俄罗斯的特点就是曲折式发展,尤其是在20世纪:十月革命后尝试走集体主义道路,而苏联解体后则是个人主义道路。"[②]

但是,金砖国家相互认同、尊重各自国家的文化特征和历史传统,并且在此基础上确认各国都认可的基本价值,即"开放、包容、合作、共

[①] 原文化部对外联络局局长谢金英在2017年金砖国家厦门峰会期间的新闻发布会上概括了金砖国家人文交流的特点:其一,金砖国家有基本价值认同。开放、包容、平等、合作、共赢、尊重文化多样性是金砖国家展现的文化和价值共识,这种内在联系为金砖国家携手谋求经济增长、完善全球治理提供了精神动力。其二,金砖国家一致认同文化对社会可持续发展有重要意义,认为文化交流合作将成为经济和社会发展的新动力,为彼此创造一个更加繁荣安全的社会,在全球范围树立一个平等而富有创造性的伙伴关系。这也正契合厦门会晤"深化金砖伙伴关系,开辟更加光明未来"的主题。其三,在五国领导人高度重视和各界积极推动下,金砖国家文化交流与合作不断取得实质性进展,为增进金砖国家人民之间相互理解和友谊,夯实民意基础发挥了重要作用。谢金英:《人文交流作为金砖国家合作三大支柱之一》,http://news.china.com/internationalgd/10000166/20170903/31269856.html,2018年5月5日最后访问。

[②] [俄]谢·卢涅夫,刘锟译:《金砖国家的合作潜力与文化文明因素》,《俄罗斯文艺》2014年第4期,第138页。

赢"的金砖精神。这些基本价值不仅来自五国的文化历史传统，也是当今世界国际合作中需要遵循和认可的价值与准则。正是因为有了对这些基本价值的认可，金砖国家之间才有了不断深入的合作与交流。此外，金砖国家还将这些基本价值作为处理国际和地区问题的准则，如历次领导人会晤后的宣言文件中多次重申对联合国和《联合国宪章》的尊重与支持，对多边主义的维护，对可持续发展的努力，对建立更加公平、公正、平等的国际秩序的推动等。

（二）人文交流覆盖领域越来越广

从上文的表4—1中可以看到，经过近十年的发展，金砖国家人文交流所涵盖的领域越来越广泛：从最初的科技、教育、卫生等领域逐步拓展到旅游、智库、社会组织、青年、互联网、体育、媒体、影视等领域，并且各领域之间的融合与共同交流越来越深，如青年科学家的交流论坛，以及政党、智库和民间社会组织的"三合一"论坛等。

金砖国家人文交流覆盖的领域之所以越来越广，首先和人文交流的目的相关。正如2018年《约翰内斯堡宣言》中所说，"我们强调金砖合作应该将人民置于中心地位"，人文交流的目的在于增进五国人民之间的了解和认识，吸引更多的人参与金砖合作，为金砖合作注入强大的动力。人文交流覆盖的领域逐渐增多，既是它自身不断发展的结果，也是为了满足人民多样化的需求。在全球一体化进程中，人们渴望了解和认识"外面的世界"，国家和政府的交流机制为人们参与全球一体化的进程提供了有效的载体和良好的基础。大多数中国人由于语言、地理和文化等方面的原因，对印度、巴西、南非等国还比较陌生，通过金砖国家人文领域之间"走出去"和"引进来"的交流方式，更多人的可以了解和认识这些国家，直观地感受这些国家的风土人情和文化传统。

其次，和人文交流的广泛性特点相关。与政治安全、经济金融两大支柱相比，"人文"本身就是一个外延较大甚至有些不确定的概念。因此，它所能涵盖的范围很广，除了美术、音乐、影视、语言等，教育、青年、卫生、体育、旅游、智库、民俗等内容也被囊括在"人文"的范畴之中。可以说，"人文交流"成为金砖国家交流内容的"兜底条款"，凡是不属于政治安全和经济金融领域的交流内容，都可以归入"人文交流"的范畴，这也使得国家之间的交流与合作不会因概念或文字表达的约束而受到限制，为金砖国家未来合作交流领域的不断扩大提供了空间和潜能。

第三，和人文交流与人民的密切联系相关。正是由于"人文"涵盖的范围较广，它与普通民众的关系也就更为密切。各个国家的普通民众对人文领域的交流合作需求更多、更明显，也能更直接和方便地感受到人文领域交流合作的成果。其中，旅游是增进了解的最直接方式，金砖国家公民相互赴对方国家旅游已经成为人文交流合作中的新亮点。全球民宿预订平台爱彼迎（Airbnb）于2017年8月31日发布的金砖国家报告显示，自2008年以来，来自金砖国家的410万游客通过该平台到其他金砖国家出行，目的地包括400多个金砖国家城市。开普敦、圣彼得堡、莫斯科、里约热内卢、约翰内斯堡、上海和北京是最热门的金砖国家游客前往目的地。[1]而据原国家旅游局的数据显示，2017年中国旅游业对GDP的综合贡献为9.13万亿元，占GDP总量的11.04%。[2]民众旅游需求的不断增强，也对各国的旅游政策产生了影响，如南非已经在酝酿放宽对来自中国的游客的签证限制。教育上的交流与合作方式也日益丰富，如接收来自其他金砖国家的留学生、建立金砖国家大学联盟、相互承认学历、在其他金砖国家设立分校等。对中国来说，在金砖国家设立孔子学院不仅是实现教育交流合作的重要方式，更是提升中国文化传播力的重要载体："全球每百所孔子学院中，就有6.6个分布在金砖国家，其中，巴西是设立孔子学院和孔子课堂最多的拉美国家，10所孔子学院和4个孔子课堂覆盖2万名学员，当地很多中小学也开始将汉语列入正式课程。"[3]而在功能上，孔子学院也不再局限于汉语的教学和传授，而发展为"综合性中外文化交流的平台"。以南非的德班理工大学孔子学院为例，其不仅开设汉语教学班，为

---

[1]《民宿共享平台报告：金砖国家旅客互访增长134%》，http://travel.people.com.cn/nl/2017/0831/c41570-29507980.html，2018年5月27日最后访问。

[2]《2017年全国旅游业对GDP的综合贡献为9.13万亿元》，http://www.ce.cn/xwzx/gnsz/gdxw/201802/06/t20180206_28087540.shtml，2018年8月5日最后访问。

[3]《［数字金砖］人文大交流 民相亲心相通》，http://news.sina.com.cn/o/2017-08-31/doc-ifykpzey3274922.shtml，2018年5月5日最后访问。

本校学生和校外中国爱好者提供汉语教学，还积极开展各类文化交流活动，并且创造性地把中国文化纳入当地的文化艺术遗产月活动中，累计已有5万多人次参与了这些交流活动。而在2017年厦门举行的金砖五国文化节中，有30多场国内外顶级艺术家的演出免费向公众开放，为中国人民提供了感受其他国家丰富文化的机会。此外，金砖国家在电影上的合作也日益成熟，合拍的首部影片《时间去哪儿了》已于2017年公映，第二部影片《半边天》也拍摄完成。2017年，中国引进的印度电影《摔跤吧！爸爸》获得接近13亿的票房和超高的口碑，习近平主席在当年上合组织阿斯塔纳峰会上也向印度总理莫迪表达了对该电影的喜爱。

（三）人文交流的方式逐步建制化

金砖国家的合作机制经过十年的发展，正在经历一个重要的转型："从一个'侧重经济治理、务虚为主'的'对话论坛'（dialogue forum）向'政治经济治理并重、务虚和务实相结合'的'全方位协调机制'（full-fledged mechanism）转型。"[①] 换言之，金砖国家的合作交流越来越注重合作的"落地"与"实施"，即能够给各国及人民以实实在在的利益与感受。受到合作机制转型的影响，诸多"接地气、惠民生"的人文交流活动也从零星举办到逐渐固定下来，成为人文交流领域的"规定动作"。正是在建制化的基础上，各方才能进一步挖掘人文交流活动的深度，让更多的金砖故事伴随着这些固定的人文交流活动得以流传，发挥人文交流的纽带作用。目前已经成建制化的人文交流活动除了表4—2中所汇总的不同领域的部长级会议外，还有：创办于2016年的金砖国家电影节已经分别在印度、中国和南非连续举办了三届；创办于2017年的金砖国家运动会已经分别在中国广州和南非约翰内斯堡举办了两届；金砖国家青年科学家论坛已经成功举办了三届；金砖国家学术论坛也已经举办了十次等。

此外，金砖国家双边之间还形成以"国家年（月）"为形式的人文交流机制。以中国为例，其和其余四国均以上述形式举办过各类双边人文交流活动：中俄两国分别举办了"2006中国'俄罗斯年'"和"2007俄罗

---

① 朱杰进：《金砖国家合作机制的转型》，《国际观察》2014年第7期，第59页。

斯'中国年'"主题活动，通过互办"主题年"活动，实现两国在文化、政治、经济、军事等各领域的有效沟通，增进中俄的互信。中国和印度把2014年共同确定为"中印友好交流年"，其间举办了各类活动，促进了两国在文化领域的更深层次的交往。2013年中国和巴西也相互举办了"文化月"活动，巴西的音乐、舞蹈、文学等在中国"巴西文化月"期间得到充分展示，使得中国民众近距离地感受到桑巴国家的热情。而在巴西"中国文化月"活动中，中国的民乐、杂技、舞蹈等东方文化也在巴西得到充分展现和传播，并受到当地民众的追捧。中国和南非互办"国家年"的共识也分别在2014年和2015年得到落实，并取得良好的成效。

当然，金砖国家的人文交流还存在需要进一步完善与改进的地方，具体体现在以下几个方面：

第一，金砖国家成员国参与程度尚不均衡，这其实与各国关注的人文交流领域的重点不同有关。目前，一些人文交流的活动是伴随着一年一度的领导人峰会举行的，因此领导人峰会的主办国在人文交流活动的内容设置、参与程度、宣传力度等方面的投入较大，而其他参会的国家却未必对主办国专门设置的人文交流议题和内容感兴趣，因此在投入的程度方面会有所差异。比如，"印度在2016年轮值主席国期间首次组织了金砖国家女议员论坛大会，而在参加会议的42名女议员代表中，仅有2名代表来自中国，3名代表来自俄罗斯"。[1] 因此，如何兼顾各国在人文领域的不同侧重和五国在人文交流方面的普遍共识，达到既求同又存异的目标，是一个非常重要的问题。

第二，金砖国家人文交流的影响力仍需进一步加强。如前文所述，金砖国家的人文交流成果是各国普通民众感受最为直接，也是需求最为直接的领域，虽然在五国的共同努力下，金砖国家之间的人文交流已经取得显著的成效，但与诸如美国文化对其他国家的影响程度相比，影响力尚有欠缺。其一，人文交流的影响程度与经济实力有较大的关系。国家经济实力不断增强，一方面可为本国文化的"走出去"提供保障和支持；另一方

---

[1] 蒲公英：《金砖国家人文交流合作机制分析》，《俄罗斯东欧中亚研究》2017年第4期，第54页。

面，也能够在一定程度上提升本国文化的影响力。在金砖五国中，中国基于目前的经济体量和经济实力，在文化的影响力上也强于其他国家。因此，金砖国家交流的三大支柱之间是相互影响的，而经济金融处于基础性地位，要通过合作不断夯实这一基础。其二，要特别注重金砖五国民间的人文交流。应该看到的是，金砖五国的诸多人文交流活动都带有明显的政府或官方色彩，这在人文交流的伊始是非常重要的，只有通过各国政府之间的合作或者得到各国政府的支持，人文交流才能够在较短时间内形成一定的影响力，并且获得更多的支持。但是，人文领域的交流是一个"润物细无声"的过程，随着交流的不断深入，仅仅依靠政府主导的活动是不够的，因此要充分发挥五国民间组织的力量，使得金砖国家的人文交流活动更加丰富和多样，并同政府主导的交流活动形成良性的互动关系，共同构成金砖国家人文交流的机制。

三、完善金砖国家人文交流机制的建议

金砖国家人文交流机制需要从以下几方面做出进一步改善。第一，高度重视并不断增强人文交流在金砖国家合作中的纽带作用。人文交流之所以能在金砖国家合作交流中发挥重要的纽带作用，一是因为它覆盖面广，能够拓展更多新的合作交流领域；它与普通民众关系最为密切，能够吸引不同阶层和群体的人们参与到金砖国家合作的大潮中，尤其是其支持民间力量在金砖国家合作中发挥作用，可增加五国人文领域沟通交流的频率。二是因为它具有柔性，更容易被五国民众所接受，进而达成共识。在政治安全、经济金融领域，五国之间除了共同遵循的政治价值和经济规律认同以外，还存在诸多政治与经济上的分歧，这些分歧并不容易在短期内消弭。而在人文领域，各国更容易达成一致，比如都追求艺术上的"美"、高质量的教育水平、更深入的学术交流等。针对各国文化的不同，"求同存异"甚至"化异"要比消弭政治与经济领域的分歧更为容易。在人文交流领域达成更多的一致性，也更有利于促进政治互信，便利经贸合作。差异性是客观存在的，国家之间的合作就是要通过机制和制度将差异转变为互补的动力。对于金砖机制而言，更是如此。来自四大洲的五国"围绕身

份认同、目标定位、议题设置、构建制度性合作框架，以及如何处理与其他多边机制关系等问题，均存在争论和博弈。对此，应构建金砖国家间利益平衡与聚同化异的合作机制，对于不同的利益诉求，应改变既往回避矛盾的惯性思维，不再一味消极地搁置争议或'存异'，而是积极地'化异'聚同。加强沟通与协调，了解彼此诉求，照顾彼此关切，在寻求利益融合点下功夫，在解决争议方式上动脑筋，努力化解分歧"。[①]

第二，注重金砖国家人文交流的品牌打造和形式创新。打造金砖国家人文交流的品牌是对已经成建制化的人文交流活动的更高要求。品牌打造的过程是对人文交流活动进行检验的过程，要将能够体现金砖国家人文交流特点的、获得市场和五国人民好评的、能够在世界范围产生影响的活动筛选出来，检验举办活动的得失与经验，进一步完善活动的各项工作，以形成品牌。品牌打造的过程是突出人文交流活动重点的过程，目前金砖国家人文交流的重点领域并不突出，这与人文交流领域的启动较晚有关，一些已成建制化的人文交流活动也是最近两三年才举办或设立的，在成熟程度和影响力方面都有限。因而，在提升金砖国家人文交流活动影响力的基础上，五国应当根据人文交流发展的趋势和各国的共同价值选取若干突出发展的领域作为金砖国家人文交流的重点领域，进而形成品牌。

此外，金砖国家人文交流的形式也要紧跟最新发展趋势，充分发挥互联网的作用，打造更多网络线上平台，探索建立统一的门户网站和移动客户端，并且提供多种语言选择，以方便不同国家的公众浏览和使用。该网络平台集人文交流活动信息发布、人文交流成果展示、各国历史文化传统介绍、申请参与或举办人文交流活动等功能于一体，以提升人文交流的便利程度。

第三，大力夯实金砖国家人文交流的基础和保障。金砖国家人文交流要发挥更大的作用，需要进一步完善人文交流的基础和保障。其中语言是人文交流的基础，也是目前各国人文交流中的障碍。虽然"艺术是无国界的"，但是没有语言的理解和相通，人文交流的效果就会打折扣。对于中

---

① 王友明：《金砖机制建设的角色定位于利益融合》，《国际问题研究》2015年第5期，第126页。

国而言，如上文所述，建于其他金砖国家的孔子学院已经成为汉语教学和推广的重要渠道，而吸纳更多来自其他金砖国家的留学生也不失为一种有效的方法。除了中文的推广与普及以外，学习其他金砖国家的语言也是非常重要的：中俄之间的地理条件和历史渊源使得俄语在中国具有一定优势；印度和南非的语言都颇为复杂，好在英语在这两国具有较大影响，可以为中国与两国的交流提供便利；巴西距离中国较远，且官方语言为葡萄牙语，中国民众对其较为陌生，需要想办法突破这一交流瓶颈。除了语言以外，各国的基本国情也是人文交流的重要基础，相较于夯实语言基础，互联网为国情认知提供了极大的便利。

而在人文交流的保障方面，制度层面的保障显得尤为重要。金砖国家目前已经形成"元首峰会——部长级会议＋专业论坛"的合作机制，其中涉及人文交流领域的具体制度有科技部长会议、教育部长会议、卫生部长会议、文化部长会议、智库论坛等，这些制度在人文交流领域发挥着重要作用。然而，随着金砖国家人文交流在金砖国家合作交流中重要程度的日益突出，基于领域划分的制度与机制建设模式应当加以调整，需要建立覆盖广泛领域、突出重点领域和品牌的人文交流保障制度，从更高层次通盘考虑和规划金砖国家的人文交流工作，使得各领域之间相互渗透与融合，由此增强人文交流的效果。

金砖国家人文交流质量保障体系构建

孙宜学*

摘 要：推动构建人文交流质量保障体系是确保金砖国家人文交流质量和实效的重要环节。金砖国家人文交流质量保障体系应以文化和谐共生为原则，在协商成立统一的人文交流机制协调管理机构，完善人文交流风险评估体系，建立跟踪监测机制等基础上开展制度化运行，从而推动形成具有世界影响力的"金砖文化"和"金砖智慧"。

关键词：金砖国家；人文交流；质量保障体系

金砖国家从概念建立到如今形成一种富有潜力和引领作用的国际合作新模式，有赖于金砖各国理智构建科学合作模式并合力推动各方利益实现互补互助，由此，金砖国家合作领域才从经济到政治、人文、科技、外交、安全，行稳且远，由蛹变蝶，从土成陶，成为名副其实的"金砖机制"，这不仅意味着世界新兴经济体国家可以引领世界经济合作新方向，而且可以发展成世界不同政体合作共赢的典范，并且能在改变世界经济结构的过程中有效地改善世界政治和文化结构，使世界命运共同体肌体康

---

* 孙宜学，同济大学国际文化交流学院副院长、教授、博士生导师。

健、血脉通畅、生机盎然。

2018年7月26日，习近平主席在金砖国家领导人约翰内斯堡会晤大范围会议上指出："金砖五国孕育出各自灿烂文明，彼此交相辉映，人文交流合作大有可为。"在金砖合作的第二个"金色十年"，怀抱着相似梦想的金砖五国人民将把"民心相通"做成一篇大文章，这篇文章的各小节分别是治国理政、电影、媒体、智库、青年、议会、教育、体育和旅游……并且不封顶，不收尾，永远在路上，永远在开放，使金砖五国的合作发展不仅着眼于金砖各国的未来，携手走向世界发展的前沿，而且服务于世界的未来，在国际舞台上发挥更加积极主动的引领作用。

事实已经证明，金砖国家要进一步团结合作，深化战略伙伴关系，行稳致远，就必须实现金砖国家之间的和谐相通，而在这之中，人文交流是起点，也是最终目标。人文交流作为金砖国家合作的重要支撑，其功能已得到金砖各国的普遍认同。近年来，五国围绕人文合作与交流相继举办了金砖国家文化部长会议，出台了《金砖国家政府间文化合作协定》《落实〈金砖国家政府间文化合作协定〉行动计划（2017—2021年）》《金砖国家加强媒体合作行动计划》《金砖国家电影人才交流培养计划》等一系列文件，金砖五国人文合作领域不断扩大，平台不断拓展，政治、经济、人文共同构成金砖合作的"三驾马车"，形成五国社会各界广泛参与的合作盛景，使金砖理念在五国国民心中不但扎下了根，而且扎得越来越深。

一、人文交流质量保障体系建设是时势所需

事实上，随着金砖国家人文合作的多元化和日趋成熟，"金砖模式"也暴露出很多问题，如随意性强、实效性弱、缺乏统一协调机制、普及化不够等。同时，"金砖模式"也受到越来越多的质疑，"金砖褪色论""金砖分化论""蜜月终结论"成为西方媒体主调。

为了保证金砖国家人文交流的效果，金砖国家必须基于推动人类命运共同体的总体规划和目标，在充分了解世界各国文化生态系统基础上，科学确定人文交流的内涵，梳理融入路径，创新传播方法，做到精准传播、精诚传播、协作传播、求同存异、有的放矢，最终构建出一个以解决现实

问题为动因，以各国文化和谐共存为目标，以相互理解和尊重为原则的金砖国家人文交流多元运行机制。

"金砖银砖都得先制砖，政府民间都要聚焦点。"筑牢金砖国家合作民意基础的"砖"是人文，人文之"砖"是各国多元合作的因，也是未来合作结出的"金砖"。要使这块"金砖"通用，适用于五国不同的土壤，"金砖"的颜色、尺寸、厚薄就要形成统一的标准。当然，标准不能只有一种，而要根据五国不同人文地理环境下的建筑特色、审美文化需求形成不同的标准，但所有标准都要追求质量第一原则，且由金砖国家共同商定、监理并督察实施，并在时机成熟时科学确立统一质量标准体系，同时协商确立可以制度化推动执行的统一的人文交流质量保障体系，从而保证人文交流的质量和实效。

二、质量保障体系应以文化和谐共生为原则

文化是血液。不论是个体还是民族，要持续保持活力，只有不断汲取外来营养，接受新的造血元素，才能使血液始终充满新鲜的元素，为肌体提供持续的生命动力。

文化交流，就犹如两个独立肌体之间输血，输出者必须明确对象并确保血型匹配，输出的对象——接受者必须为输出者提供合适的渠道，并且保证在接受到适量的输血后能借以再造自身生命延续所需的新血。换言之，任何文化，若要在异域文化环境下生存与发展，必然首先在异域获得生存的土壤和发展的空间，依托所在国本土的政治、人文、社会、生活等资源，以"传"本民族文化之血，"引"异域肌体再造包含本民族文化元素之血，并在时机成熟时促进新血倒流，反哺本民族文化母体，使母体生命成为世界共有之生命载体，然后用新的世界之血反哺世界，从而实现本民族文化与其他民族文化之间输血→造血→再输血的循环。这也是世界各国文化创造性转化、创造性发展的循环，是中外文化交流的最高阶段和最高境界，是各民族文化在交流中获得世界价值和永恒价值的根基。因为只有实现了这种循环，本民族文化才能真正与其他国家的世界观、与全世界的多元文化实现共生。

金砖国家人文交流机制涉及的国家多，文化也多元。因此，金砖五国应联合调研不同国家文化的构成，具体分析不同国家的国情舆情现状，据以确立具有明确针对性的相互交流策略和路径，推动各国文化实现有效融合、和谐共存，使金砖五国不但能分享彼此经济发展的红利，而且能基于互利共生原则，推动互信合作，深度融合，共享和平，共同发展，和谐发展，从而保证金砖人文交流机制在各国顺利落地、扎根，进而获得可持续发展。

"兵马未动，粮草先行。"要保证金砖国家人文交流的质量，最基础也最关键的工作是尽快为各国人文交流和谐进展提供行之有效的政策支持和"后勤保障"，建立符合实际的综合质量保障体系。质量保障体系应以最具针对性、最重实效性的宏观决策为基础，以不同文化的丰富内涵应对世界各国文化的复杂形态，以传播方法的多元应对各国文化结构的多元，以不断创新的新技术应对各国不断增加的新需求，以真诚的态度赢得各国真诚的尊重，以良善之心应对万变之势，以自省的心胸容纳各色异见，以积极的行动应对消极的怀疑……同时，基于互信互认原则，合力协调相关力量进行系统整体研究，从内容、方法、目标等方面集中规划，以保证五国的人文交流实践服务于统一话语体系、统一发展道路、统一实施目标、统一评估标准，最终形成具有金砖国家特色的人文交流话语体系，推动金砖国家人文交流合作以多元文化和谐共生为原则，推动优化各自的生存空间，实现更合理的资源分配，进而推动实现世界不同文化之间的互利共生。

三、质量保障体系制度化运行的关键

金砖国家的人文交流要推进不同文化和谐共生，首先就要求各个国家发自内心地认识到"和而不同""求同存异"是五国之间坦诚合作、共同可持续发展的前提。为了保证这一共生生态的健康持续，人文交流质量保障体系首先应完善几个关键基础。

（一）协商成立统一的人文交流机制协调管理结构

目前，金砖国家各自建有专门宣传和传播本国文化的官方机构与有官方背景的民间机构，负责本国文化的传承和国际传播，并且基于自身需要，多采取趋利性的传播政策，使人文交流粘附着强烈的功利色彩。

金砖合作具有巨大的潜力，可能会再造五国崭新的未来，而中国作为有世界担当的大国，则有责任通过金砖合作再造一个世界，成为名副其实的领导型大国。目前，金砖各国对待外来文化的态度各不相同，立法也不健全，统一协调的难度很大。但金砖各国可以秉持文化平等原则，以各国已有国际人文交流机构为基础，通过平等协商，成立推动各国文化之间平等交流的统一协调管理结构，为实现各国文化平等和平交流服务。这一机构可遵照自愿加入、权利平等、互惠互利原则，通过协调平衡不同文化之间的矛盾冲突，共同决定各国文化国际传播的内容和方式，指导各国分别承担机构统一安排的文化传承与传播工作并行监督之责。

（二）完善人文交流风险评估体系

金砖五国之间的人文交流虽然秉持平等合作、互利共生原则，但事实上不可能做到绝对平衡。一方面，人文交流意味着文化之间一定要产生接触，接触就可能发生碰撞甚至冲突，最重要的是，一国文化必须依托于异国社会环境才能获得生存和发展，传播者和传播对象之间没有绝对的利益平衡。另一方面，从交流双方的动机来说，一般是传播者更主动，所以获益通常较大；而传播对象一般相对被动，更趋于静态防守，获益较少。在人文交流过程中，平衡是暂时的，冲突是永恒的，这是人文交流的自然状态，若不经过这个过程，传播行为就不可能完成，交流目的也不会实现。

每种文化皆具有扩张性生存本能，都希望占据越来越大的生存空间，获取越来越多的资源，以实现自身的进一步繁衍发展。传播者和传播对象对此都必须有清醒的认识。金砖五国首先要认识到人文交流中的这种不平衡现象属正常现象，并能科学理解、客观认同这种人文交流机制的形成过程，这对于构建金砖五国人文交流共生机制具有决定性意义。

目前，世界各国对待外来文化一般采取防御策略，对外来文化在本国的传播一般会进行官方或民间的风险评估，以保证自身文化的安全，甚至将之上升到国家安全的层面。这是常态，也属常理，金砖各国不但不应回避或反对，而且要主动配合，或直接参与所在国的人文交流风险评估，双方或多方应联合制定人文交流的顺序和步骤，共同协调传播的节奏。经过风险评估后的文化将会由所在国主动引入，并且得到所在国的充分尊重，传播质量也更易得到保证。

金砖五国的人文交流风险评估是一个科学完善的体系，即基于具体问题、文化差异、互惠互利原则，设计评估标准，得出科学结论，确定评估等级。这种风险评价体系可以保护所在国的价值观生态系统不会受到传播者的强势攻击，也能在较大程度上避免一些危害所在国生态系统的价值观被引进。

（三）建立跟踪监测机制以保证人文交流效果

人文交流是一个动态的持续过程，总是时时处于发展变化之中，如果不进行跟踪监测，就无法掌握其中的变化及原因，也就无法及时做出调整，以保证交流的节奏和质量。

建立人文交流跟踪监测制度不但可使金砖国家之间的人文交流更科学、合理、有序、有效，还会促使彼此认识到他国文化在本国的传播处于双方可控范围内，不会对本国的文化生态安全、国家安全造成威胁，从而更加主动地配合外来文化在本国的交流与传播。

（四）科学设定人文交流风险评估指标

要想保证人文交流风险评估的准确性和科学性，就应建立相应的风险评估指标体系。风险评估指标的确立应基于对所在国的"生理机制"、繁殖和传播能力、亲缘关系等各种信息的全面掌握，发挥一切相关部门的积极能动作用，应对人文交流泛在共生的"无所不在性"，据此确定金砖各国文化、价值观之间的合作交流已经处于何种平衡状态、应该处于何种平衡状态，从而保证各国人文交流实现有序、有据、有效发展，达成和谐共生。

人文交流的效果具有不确定性、弥漫性、综合性与混合性，评估标准很难量化，也难以形成具有广泛认同性的统一评估标准。但人文交流的效果同时具有阴性和显性特征，基于人文交流效果的显性特征，可以基本判断人文交流效果的广度和深度，判断传播者与宿主之间共生关系的融合度和分离度，并据此确定人文交流的角度和深度。这是人文交流效果评估标准或指标的现实基础。具体指标可包括：

人文交流机构的数量。据此可判断两种或多种文化相互需求的度和量，也能据此了解各自人文环境的生态结构。

国际学生人数。即所在国接受的外国留学生人数，学习异域文化的所在国国民人数以及类别，学成归国人数与留在所在国的人数之比等。

所在国国民教育体系内开设其他语言与文化课程的学校、院系的数量和等级。

语言考试的普及度。针对外国人的语言考试机构的数量、类别、年考试次数等。

外文出版物的翻译量和发行量。面向所在国翻译发行的出版物的数量和类别，以及国内外译者的比例。

海外本国族裔和本民族语言学校、媒体的数量。海外族群既是本国文化的传播对象，也是传播者。海外语言学校和媒体则是海外本国文化传播的主要平台，可以打通人文交汇的障碍，培育文化多元和谐共生的人文生态环境，为金砖五国的人文交流营造更便捷的交流途径和生存环境。

海外企业、社会机构数量。通过分析本国企业在其他国家的数量和产值及本土化程度，可以判断本国文化在所在国本土的生存能力和生存现状。

金砖各国政治生态不一，经济水平差异大，地缘政治复杂多变，社会与文化机制不同，应进一步规范多边合作机制，共同应对风险，分享机遇，在实践中摸索建立、完善科学的人文交流风险评估体系，并基于具体问题、文化差异、互惠互利原则，设计评估标准，得出科学结论，确定评估等级。这种风险评价体系既能保护各国的人文生态系统不受到外来文化的强势攻击，也能在一定程度上形成统一的金砖国家人文交流风险规避机动体制。以此为基础，金砖国家可相互尊重，联合制定人文交流的顺序和步骤，共同协调交流节奏，使人文交流充满人情味。

综上，在当今世界格局越来越围绕人类命运共同体优化组合的趋势下，金砖机制必将发挥越来越积极的引领作用，人文合作的功能也会越来越受到重视。但人文交流涉及人类生活的各个方面,任务重,头绪复杂,障碍多。金砖国家作为世界人文合作交流的典范,应在相互充分了解和理解的基础上,建立具有金砖国家特色、世界价值的文化传播话语体系、运行机制、质量保障体系,从而更好地服务于新世界的新要求,共同推动各自灿烂的文化形成合力,惠泽世界,润濡世界,主导世界先进文化发展,在推动世界各国文化相互融合的过程中形成具有世界影响力的"金砖文化""金砖智慧",进而推动世界共同建设一个繁荣发展的人类命运共同体。

参考文献

1.《金砖国家领导人厦门宣言》,《人民日报》2017年9月5日。

2. 蒲公英:《金砖国家人文交流合作机制分析》,《俄罗斯东欧中亚研究》2017年第4期。

3. 张志洲:《金砖机制建设与中国的国际话语权》,《当代世界》2017年第10期。

4. 韩业庭:《以文化为媒 促合作交流——"一带一路"人文交流与合作取得新进展》,《光明日报》2017年4月14日。

5. 骆嘉:《金砖国家智库合作的现状、困境与策略》,《智库理论与实践》2018年第2期。

6. 徐秀军:《金砖国家人文交流机制建设:作用、调整及对策》,《当代世界》2018年第8期。

金砖国家高等教育合作问题与前景分析*

蒲公英**

摘　要：金砖国家作为世界人口大国和地区大国，在高等教育领域更具优势与特色。在全球化不可逆转的背景下，随着金砖国家和新兴经济体国家粗放式高增长经济阶段的逐渐结束，以人力资本驱动的经济发展阶段必将到来，金砖国家高等教育合作的重要性与必要性愈加凸显。为了充分开发和利用高等教育资源，金砖国家成员国之间已经开始尝试搭建相关合作机制，但金砖国家能否突破各自教育理念中的偏见，实现高等教育体系的相互认可，是金砖框架下推动高等教育深化合作的关键问题。与此同时，金砖国家在教育国际化优先方向上的分歧，当前以项目合作为主的趋势以及面临的经费问题，是阻碍高等教育合作机制化发展的重要因素。据此，在金砖国家框架下，中国可主动推动金砖国家高等教育合作的开展，充分发挥金砖国家的组织优势和资源禀赋，努力构建新型教育国际化合作关系，充分融合中国的市场优势和奖助学金制度，吸纳金砖各国的优秀人

---

* 本文系重庆市社科规划博士培育项目"镜鉴与启示：俄罗斯软实力外交研究"（项目批准号：2016BS062）与四川外国语大学年度科研项目青年项目"俄罗斯软实力政策及对我国的启示研究"（项目批准号：sisu201621）的研究成果。

** 蒲公英，四川外国语大学俄语系副教授，金砖国家研究院研究员。

才参与到高等教育合作当中，同时努力激活金砖国家各级教育主管机构和教育研究人员的沟通渠道，在合作项目上积极创新，为金砖国家高等教育的机制化合作创建良好基础。

关键词：金砖国家；高等教育；机制化合作

在知识经济崛起与全球化不断深化的时代，高等教育竞争力水平是一国综合国力的重要标志。在新经济时代，高等教育水平可以决定该国创新能力、产业升级和高新技术实力的分布态势，被更多的国家视为与国家竞争力直接挂钩的重要因素。当前金砖国家已由最初的一个概念逐步发展成不容世界忽视的全球新兴国家共同体，其合作成效正逐步凸显在经济、金融、政治、外交等很多领域。作为新兴经济体的"火车头"，金砖国家在世界经济发展中的突出表现引人关注，人文领域的合作也在迎头赶上。2016年10月，习近平主席在金砖国家领导人第八次会晤大范围会议上着重指明了人文交流对于金砖国家共同建设开放世界与深化伙伴关系的重要性——"要加强人文交流，促进民心相通，夯实金砖国家合作的民意基础"。作为人口大国和地区大国，金砖成员国在高等教育领域拥有庞大的教育群体、发达的体系和雄厚的资源，如何更加积极有效地推动金砖国家间的高等教育合作，将是该共同体在未来深化人文交流合作的必然选题。

一、金砖国家高等教育合作的发展现状与特点

近年来，金砖国家的高等教育合作问题逐步得到关注，金砖国家内部也开始推动建立相应的机制。金砖国家拥有丰富的高等教育资源：作为人口大国，金砖五国人口总数占世界人口总数的42%，而作为发展快速的新经济体，2017年金砖五国的GDP总量占全球GDP总量的27%。[1] 庞大的人口和充满活力的经济，是金砖国家发展高等教育的良好先决条件。从数量上看，金砖国家高等教育的入学规模与世界其他国家相比占有绝对优

---

[1] 李胜利、解德渤：《金砖国家高等教育质量比较——基于2009—2015年〈全球竞争力报告〉的分析》，《高等教育研究》2016年第10期。

势，其中中国的高等教育入学人数位居全球第一，印度高等教育入学人数位居第二。中国高等教育机构数量位居全球第二，印度高等教育机构数量位居第一。俄罗斯高等教育毛入学率为76.1%，全球排名第18位，而其他四个国家则在毛入学率上还存在很大的提升空间。

表6—1　金砖国家义务教育持续时间与2018年本科毕业生数量

	2018年本科毕业生数量（万人）	义务教育持续时间（年）
中国	820	9
俄罗斯	71.6	11
巴西	85	14
印度	650	8
南非	70	9

资料来源：笔者根据公开资料整理。

总体上看，金砖国家的高等教育各有优势：俄罗斯提供了较为完善的分类教育，高等院校在理工实验设备和创新基础设施方面，拥有大规模和成体系的优势。印度依托英联邦国家良好的高等教育传统，实施灵活的全英文授课模式，其信息工程和管理类的大学毕业生受到国际市场的青睐。中国在高等教育规模和高等教育投入方面位居世界前列，对高层次人才吸引力不断增强，人才培养的专业化设置较好。南非在依托英联邦教育资源的同时，利用其较为自由的市场经济环境，在培养商业人才方面独具优势。巴西在高等教育方面有独特的多样性设置，利用其与欧洲和北美的特殊联系，在培养精英人才方面独具优势。[1]

为了充分利用高等教育资源，金砖国家成员国之间已经开始尝试搭建相关合作机制。2013年11月，金砖国家召开首届教育部长会议。在政府间层面，从金砖国家领导人峰会发表的联合宣言来看，在2014年之前，

---

[1] 唐晓玲：《"金砖国家"高等教育竞争力研究——基于巴西、俄罗斯、印度、中国的数据比较》，《现代教育管理》2018年第9期。

金砖国家还只是把高等教育合作视为人文合作的一部分。2014年的福塔莱萨峰会和随之提出的福塔莱萨行动计划，首次将教育部门之间的合作列为长期化机制。2015年金砖国家领导人第七次会晤发表的《乌法宣言》中，首次将高等教育作为成员国之间开展合作的方向之一，并明确了高等教育合作的具体落实方向："呼吁在承认大学文凭和学位方面加强交流，要求金砖国家相关部门就学位鉴定和互认开展合作，支持建立金砖国家网络大学和大学联盟的倡议。"①

在政府领导人的推动下，外交层面以下各个轨道也开展了积极的高等教育合作：2011年，俄罗斯总统梅德韦杰夫推动金砖国家间成立金砖问题国家间研究委员会，由俄罗斯科学院和俄罗斯外交部具体负责落实推动金砖国家间科研院所的合作。② 2012年，在俄罗斯的推动下，金砖国家首脑峰会决定在俄罗斯莫斯科大学公共管理学院的基础上建立金砖国家院系间协调委员会，由莫大公管学院负责推动金砖国家高校院系之间的合作工作。2015年10月，中国推动金砖国家建立大学校长间《北京共识》，并依托北京师范大学成立金砖国家大学联盟。2015年俄罗斯在莫斯科主导建立了金砖国家网络大学。这两项机制被金砖国家首脑联合宣言评价为"促进金砖国家在高等教育领域的合作和伙伴关系"。2016年12月俄罗斯国立管理大学在莫斯科主持召开了金砖国家高校间"人工智能与数字经济"国际论坛，并签署了发展数字社会的相关协议，金砖国家高校间将开展联合研究，建立联合实验室和研究中心。

二、金砖国家高等教育合作的重要意义

（一）积累面向未来的人力资本

与其他领域不同，金砖国家高等教育合作具有典型的"发展投资"性

---

① 2016年之前金砖国家领导人峰会的历次联合宣言可见金砖国家联合体信息门户网站：http://infobrics.org/。

② М. С. Липоватая, Вопросы Сотрудничества Стран Брикс в сфере высшего образования, вестн. моск. ун_та. сер. 27. глобалистика и геополитика. 2017. No 4.

质。世界经济论坛发布的《人力资本报告》显示，在人力资本开发方面，世界各国都面临严峻的挑战，尤其是人口数量较多的金砖五国。在该报告列出的最重要的"人力资本指数"数据中，俄罗斯最高，排在第26位，中国在第64位，巴西在第78位，南非和印度已经在90位以外。[1] 显然，金砖五国庞大的人口基数并未转化成适应全球化经济发展的优势人力资本，这种人才资源与人口供给之间的结构性缺位，将构成金砖国家未来多年主要的发展挑战。

对于金砖国家来说，随着粗放式高增长经济阶段的逐渐结束，任何国家都会进入一个人力资本驱动的经济发展阶段。在这个阶段，国家内部需要进行艰难的产业结构调整与升级，而人力资本是支撑产业调整最重要的资源。[2] 与其他经济要素不同，人力资本的投入产出必须通过高等教育来实现。相关研究表明，中国增加教育和培训投入，将给中低速阶段的中国经济带来0.1个百分点的潜在增长率。[3] 国际研究也指出，低水平的人力资本无法对经济增长产生显著影响，只有通过高等教育的途径提升劳动者的受教育水平和技能积累，才能显著改善经济发展面貌。因此，发展高等教育是金砖国家为代表的新兴经济体在未来必须加强的领域。

（二）重新构筑全球化发展的基石

当前，经济结构和收入分配等方面的问题长期得不到解决，逆全球化和民粹化等反全球化的意识不断投射到发达国家的政治态势当中，进而影响欧美等国家的相关对外决策，对经济全球化构成严峻的挑战。与以往在具体政策和机制方面遭受质疑不同，当前的经济全球化遭受的最大质疑是就业问题，很多人质疑其无法给参与者带来明确的职业获得感。依靠经济

---

[1] Human Capital Report 2015: Employment, Skills and Human Capital, Global Challenge Insight Report, World Economic Forum.

[2] Aoki, M. (2012) Five Phases of Economic Development and Institutional Evolution in China, Japan and Korea, Part I, in Aoki, M., T. Kuran and G. R. Roland, eds, Institutions and Comparative Economic Development, Basingstoke: Palgrave Macmillan.

[3] Lu, Y. and F. Cai (2014) China's Shift from the Demographic Dividend to the Reform Dividend, in L. Song, R. Garnaut and F. Cai (eds), Deepening Reform for China's Long Term Growth and Development, ANU E Press, Canberra, pp. 27 - 50.

政策去解决就业问题是一项非常复杂的内外政策博弈行动，特朗普政府在该问题上的行动表明国家很难通过经济政策妥善解决就业问题，而教育是解决就业问题的一种有效途径。南非教育部长布莱德·恩齐曼德认为，教育培训可以给年轻人带来更多的机会，更好地解决失业和不平等，是金砖国家合作的"战略领域"。[1]

高等教育水平的提升，一方面依靠物质资本的投入与积累，另一方面需要不断深化的教育国际化。改革开放后，中国教育国际化的步伐与国家经济发展速度基本一致。随着2018年美国在多份战略安全报告中将中国明确列为主要战略竞争对手，美国和欧洲国家开始以防止高新技术被窃取为理由，强化了对中国留学和访学人员的审核。然而，由于2008年金融危机造成的债务问题，中国教育国际化的主要合作伙伴国——美国、英国、加拿大、新西兰和澳大利亚——近年来不约而同地大幅提升中国留学人员的学费门槛。中国的教育国际化格局亟需重构，这种现象不仅出现在中国，也深刻影响着其他金砖国家。由于教育国际化的萎缩，世界各国的青年群体开始从支持全球化逐步过渡到反感全球化。例如，美国大学生因为高昂的学费和助学贷款负担，转而对中国的负面看法不断增多。因此，加强金砖国家间的高等教育合作，有利于巩固相关国家的青年群体，并构筑全球化发展的基石。

三、金砖国家高等教育合作面临的问题与挑战

金砖国家高等教育合作尽管前景光明，但是仍面临较为复杂的问题与挑战。

（一）金砖国家围绕高等教育的共识还有待建立

笔者认为，在教育领域有必要关注国家的教育理念，如果两个国家间的教育理念无法弥合，则双边教育合作很难持久和深化。尽管金砖国家的合作机制有效地促进了五个国家间的外交关系发展，但是因为金砖五国存

---

[1] 余燕：《金砖国家教育部长：加强教育培训与合作》，《世界教育信息》2016年第3期。

在不同的教育理念,目前还很难深化彼此间的高等教育合作。

中国的高等教育理念以大众化教育为主,中华人民共和国建立以来,构筑了世界上规模最大的教育体系。中国把高等教育既视为培养人才的主要途径,也视为构建社会文明的重要手段。近年来,中国高等教育更多强调专业化教育,但是高等教育服务于大众的理念并未改变。俄罗斯的教育理念与中国较为接近,也以大众化高等教育为主,但是近年来随着教育市场化改革,其高等教育部分开始向精英教育方向转变,尤其是参与教育国际化的高等院校,已把主要工作集中在与欧美联合培养精英的方向上。

印度和南非秉承英式"精英教育"的理念,在实际的高等教育体系中造成人才培养的两极分化:高端人才可以达到国际最高水平,但是培养数量不足,远远不能满足国家发展的需求。而产业经济发展所需的中低级人才则明显供给不足,并在国内就业市场上造成大量低端劳动力失业的现象。[①] 巴西更多地学习美国的"教育自治"理念,政府在教育体系中只负责相关的政策指导,把具体的办学权利和办学监督都通过民选制度转移给民间专业人士和专业机构,这也是其学费高昂的主要原因。

在未来推进金砖国家高等教育合作方面,如何弥合教育理念方面的分歧,可能成为最大的挑战。考虑到教育对每个成员国都兼具经济发展和意识形态塑造的双重功能,金砖国家能否突破各自教育理念中的偏见,实现高等教育体系的相互认可与谅解,是金砖框架下推动高等教育深化合作的关键问题。

(二)短期内难以从"项目化"合作转向"机制化"合作

高等教育合作的最高境界是"机制化"合作,这方面的主要代表是欧盟发起的《索邦宣言》和"博洛尼亚进程"(Bologna Process)。为了推动欧盟内部的高等教育机制合作,1998年5月法国、德国、意大利和英国的教育部长率先在法国索邦大学聚会,研究如何加速推动高等教育人员流动和资历互认工作。会间,他们共同签订了一个旨在促进四国高等教育体系

[①] 高巍、黄世英、吴琼:《金砖国家教育的比较研究》,《教育教学论坛》2015年第12期。

相互协调的协议，即《索邦宣言》。《索邦宣言》的主要内容为：循序渐进地推动欧洲高等教育学位和学制总体框架的建立；建立共同的学制和学历；加强并促进师生流动；清除学术人员流动的障碍并促进学历资格的承认；要面对劳动力结构化短缺和智能化带来的失业问题。博洛尼亚进程是29个欧洲国家于1999年在意大利博洛尼亚提出的欧洲高等教育改革计划，该计划的目标是整合欧盟的高教资源，打通教育体制。博洛尼亚进程的发起者和参与国家希望，到2010年，欧洲博洛尼亚进程签约国中的任何一个国家的大学毕业生的毕业证书和成绩，都将获得其他签约国家的承认，大学毕业生可以毫无障碍地在其他欧洲国家申请学习硕士阶段的课程或者寻找就业机会，以实现欧洲高教和科技一体化，建成欧洲高等教育区，为欧洲一体化进程做出贡献。

从长远来看，金砖国家高等教育合作只有达到博洛尼亚进程的程度，才能真正实现机制化合作。但是，当前制约金砖国家实现机制化合作的条件还有很多。

一是不同教育理念带来的教育体制区别很大，金砖五国教育主管部门和教育执行机构之间还需要较长时间去熟悉对方的机制。例如，俄罗斯的研究生教育学制与其他金砖国家明显不同，要想展开学分互相承认和互换，首先需要金砖国家之间围绕俄罗斯的教学学制达成一致性意见。而印度和南非的本科教育与中国的本科教育在基础科目上存在较大差别。巴西国内高度自治的教育体制，也让其他国家对接巴西教育体系产生很多困难。

二是各国在教育国际化优先方向的选择上还存在分歧：中国希望优先展开高新技术领域的高等教育合作；俄罗斯希望其他金砖国家能够更多地利用俄罗斯较为过剩的高等教育资源；印度担忧较深地涉足金砖国家高等教育合作可能导致英美核心教育资源对自己的疏离；南非国内教育界则对中俄高等教育体系在教育平权和公平选拔机制方面隔阂较深，担心己方的黑人学生可能会遭遇种族歧视。

三是金砖各国政府当前的外交表态以鼓励"项目化"合作为主。目前，高等教育系统已深刻嵌入一国的意识形态和精英群体的塑造当中，因此各国政府对于充分开放高等教育之间的机制化合作较为忌惮。综合金砖各国和领导人联合宣言的表态，我们可以看到金砖各国政府高层都以鼓励"项目化"合作为主。中国政府鼓励开展联合学位培养和建设中外联合大学，俄罗斯政府鼓励开展联合科研项目，南非和印度政府则重点参与通识教育和技能教育方面的合作。对于金砖国家政府来说，开展"项目化"合作面对的政策阻力和国内质疑较少，而且参与者有数量限制和明确分工，可以在短时间内取得成效，给提倡合作者更多的信心。

四是高等教育经费问题尚未达成原则性意见。高等教育若想深化国际合作，金砖国家需要就经费问题形成原则性意见。当前，金砖国家之间的合作以"项目化"合作为主，所以经费问题能够通过双边渠道解决。如果在未来要实现金砖国家间的多边国际合作，则成员国需要在金砖国家框架下就经费问题达成原则性意见。考虑到当前部分成员国背负沉重的政府债务，为多边合作寻求合适的经费来源将是一个较大的挑战。

四、中国与金砖国家高等教育合作前景

中国近年来在高等教育领域取得瞩目的成就，总体竞争力水平在金砖国家中位于前列，但是中国高等教育"大而不强"的格局还将持续多年。在中美竞争态势日益凸显的背景下，主要依靠欧美合作的中国高等教育国际化道路面临巨大挑战。中国需要依托金砖国家这样的非欧美国家多边机制，推动自身的教育国际化在另一个方向发展壮大，以实现国家提升教育竞争力的战略目标。展望未来，中国可以在以下领域主动作为，推动金砖国家高等教育合作的开展。

一是充分发挥金砖国家的组织优势和资源禀赋，努力构建新型教育国际化合作关系。金砖国家在高等教育合作方面具有成员国资源禀赋不同和去中心化的组织形式等特点。在当前世界地缘竞争日趋激烈的背景下，中国应该充分发挥金砖国家的比较优势，推动新一轮教育国际化的发展。

二是将中国的市场优势与奖助学金制度充分融合，尽力吸纳金砖各国的优秀人才参与到高等教育合作当中。中国的经济实力在金砖国家当中居于领先地位，国内发达的消费市场也吸引着各国投资者和劳动者。当前中

国已经为金砖各国学生提供了数量不一的奖助学金，但是相关的奖助学金制度还未能与外国人就业制度联动，降低了相关学生来华学习和发展的意愿。中国可以考虑从顶层设计的角度，把国内人才需求与奖助学金制度结合起来，在金砖国家内部推动高等教育人才的新型来华访学留学制度，中国充分利用金砖国家高等教育发展带来的红利。

三是与金砖国家各级教育主管机构和教育研究人员充分沟通和讨论，在"人类命运共同体"理念的指引下，设法寻找各国在教育理念上的共同交集，推动金砖国家早日在教育领域发表联合宣言。中国可与金砖国家在高等教育涉及的社会治理、经济发展和人权保护方面，尝试酝酿出适合金砖国家自身情况的共同原则。

四是在合作项目上积极创新，中国可以根据每个金砖国家的具体情况，推出相应的合作项目。中国可以面向全部金砖国家开放高校中国际学生和国际教师的比例，鼓励符合资质的学院招收大量来自金砖国家的不同背景和文化的学生，国际教师不仅可在华授课，还可以开展全球性研究项目，并可在金砖国家范围内进行实证研究和联合实验。中国还可与印度、南非和巴西等较有特色的教育系统合作，在高校专业课中增加富有地区特色的内容，并引导学生多去观察和发现金砖国家之间对于不同知识的理解差别，同时更多地鼓励中国高校与俄罗斯和印度高校开展国际交换生项目，考虑到赴这两个国家的国际旅费和生活费用并不高，应该推荐更多的中国高校学生前往俄印两国进行交换学习。依托高校资源，金砖国家之间可以组织短期访学团，集中组织相关学生、老师以及相关行业的从业人员赴各金砖国家学习和访问交流。基于金砖国家框架下工商合作较为活跃的特点，中国还可以组织相关高校开展国际实习合作，赴金砖国家中的优秀企业实习，增进相互了解，并帮助学生获得更好的国际化经验。中国还可以考虑与金砖国家联合成立研究中心，并在相关国家建立海外校区。研究中心主要帮助高校的科研人员和学生更好地了解最新的学术进展，并帮助他们与当地的学术机构、校友和实业家建立关系，海外校区的建立将有利于推动中国与驻在国的双边关系，并为希望前往这些国家开展学习、交流和访问的学生与学者提供可靠的基础设施与环境。

高等教育是一个关乎金砖国家未来可持续合作的重要领域，将为金砖国家共同推动全球治理提供重要的人才保障。中国在推动本国教育重心从"知"转到"行",实现人才强国战略目标的同时,更应考虑在全球视野下不断整合与凝聚金砖国家和世界发展中国家的高等教育资源,从而为人类命运共同体的构建提供更为坚实的人才基础。

中国与金砖国家人文交流[*]

朱天祥[**] 张铭瑶[***]

摘　要： 中国是金砖国家人文交流的推动者和引领者，在促进人文交流成为金砖国家合作支柱的问题上发挥了积极且重要的作用。中国认为，金砖国家人文交流兼具可能性与可行性，应秉持平等、开放和包容的原则，深入推进在文化、教育、卫生、体育、旅游、地方等领域的合作，既重视政府引导，更注重民间参与，同时还要做到持之以恒，从而在实现文化大交流目标的基础上，达到便利金砖国家全方位合作的目的。为此，中国在金砖国家人文交流领域不断贡献中国方案和中国力量，特别是通过与俄罗斯、南非、印度建立双边高级别人文交流机制夯实金砖国家人文交流基础。在此背景下，创建中国—巴西高级别人文交流机制，实现中国与其他金砖成员的机制全覆盖，也是中国对金砖国家人文交流的重要贡献。

关键词： 金砖国家；人文交流；中国；立场；实践

习近平主席指出："中国是金砖机制的坚定支持者和参与者，把金砖

---

[*] 本文是2018年度重庆市社科规划培育项目"中国特色大国外交的'一对多'整体合作模式研究"的阶段性成果，项目编号2018PY06。
[**] 朱天祥，四川外国语大学金砖国家研究院对外关系研究所所长。
[***] 张铭瑶，四川外国语大学国际关系学院比较制度学专业硕士研究生。

国家合作作为中国外交的重要方向。"① 为此，中国在金砖国家合作伊始就积极贡献中国方案，② 并在迄今为止先后主办的两场金砖国家领导人会晤中提出具有中国特色、世界眼光、金砖情怀的诸多重要理念与务实举措。尤其是2017年厦门峰会期间，习主席提出的"平等相待、求同存异""务实创新、合作共赢""胸怀天下、立己达人"三条重要启示，为未来的金砖合作指明了方向。其中特别值得一提的是，"人文交流作为后起之秀，成为金砖中国年的一大亮点"，并在中国的力推之下发展成"金砖合作的新支柱"。③ 可以说，中国对金砖国家人文交流表现出格外的关注和重视。在此背景下，探讨中国关于金砖国家人文交流的立场，梳理中国在金砖国家人文交流领域的实践，对中国参与金砖国家人文交流的特点进行总结，具有十分重要的现实意义。

一、中国关于金砖国家人文交流的立场

尽管中国政府并没有出台一个专门的文件宣示其关于金砖国家人文交流的立场，但是中国国家领导人在历次金砖峰会上的发言仍然可以作为了解其官方政策的一个重要渠道。2009年6月16日，时任国家主席胡锦涛指出，鉴于金砖四国"历史文化悠久、人文底蕴深厚、人民友谊源远流长"，金砖国家应该"积极拓展文化、教育、卫生、旅游、体育等领域交流合作，促进人民相互了解，推动各界成为好朋友、好伙伴，为深化全方位合作打下坚实社会基础"。④ 2010年4月15日，胡主席再次指出，金砖

---

① 习近平：《坚定信心 共谋发展——在金砖国家领导人第八次会晤大范围会议上的讲话》，2016年10月16日，https://www.fmprc.gov.cn/web/gjhdq_676201/gjhdqzz_681964/jzgj_682158/zyjh_682168/t1406096.shtml。

② 2009年6月16日，时任国家主席胡锦涛在首届"金砖四国"领导人会晤时就曾建议，金砖国家可以从"增强政治互信""深化经济合作""推进人文交流""提倡经验互鉴"四个方面开展合作。参见胡锦涛：《在"金砖四国"领导人会晤时的讲话》，2009年6月16日，https://www.fmprc.gov.cn/web/gjhdq_676201/gjhdqzz_681964/jzgj_682158/zyjh_682168/t568042.shtml。

③ 参见《杨洁篪就金砖国家领导人第九次会晤和新兴市场国家与发展中国家对话会接受媒体采访》，2017年9月6日，https://www.brics2017.org/dtxw/201709/t20170906_2010.html。

④ 参见胡锦涛：《在"金砖四国"领导人会晤时的讲话》，2009年6月16日，https://www.fmprc.gov.cn/web/gjhdq_676201/gjhdqzz_681964/jzgj_682158/zyjh_682168/t568042.shtml。

四国的"政治体制、发展方式、宗教信仰、文化传统不尽相同,却能成为好朋友、好伙伴",其缘由之一即在于不同历史文明的相互借鉴、不同文化传统的相互交流。① 2011年4月14日,胡主席在倡议维护世界和平稳定时强调,金砖国家应"尊重文明多样性,在交流互鉴、取长补短中相得益彰、共同进步"。② 2012年3月29日,胡主席再次呼吁金砖国家"努力使各领域合作发挥应有作用,巩固金砖国家合作的经济、社会、民意基础"。③

2013年3月27日,习近平主席提出,"要用伙伴关系把金砖各国紧密联系起来",下大气力推进人员往来领域的合作,并朝着"文化大交流"的目标前进。④ 2014年7月15日,习主席在阐释金砖国家独特的合作伙伴精神时就将"不同文化文明互鉴"视为包容精神的重要内涵之一。⑤ 2015年7月9日,习主席提议将"构建弘扬多元文明的伙伴关系"作为加强金砖国家伙伴关系的重要方面。他指出,"金砖国家合作的成功充分证明,不同社会制度可以相互包容,不同发展模式可以相互合作,不同价值文化可以相互交流。我们要坚持开放包容,在交流互鉴中取长补短,在求同存异中共同前进"。⑥ 2016年10月16日,习主席再次强调,金砖国家要"加强人文交流,促进民心相通,夯实金砖国家合作的民意基础",以此实

---

① 参见胡锦涛:《合作 开放 互利 共赢——在"金砖四国"领导人会晤时的讲话》,2010年4月15日,https://www.fmprc.gov.cn/web/gjhdq_676201/gjhdqzz_681964/jzgj_682158/zyjh_682168/t682096.shtml。

② 参见胡锦涛:《展望未来 共享繁荣——在金砖国家领导人第三次会晤时的讲话》,2011年4月14日,https://www.fmprc.gov.cn/web/gjhdq_676201/gjhdqzz_681964/jzgj_682158/zyjh_682168/t815150.shtml。

③ 参见胡锦涛:《加强互利合作 共创美好未来——在金砖国家领导人第四次会晤大范围会谈时的讲话》,2012年3月29日,http://www.gov.cn/ldhd/2012-03/29/content_2102681.htm。

④ 参见习近平:《携手合作 共同发展——在金砖国家领导人第五次会晤时的主旨讲话》,2013年3月27日,https://www.fmprc.gov.cn/web/gjhdq_676201/gjhdqzz_681964/jzgj_682158/zyjh_682168/t1025978.shtml。

⑤ 参见习近平:《新起点 新愿景 新动力——在金砖国家领导人第六次会晤上的讲话》,2014年7月15日,https://www.fmprc.gov.cn/web/gjhdq_676201/gjhdqzz_681964/jzgj_682158/zyjh_682168/t1174958.shtml。

⑥ 参见习近平:《共建伙伴关系共创美好未来——在金砖国家领导人第七次会晤上的讲话》,2015年7月9日,https://www.fmprc.gov.cn/web/gjhdq_676201/gjhdqzz_681964/jzgj_682158/zyjh_682168/t1280127.shtml。

现"共同深化伙伴关系"的目标。①

2017年9月4日，习主席就全面深化金砖伙伴关系，开启金砖合作第二个"金色十年"进一步呼吁，金砖国家须"致力于促进人文民间交流"。他强调，"国之交在于民相亲。只有深耕厚植，友谊和合作之树才能枝繁叶茂。加强我们五国人文交流，让伙伴关系理念扎根人民心中，是一项值得长期投入的工作。这项工作做好了，将使金砖合作永葆活力"。他还希望，在金砖五国领导人的共同关心和推动下，现有的人文交流合作活动"能够经常化、机制化，并努力深入基层，面向广大民众，营造百花齐放的生动局面"。② 2018年7月26日，习主席在巩固"三轮驱动"合作架构的原则下，继续倡议金砖国家"深入拓展人文交流合作"。在他看来，"金砖五国孕育出各自灿烂文明，彼此交相辉映，人文交流合作大有可为"。金砖国家应当"继续以民心相通为宗旨，广泛开展文化、教育、卫生、体育、旅游等各领域人文大交流，筑牢金砖合作民意基础"。为此，中方还提出诸如"举行金砖博物馆、美术馆、图书馆联盟联合巡展"，"加强文化创意产业、旅游、地方城市等领域合作"，"讲述更多精彩动人的金砖故事"等具体建议。③

总的来讲，中国关于金砖国家人文交流的立场可以粗略地分为两个时期。第一个时期是从2009年至2012年。此时，中国政府更多强调的是人文交流的"为何"问题，也就是通过说明人文交流的好处来动员金砖国家加大对人文交流合作的投入。第二个时期是从2013年起至今。相对而言，这一阶段除了继续关注"为何"问题外，中国政府还越发注重人文交流的"如何"问题，也就是通过提出具有操作性的政策措施来吸引金砖国家扩大对人文交流合作的参与。不仅如此，2013年以来中国政府的立场还具备

---

① 参见习近平：《坚定信心 共谋发展——在金砖国家领导人第八次会晤大范围会议上的讲话》，2016年10月16日，https://www.fmprc.gov.cn/web/gjhdq_676201/gjhdqzz_681964/jzgj_682158/zyjh_682168/t1406096.shtml。

② 参见习近平：《深化金砖伙伴关系 开辟更加光明未来——在金砖国家领导人厦门会晤大范围会议上的讲话》，2017年9月4日，https://www.brics2017.org/dtxw/201709/t20170904_1892.html。

③ 参见习近平：《让美好愿景变为现实——在金砖国家领导人约翰内斯堡会晤大范围会议上的讲话》，2018年7月26日，http://cpc.people.com.cn/n1/2018/0727/c64094-30173944.html。

一个显著的特征，即将人文交流置于金砖国家伙伴关系的大框架下，努力推动其成为金砖国家伙伴精神的重要体现、金砖国家伙伴关系构成的重要支柱以及金砖国家伙伴关系全面深化的重要保障。此外，通过前后对比也可以发现，中国的立场逐渐呈现出一种在顶层设计上更加系统化、在具体实施上更加专门化的大趋势。

具体而言，中国关于金砖国家人文交流的立场还可以概括为以下几个方面：

第一，关于人文交流的可能性与可行性。中国政府认为，金砖国家各自均为特定文明的主要代表，且这些文明大多历史悠久、底蕴深厚，具备相互吸引的巨大潜力。与此同时，金砖各国所代表的文明和文化不仅在地理上界限分明，而且在谱系上特点各异，因而具有相互学习、相互借鉴的良好前景。

第二，关于人文交流的目标与目的。中国政府认为，金砖国家人文交流的直接目标是推动全方位、多领域、立体化的文化大交流，进而打造基于多元文明的金砖国家伙伴关系。其根本目的在于为金砖国家合作奠定坚实的社会和民意基础，经由民心相通增进政治互信，便利经贸合作。

第三，关于人文交流的基本原则。中国政府认为，金砖国家人文交流首先应是平等的交流。国与国、人与人、文明与文明、文化与文化之间不存在任何高低贵贱之分，各自都有权利得到其他各方的充分尊重。其次应是开放的交流。金砖各国既要有文化自信的勇气，也要通过实实在在的政策举措便利民众之间的相互往来。最后应是包容的交流。金砖各国既不要文化自傲，也不要文化自卑，而要有求同存异、取长补短的阳光心态。

第四，关于人文交流的主要内容。中国政府认为，金砖国家人文交流的主要领域可以包括文化、教育、卫生、体育、旅游、地方等。其中，每个领域还可细化出更多的合作议题。比如，文化领域的合作可以涉及文化创意产业以及博物馆、美术馆、图书馆联盟的联合巡展等。

第五，关于人文交流的方式方法。中国政府认为，一方面金砖各国政府要积极推动金砖国家人文交流机制走深走实，要通过搭建平台，制定政策，排除障碍，营造氛围，起到引领民众交流的积极作用；另一方面金砖国家要特别重视"接地气"的人文交流活动，要想办法让更多更好的人文交流深入基层，惠及普通民众。

第六，关于人文交流的注意事项。中国政府认为，相对于金砖国家在政治和经济领域的合作，人文交流的投入更大，见效更慢，但一旦形成良好效应，则必将发挥积极作用。因此，在对待人文交流的问题上，金砖国家要有耐心，有信心，有恒心，要以战略眼光和系统思维排除短期利益和局部利益的干扰，使得金砖国家人文交流行稳致远，形成良好效应，发挥积极影响。

二、中国在金砖国家人文交流领域的实践

2017年9月3日，习近平主席在金砖国家工商论坛开幕式上指出："金砖国家不是碌碌无为的清谈馆，而是知行合一的行动队。我们五国以贸易投资大市场、货币金融大流通、基础设施大联通、人文大交流为目标，推进各领域务实合作，目前已经涵盖经贸、财金、科教、文卫等数十个领域，对合作共赢的新型国际关系做出生动诠释。"[①] 其中，就推动金砖国家人文交流而言，中国除了积极参与其他金砖国家举办的各种活动外，还主办或承办了一系列特色鲜明的人文交流活动，真心实意地为金砖国家贡献了中国方案和中国力量。

表8—1　中国主办或承办的金砖国家人文交流活动一览表（截至2019年6月）

时间	地点	活动名称	主要内容
2011年12月2—3日	三亚	首届金砖国家友好城市暨地方政府合作论坛	论坛围绕"展望未来、共享繁荣、发展友城、推动合作"这一主题，探讨金砖国家友好城市和地方政府如何应对发展过程中所面临的问题与挑战，主要涉及粮食安全、金融危机、城市发展与低碳环保、能源战略、文化交融等议题

---

① 参见习近平：《共同开创金砖合作第二个"金色十年"——在金砖国家工商论坛开幕上的讲话》，2017年9月3日，https://www.brics2017.org/dtxw/201709/t20170903_1878.html。

续表

时间	地点	活动名称	主要内容
2012年9月26—27日	重庆	2012年金砖国家智库论坛	论坛议题包括："国际金融危机背景下金砖国家发展模式的调整""创建金砖国家开发银行的可行性""进一步推动金砖国家之间经贸合作"
2013年9月11日	上海	金砖国家信息共享与交流平台	平台正式成立并开通运转，通过金砖国家工商理事会中方理事秘书处同复旦大学金砖国家研究中心的共同建设和运营，不断自我完善，为推进金砖国家合作参与全球治理提供高质量的信息服务
2014年11月6日	北京	首届金砖国家经济智库论坛	论坛旨在探讨金砖国家如何通力合作应对挑战，谋求改革国际金融体系
2015年10月18日	北京	金砖国家大学联盟	来自俄罗斯、巴西、印度、南非和中国的50多所著名大学校长在北京师范大学宣告联盟成立并达成《北京共识》
2015月12年1日	北京	首届金砖国家媒体峰会	峰会旨在建立一个金砖国家主流媒体高端对话交流平台，推动五国媒体业的创新发展，增进世界人民对金砖国家的了解，以及金砖国家人民之间的友谊
2017年3月22日	北京	"深化金融合作 共促金砖发展"金砖国家智库研讨会	研讨会主题包括："全球经济治理与金砖国家角色""金砖国家金融合作：进程评估和未来前景""金砖国家金融合作与中国"
2017年5月30日至6月3日	北京	第三届金砖国家青年外交官论坛	论坛以"深化金砖伙伴关系，开辟更加光明未来"为主题，下设"新兴市场和发展中国家国家共同发展""金砖国家经贸务实合作""金砖国家互联互通"等议题。其间，围绕"金砖国家人文大交流"这一主题，金砖国家青年外交官还与北京师范大学师生代表进行了座谈

续表

时间	地点	活动名称	主要内容
2017年6月7—8日	北京	金砖国家媒体高端论坛	论坛以"深化金砖国家媒体合作,促进国际舆论公平公正"为主题,包括"全媒体创新与媒体发展"和"媒体义务与社会责任"两项议题。会后还发表了《金砖国家加强媒体合作行动计划》
2017年6月10—12日	福州	金砖国家政党、智库和民间社会组织论坛	金砖国家政党对话以"发挥政党作用,引领合作方向"为议题;金砖国家学术论坛以"凝聚思想智慧,创新合作思路"为议题;金砖国家民间社会组织论坛以"增进民心相通,夯实合作根基"为议题;会议通过《福州倡议》,并就《金砖国家第九次学术论坛对金砖国家领导人厦门会晤的建议》达成一致
2017年6月17—21日	广州	首届金砖国家运动会	运动会共设3个大项、10个小项,既有鲜明中国特色的武术项目,也有普及性高、影响力大、兼具竞技性和观赏性的篮球与排球项目
2017年6月23—27日	成都	2017年中国成都·金砖国家电影节	电影论坛以"金砖国家电影合作之路"为主旨,重点探讨金砖国家之间合作拍片的方法模式。国家电影日活动以"不同文化,一样精彩"为主题,以"每一天,一个国家,一种电影文化"的方式,专题展映每个国家的电影,全方位彰显金砖各国的电影文化,让更多观众有机会感受不同国度的文化魅力。另外,由来自金砖国家的大师级导演合作完成的影片《时间去哪儿了》也在电影节期间举行了首映

续表

时间	地点	活动名称	主要内容
2017年7月1—3日	郑州	2017年金砖国家网络大学年会	年会以"国际化办学与务实合作"为主题。会后共同签署《金砖国家网络大学国际管理董事会章程》《2017—2018年金砖国家网络大学行动计划》《2017年金砖国家网络大学年度会议郑州共识》等重量级文件，达成一系列多边和双边合作协议
2017年7月5日	北京	第五届金砖国家教育部长会议	会议以"金砖国家教育合作：促进卓越和公平"为主题，通过了《第五届金砖国家教育部长会议北京教育宣言》等成果文件，就金砖国家教育未来合作达成系列共识
2017年7月6日	天津	第七届金砖国家卫生部长会暨传统医药高级别会议	会议通过《天津公报》，旨在加强金砖国家在全球卫生治理中的作用，积极分享改善卫生体系、提高卫生服务质量的有益经验，促进实现健康相关的可持续发展目标
2017年7月6日	天津	第二届金砖国家文化部长会议	五国代表共同签署了《落实〈金砖国家政府间文化协定〉行动计划（2017—2021年）》，并一同见证了金砖国家图书馆联盟、博物馆联盟、美术馆联盟和青少年儿童戏剧联盟签署成果文件
2017年7月12日	成都	2017金砖国家友好城市暨地方政府合作论坛	论坛以"联动发展、共创共享"为主题，包括省市首长高端访谈以及城市国际化和教育交流等主题论坛，并发布了《成都倡议》，推动了金砖国家地方交流与合作的机制化
2017年7月12—14日	杭州	第二届金砖国家青年科学家论坛	论坛主题为"共同打造青年科学家的科技创新领导力"，设立了能源、材料和生物医药三个主题学科分论坛与一个交叉学科分论坛

续表

时间	地点	活动名称	主要内容
2017年7月18日	杭州	第五届金砖国家科技创新部长级会议	会议就科技创新政策交流、专题领域合作、联合资助多边研发项目、青年创新创业、青年科学家交流、科技园区合作等达成多项重要成果。会后发表了《杭州宣言》《金砖国家创新合作行动计划》和《金砖国家2017—2018年科技创新工作计划》
2017年7月24—25日	北京	第六届金砖国家工会论坛	论坛以"可持续发展与工会作用"为主题，包括"可持续发展：劳动世界面临的机遇和挑战""推进2030议程：工会的历史任务""开启新的金色十年：加强金砖国家劳动世界的交流合作"等议题，并通过了《金砖国家工会论坛宣言》《金砖国家工会致金砖国家劳工就业部长会议联合声明》《金砖国家工会论坛暂行规则》等文件
2017年7月25—27日	北京	2017年金砖国家青年论坛	与会代表围绕"新时期各国青年政策重点和特点""金砖国家青年创新创业"等议题进行深入探讨，并最终形成《2017年金砖国家青年论坛行动计划》
2017年8月15—22日	莆田	2017年金砖国家少年足球邀请赛	来自金砖国家的24支球队共计600余名运动员参加了本次比赛
2017年8月22—26日	杭州	金砖国家技能发展与技术创新大赛——3D打印与智能制造技能大赛	3D打印造型技术大赛+智能制造生产线运营与维护大赛
2017年9月15—22日	厦门	金砖国家文化节	以"文明相融、民心相通"为主题，邀请来自金砖五国的210多位艺术家举办现场演出、户外演出、艺术大师课、主题展览和金砖国家电影展映等30余场相关活动

续表

时间	地点	活动名称	主要内容
2017年9月21日	北京	《金砖国家青年对中国文化认知》调查	旨在了解金砖国家青年对中国文化符号认知与偏好、中国文化接触意愿与渠道、中国文化产品与文化活动偏好，由北京师范大学文化创新与传播研究院课题组对俄罗斯、印度、巴西、南非4国青年展开调研
2018年5月6—7日	北京	"深化金砖伙伴关系 促进新型国际发展合作"——金砖国家智库国际研讨会暨第十七届"万寿论坛"	论坛议题包括："人类命运共同体与新国际发展观""金砖合作的新机制与新路径""金砖合作与实现国际可持续发展""国际发展与合作：来自金砖国家的最佳经验"
2018年6月9日	重庆	"金砖国家人文交流：政府引导与民间互动"——2018年金砖国家智库国际研讨会暨第21届万寿论坛	论坛议题包括："金砖国家人文交流机制创新与协同发展的思路与举措""金砖国家人文交流促进五国民心相通的路径与方式"
2018年7月10—13日	杭州	2018"一带一路"暨金砖国家技能发展与技术创新大赛——首届模具数字化设计和智能制造技能大赛	旨在促进金砖国家技能发展和技术交流，落实金砖五国共同签署的有关人才发展合作的备忘录，并搭建"一带一路"暨金砖国家职业技能发展、工程能力培养和智能技术创新的人才国际合作平台

续表

时间	地点	活动名称	主要内容
2018年7月20日至8月22日	北京	金砖国家青少年儿童戏剧联盟系列活动	活动涵盖"金砖五国"儿童戏剧展演、金砖国家青少年儿童戏剧联盟会议等活动
2018年10月25日	北京	首届金砖国家博物馆联盟大会	来自巴西博物学院、巴西皇家博物馆、俄罗斯国家历史博物馆、印度国家博物馆、中国国家博物馆、南非迪宗博物馆等的代表共同见证了金砖国家博物馆联盟成立,共商金砖国家博物馆合作共赢大计
2018年11月1日	北京	2018年金砖国家智库国际研讨会第25届万寿论坛暨首届沃德论坛	论坛以"推动金砖国家传统医药合作,共建人类健康共同体"为主题,设置了"全球健康形势与传统医药发展战略""第四次工业革命与传统医药创新发展""健康城市建设与传统医药发展"等多个议题
2019年5月10日	北京	电影《半边天》首映式	由中国导演贾樟柯监制的第二部金砖五国合作影片《半边天》于5月10日上映。该片由五国女导演携手合作,以"当代女性情感与社会"为主题,从女性视角发声,去理解女性,倾听女性,关注女性自我价值的实现
2019年5月26日	上海	2019年金砖国家大学联盟首届全体大会	大会聚焦金砖国家教育务实合作,期望切实推进成员高校间的合作与交流,共同讨论金砖国家大学联盟的可持续发展战略
2019年6月29日	北京	2019年金砖国家智库国际研讨会	研讨会以"全球治理与多边主义"为主题,分议题包括:"金砖国家如何在单边主义抬头的趋势下捍卫多边主义""金砖国家在全球发展治理中的责任与作用""金砖国家如何引领全球经贸体系规则重塑""在新工业革命背景下,金砖国家在全球治理新疆域中的作为"

资料来源:互联网公开资料,表格为笔者自制。

虽然上述信息没有穷尽中国过去十年在金砖国家人文交流领域的所有实践，但我们仍然可以从这些具有代表性的活动中发现，中国在金砖国家领导人会晤开启后的很长一段时期内对人文交流的实际投入是相当有限的。当然，这与金砖国家合作机制自身的发展演变密切相关。在当时只是强调金砖合作的政治经济双轮驱动架构的背景下，中国过多地介入人文交流事务反而会显得有些不合时宜。同理，当金砖国家日益发现人文交流的潜在价值和重大影响并将其正式确定为金砖合作的第三根支柱时，金砖国家对人文交流的重视程度和投入力度自然也就不一样了，更何况正值中国主办金砖国家领导人第九次会晤之际。因此，2017年由中国举办的人文交流活动异常丰富，不仅包括对之前机制化活动的继承，而且有一些充满中国智慧的创新之举。尽管人文交流的大部分活动都由峰会主办国承办，但是中国在非主办时期同样对金砖国家人文交流保持了一个较为积极的姿态。

三、中国促进金砖国家人文交流的双边模式

金砖五国是金砖国家合作的基础，处理好与其他四国的双边关系是每一个金砖成员的责任和义务，也是推动和保障金砖国家合作顺利开展的重要前提。从这个意义上讲，与俄罗斯、南非、印度和巴西分别建立人文交流机制同样是中国促进金砖国家人文交流的重要途径。迄今为止，除巴西以外，中国已经与俄罗斯、南非和印度先后创建了高级别人文交流机制。其中，最早确立的双边人文交流机制即是中俄人文合作委员会。2000年7月18日，时任国家主席江泽民和俄罗斯总统普京在北京签署了《中华人民共和国和俄罗斯联邦北京宣言》。宣言提出"应加强和扩大两国科技、教育、文化和体育领域的合作"，并强调"两国人民世代友好是中国人民和俄罗斯人民的共同心声。实现这一目标，不仅需要两国政府，而且也需要两国人民的广泛参与和不懈努力。为此将积极支持中俄友好、和平与发展委员会的工作，并鼓励两国其他形式的民间交往"。[①] 在此背景下，中俄

---

① 参见《中华人民共和国和俄罗斯联邦北京宣言》，2000年7月18日，https://www.fmprc.gov.cn/web/gjhdq_676201/gj_676203/oz_678770/1206_679110/1207_679122/t6787.shtml。

教文卫体合作委员会于同年11月正式成立。

2001年7月16日,中俄双方在莫斯科正式签署《中俄睦邻友好合作条约》。该条约的第十六条规定:"缔约双方将大力促进发展文化、教育、卫生、信息、旅游、体育和法制领域的交流与合作。"随后,中俄之间的人文交流得以大幅增加,其交流与合作的领域也远远超出教育、文化、卫生和体育的范畴。因此,2007年7月13日,双方正式将教文卫体委员会更名为中俄人文合作委员会,下设教育、文化、卫生、体育、旅游、媒体和电影等7个分委会以及档案合作工作小组。[①] 截至2018年10月,中俄人文合作委员会已经召开了19次会议,而两国在此框架下开展的诸如青年交流、媒体论坛、文化节、青少年运动会、电影节、传统医药合作、旅游年等人文交流活动,都对金砖国家人文交流的规划与设计产生了重要影响,并在金砖国家人文交流活动的具体实施过程中得到相应的体现。与此同时,随着金砖国家人文交流氛围的日益浓厚,中俄双边人文交流机制的成功实践也为中国推动与其他金砖国家建立相应机制提供了重要的参考和借鉴。

2015年12月4日,习近平主席在中非合作论坛约翰内斯堡峰会开幕式上致辞时提出,"将中非新型战略伙伴关系提升为全面战略合作伙伴关系,并为此做强和夯实'五大支柱'"。其中,第三根支柱即是"坚持文明上交流互鉴"。习主席希望"加强中非两大文明交流互鉴,着力加强青年、妇女、智库、媒体、高校等各界人员往来,促进文化融通、政策贯通、人心相通,推动共同进步,让中非人民世代友好"。[②] 在两国元首的直接推动下,2017年4月24日,中国—南非高级别人文交流机制正式建立。该机制是中国与非洲国家建立的首个高级别人文交流机制,其宗旨之一就是"为发展和丰富现有的双边、多边合作交流机制与项目而创造新的机遇"。[③] 正如习主席在发给该机制首次会议的贺信中所说的那样,"机制的启动将

---

① 参见李亚男:《论中俄关系发展进程中的人文交流与合作》,《东北亚论坛》2011年第6期,第115页。

② 参见习近平:《开启中非合作共赢、共同发展的新时代——在中非合作论坛约翰内斯堡峰会开幕式上的致辞》,2015年12月4日,http://www.xinhuanet.com/world/2015-12/04/c_1117363197.htm。

③ 参见《中南高级别人文交流机制》,http://www.moe.gov.cn/s78/A20/s3117/moe_854/201707/t20170731_310399.html。

夯实中南关系的民意基础,有力推动两国人文交流"。而"中国和南非同为发展中大国和金砖国家成员",中南两国的人文交流必将有助于金砖国家人文交流的进一步扩大和深化。从某种意义上讲,中国—南非高级别人文交流机制的创建也是为了更好地烘托和支持作为厦门峰会主办方的中国力推人文交流正式成为金砖合作的新支柱。

2017年6月18日,印度边防部队越界阻拦中国在中印边境的洞朗地区修建公路,从而引发了双方长达两个多月的对峙事件。此时正值中国主办金砖国家领导人第九次会晤,因此莫迪总理是否会正常出席厦门峰会,也被打上了一个大大的问号。虽然印军在8月28日将越界人员和设备全部撤回印方边界一侧,印度政府也在几乎最后一刻宣布了莫迪将如期出席金砖峰会的消息,但此次事件表明中印两国在边境地区的领土争端和主权纠纷已经在事实上影响到金砖合作的正常开展。可以说,在边界问题彻底解决尚无明确时间表的情况下,军事上的共同管控和政治上的相互尊重将成为一种常态。其实,除此之外,人文方面的沟通与交流也是缓解竞争和冲突恶性影响的一剂良药。

为此,习近平主席在2018年4月同莫迪总理进行武汉会晤时就特别强调,要将促进更加广泛的人文交流作为下一阶段两国全方位合作规划的重要内容之一。也正是在此次会晤期间,两国领导人一致同意建立两国高级别人文交流机制。而特别有意思的是,中方将会晤地点定在武汉的原因之一就在于武汉自身的深厚历史底蕴及其同印度之间自春秋时期就开始形成的历史渊源。[①] 2018年12月21日,中国—印度高级别人文交流机制正式确立。中印双方一致认为,应积极参与包括金砖国家在内的各种多边机制的人文交流,从而为促进地区和世界的和平与发展做出积极贡献。[②]

迄今为止,在金砖国家范围内,中国唯独没有与巴西建立高级别人文交流机制。然而,这并不意味着中巴之间没有开展过人文交流与合作。事实上,提起中巴人文交流,300多名中国茶农在1812年应葡萄牙摄政王若

[①] 参见《外交部副部长孔铉佑就中印领导人非正式会晤举行媒体吹风会》,2018年4月24日, http://www.xinhuanet.com/world/2018-04/24/c_1122736469.htm。
[②] 参见《中印高级别人文交流机制首次会议达成一系列共识》,2018年12月22日, http://world.people.com.cn/n1/2018/1222/c1002-30482144.html。

昂六世之邀赴里约热内卢培育茶树的往事一直是中巴双方津津乐道的人文交流源头。① 此后，中巴人文交流循序渐进，在各领域取得良好的进展。2014年7月17日，中巴双方发表的关于进一步深化中巴全面战略伙伴关系的联合声明强调，"应进一步加强两国政府、立法机构、政党、社会团体、地方等往来"。② 2015年5月19日，李克强总理在对巴西进行正式访问时又与时任巴西总统罗塞芙发表联合声明指出，双方将通过扩大在教育、研究和智库方面的合作加深相互了解。③ 2017年9月，时任巴西总统特梅尔访华。习近平主席在与特梅尔总统会谈时就曾指出，中巴双方要扩大文化、新闻、旅游、体育等领域的交流合作。对此，特梅尔总统也表示愿意扩大上述交流，增进两国人民的相互了解和友谊。④ 巴西驻华大使更是强调，"和过去的巴西总统访问相比，此次特梅尔总统对中国的访问加入了相当比重的人文交流与合作的内容……人文交流与合作为中巴关系注入了新鲜血液，并拓展了两国关系的内涵"。⑤

2019年10月25日，巴西总统博索纳罗访华，除了提出务实利民，打造合作新高地之外，更强调促进民心相通，全面加强人文等领域合作。其实，早在2019年初，巴西公民和社会行动部部长特拉就曾明确表示，"中国是巴西的重要合作伙伴，巴西希望加大与中国的人文交流，通过在文化、体育、艺术、青年、社会等领域合作，促进两国关系持续向前发展"。⑥ 种种迹象表明，中国与巴西建立高级别人文交流机制的条件已经成

---

① 参见《中国—拉美人文交流应深耕细作》，2015年5月26日，http://www.gov.cn/xinwen/2015-05/26/content_2868913.htm。

② 参见《中国和巴西关于进一步深化中巴全面战略伙伴关系的联合声明》，2014年7月18日，https://www.fmprc.gov.cn/web/gjhdq_676201/gj_676203/nmz_680924/1206_680974/1207_680986/t1175756.shtml。

③ 参见《中华人民共和国政府和巴西联邦共和国政府联合声明》，2015年5月20日，https://www.fmprc.gov.cn/web/gjhdq_676201/gj_676203/nmz_680924/1206_680974/1207_680986/t1265272.shtml。

④ 参见《习近平同巴西总统特梅尔举行会谈》，2017年9月1日，http://www.xinhuanet.com/politics/2017-09/01/c_1121588439.htm。

⑤ 参见《巴西驻华大使：特梅尔总统访华成果显著 人文交流成为新亮点》，2017年9月4日，https://news.china.com/news100/11038989/20170904/31280870.html。

⑥ 参见《巴西希望加大与中国的人文交流》，2019年1月29日，http://world.people.com.cn/n1/2019/0129/c1002-30597536.html。

熟。中国应充分利用博索纳罗总统访华之机力推该机制的成功落地，从而为 2019 年 11 月在巴西利亚举行的金砖国家领导人第十一次会晤营造更加浓郁的人文交流氛围。

四、结语

2017 年 7 月，中央全面深化改革领导小组审议通过了《关于加强和改进中外人文交流工作的若干意见》。该意见明确指出，"中外人文交流是党和国家对外工作的重要组成部分，是夯实中外关系社会民意基础、提高我国对外开放水平的重要途径"，并提出"将人文交流与合作理念融入对外交往各个领域"。[1] 从时间节点上看，这与同年 9 月举办的金砖国家厦门峰会突出强调人文交流，力推人文交流支柱化具有十分密切的关系。可以说，中国以开创之举和实际行动促进金砖国家人文交流正是中国进一步落实中外人文交流工作的重要体现。2019 年 7 月 26 日，国务委员兼外交部长王毅在出席金砖国家外长正式会晤时表示，金砖国家要"全面平衡推进经贸财金、政治安全、人文交流'三轮驱动'，不断为金砖合作注入强劲动力，也为不同文明之间包容互鉴、和谐共生走出一条新路"。[2] 可以预见，中国将一如既往地支持金砖国家人文交流，并在金砖国家人文交流中发挥引领者的作用，从而通过人文交流保障金砖国家全方位合作的稳步推进。

---

[1] 参见《中共中央办公厅、国务院办公厅印发〈关于加强和改进中外人文交流工作的若干意见〉》，2017 年 12 月 21 日，http://www.gov.cn/zhengce/2017-12/21/content_5249241.htm。

[2] 参见《王毅出席金砖国家外长正式会晤》，2019 年 7 月 27 日，https://www.fmprc.gov.cn/web/wjbzhd/t1683857.shtml。

学术书评

BRICS: Construir a educação para o futuro-prioridades para o desenvolvimento nacional e a cooperação internacional 书评

刘梦茹[*]

一、内容简介

教育乃国之根本，是社会经济发展的支撑。金砖国家教育部长会议机制的正式确立，不仅为金砖五国未来教育领域的合作提供了更多机会，还将为全球经济的可持续发展做出贡献。在此背景下，2014年联合国教科文组织（UNESCO）出版了有关金砖国家未来教育的报告书——《BRICS: Construir a educação para o futuro-prioridades para o desenvolvimento nacional e a cooperação internacional》（《金砖国家——建立面向未来的教育》）。[①]

---

[*] 刘梦茹，四川外国语大学西葡语系葡萄牙语讲师、葡萄牙语言学在读博士。

[①] 《BRICS: Construir a educação para o futuro-propriedades para o desenvolvimento nacional e a cooperação internacional》是2014年由联合国教科文组织出版的《BRICS-Building education for the future: priorities for national development and international cooperation》的葡语版，由玛利亚·安吉利卡·贝阿尔维斯达席尔瓦（Maria Angélica B. Alves da Silva）翻译。原版主要作者为弗郎索瓦·勒克莱克（François Leclercq）。凯特琳娜·亚纳尼亚多（Katerina Ananiadou）和伯尼恩·卡克伦（Borhene Chakroun）提供第三章中涉及的数据信息。阿尔伯特·默提瓦斯（Albert Motivans）和帕特里克·蒙祖里德斯（Patrick Montjouridès）提供有关工作的数据信息。铁奥帕尼亚·查瓦特齐亚（Theophania Chavatzia）提供协助。安德鲁·乔斯顿（Andrew Johnston）编辑报告。卡拉·戴维斯（Cara Davis）在迪艾拉·麦克马洪（Tierra McMahon）的帮助下管理报告制作。

这份报告书介绍并分析了金砖五国的教育机制与政策、技能发展与职业教育的政策以及在教育与技能发展领域的合作，并对未来的合作提出一些建议，向金砖国家提供了一个相互学习和交流经验的平台。其中特别强调了教育发展注重质量与平等的趋势，还提到专业技能的发展特别是职业教育与技能培训，是实现可持续发展与包容性增长的关键因素。

此报告书收集已有数据进行现状分析后提出，金砖国家的教育需要注重学前教育与高等教育的普及和发展。对于职业教育和技能发展而言，需要将重点放在提升专业技能、制定标准要求、加强与劳动力市场的联系、消除不平等、提供弱势群体的培训并提升其就业能力上。金砖五国基于各自国情制定的教育体制、教育策略、技能发展计划具有借鉴意义和代表性，能为世界各国未来教育的发展和合作提供宝贵的经验和非常有价值的数据信息，并为未来教育的发展铺设新的道路。

报告书分四个章节，分别涉及金砖国家的教育机制、金砖国家职业教育和技能发展与政策、金砖国家在教育与技能发展领域的国际合作以及未来的合作建议。

二、主要观点简述

报告书中指出，近年的数据显示出印度与南非学前教育的普及率、各国的高等教育人数均呈现出不同程度的增长。金砖国家正在关注如何提升教育质量，让学生在生活和工作中有所成就，从而为经济发展做出贡献。

事实上，尽管教育发展迅速，高等教育的接受率却仍然较低，正规职业教育与培训机构的教学质量也不尽如人意。这也使得很大一部分青少年与成人因缺乏专业技能而就业能力不强，阻碍了社会发展与进步。据此，报告书中提出应提升基础教育质量，并制定弱势群体的扫盲计划与职业技能发展计划。

为实现公平的经济增长与可持续发展，报告书中还提出在基础教育、高等教育与技能发展领域应采取一系列措施，具体包括：1）基础教育方面：巴西、中国、印度与南非应实现中小学教育的普及，注重优质教育与学前教育。（2）高等教育方面：金砖国家应扩大高等教育的覆盖范围，并成立世界一流的教学研究中心。(3) 技能发展方面：金砖国家应创建综合技能发展机制，以使其经济基础多样化；设定并实施国家资格框架标准，对技能进行资格判定；扩大中高等职业技术道路；鼓励公司培训员工；拓展弱势青年与成年人的培训计划。[1]

三、章节主要内容简述

（一）金砖国家教育体制的分析及政策建议

书中指出，在基础教育方面，金砖五国因其国情不同而分别存在不同的问题。其中特别提到，印度除了要扩大基础教育的覆盖范围之外，还需要加大投资，以改善农村地区学校的基础设施。对比金砖五国基础教育的情况及其采取的政策措施后可以看出，五国均力求普及学前教育和高中教育，但学前教育在五个国家中差异较大。其中，俄罗斯的学前教育机制达到三年到四年，而南非则不到一年，主要原因在于印度和南非在保障幼儿健康与营养方面临着巨大挑战。[2]

金砖五国通过宪法均保障了各国儿童的受教育权，儿童都必须接受九年的小学和初中教育（印度为八年）。[3] 基础教育机构大多是国家公立机构，私立机构相对较少，且政府须介入以确保其符合要求。在中国和巴西，相比基础教育的私立机构，学前教育的私立机构更为普遍。

另外，金砖五国也制定了符合各国教育现状的国家计划，还指出当前面临的教育问题，提出解决方案。这些计划都旨在普及学前教育、高等教

---

[1] François Leclercq, et al., Maria Angélica B. Alves da Silva（tradutora da versão em português）, *BRICS-Construir a educação para o futuro: Propriedades para o desenvolvimento nacional e a cooperação internacional*, Escritório da UNESCO em Brasília, 2014, p. 3.

[2] François Leclercq, et al., Maria Angélica B. Alves da Silva（tradutora da versão em português）, *BRICS-Construir a educação para o futuro: Propriedades para o desenvolvimento nacional e a cooperação internacional*, Escritório da UNESCO em Brasília, 2014, p. 6.

[3] François Leclercq, et al., Maria Angélica B. Alves da Silva（tradutora da versão em português）, *BRICS-Construir a educação para o futuro: Propriedades para o desenvolvimento nacional e a cooperação internacional*, Escritório da UNESCO em Brasília, 2014, p. 12.

育，提升学习成绩，拓展技能与高等教育发展计划，以满足知识型经济发展的需求。

据相关数据及信息显示，针于学前教育的普及，金砖五国根据各自不同国情制定了如下政策：巴西计划在2016年前实现两年学前教育的普及；中国计划在2020年前实现一年至三年学前教育的普及，并在农村新建教室、教学楼，向农村留守儿童提供上学机会；印度订立目标，为所有儿童提供至少一年学前教育的资助；俄罗斯恢复学前机构的基础设施，并向就读私立幼儿园的家庭提供补偿；南非将学龄前儿童的教育视为重中之重，并采取一系列措施解决健康、营养和教育问题。[1]

此外，五国还将推动发展高等教育视为首要任务。巴西计划在2020年前实现每年培训6万名硕士和2.5万名博士的目标；中国侧重于将大学发展成世界一流水平的高等教育机构，提高其全球竞争力，还鼓励学生参与研究，加强高校与企业之间的合作，重组课程与学科，并极力消除各区域之间的不平等性；印度计划通过新建机构、扩大现有机构、改善基础设施、建立国家高等教育委员会的方式，来实现高等教育的普及，保证其公平性与质量；俄罗斯成立联邦大学，优化各地区可用资源，加强高校、经济与社会之间的联系；南非则计划向穷人提供免费高等教育，加强大学的科研创新能力。[2]

金砖五国也为学生交流做出重大贡献。巴西政府于2011年启动了"无国界科学"项目，实现在2015年前为在国外高校学习科技、工程与数学课程的巴西学者提供10万份奖学金。[3] 与此同时，金砖国家也成为越来越有吸引力的目的留学国。但是，目前金砖国家之间的学生交流状

---

[1] François Leclercq, et al., Maria Angélica B. Alves da Silva（tradutora da versão em português），*BRICS-Construir a educação para o futuro: Propriedades para o desenvolvimento nacional e a cooperação internacional*, Escritório da UNESCO em Brasília, 2014, pp. 19 - 20.

[2] François Leclercq, et al., Maria Angélica B. Alves da Silva（tradutora da versão em português），*BRICS-Construir a educação para o futuro: Propriedades para o desenvolvimento nacional e a cooperação internacional*, Escritório da UNESCO em Brasília, 2014, pp. 20 - 21.

[3] François Leclercq, et al., Maria Angélica B. Alves da Silva（tradutora da versão em português），*BRICS-Construir a educação para o futuro: Propriedades para o desenvolvimento nacional e a cooperação internacional*, Escritório da UNESCO em Brasília, 2014, p. 21.

况并不理想。

报告书中指出，金砖国家面临的主要挑战是公共政策的制定。只有制定了合适的政策方针，高等教育体制才能不断满足需求，才能为不同的学生群体提供高质量的教育。全球化的不断发展和深化，意味着有必要建立国际高等教育准则，以对高等教育进行规范。对此，联合国教科文组织积极倡导批准并实施了认可高等教育资格的《区域性公约》。[1]

报告书中还提到，在实现教育普及的进程中，社会环境与经济发展的差异导致了教育的不平等性。具体来说，农村与经济不发达地区的教育水平和教育设施较差，而城市与经济发达地区的教育水平和教育设施较为优越。这一差异反过来又加大了经济发展的差异，使得不平等性更为显著，从而对社会凝聚力构成严重威胁。对此，金砖国家正制定计划与政策，努力提高教育的公平性。与此同时，各国也在根据自身的教育发展情况，完善教育考核制度，制定明确的教育目标。

总的来看，金砖国家的不同教育体制提供了相互学习、借鉴和相互合作的机会。五国都比较关注的是：提高义务教育质量与公平性、普及学前教育与高等教育、实现不同环境下对教育的有效管理与资助。[2]

综上，报告书提出以下政策建议：改善教育管理与资助，以确保公立学校的教育质量与公平性；制定并实施国家教育考试的总体标准；提高教育质量；加强高等教育学生的流动性，特别是促进金砖国家高等教育机构之间的学生交流。[3]

（二）金砖国家职业教育的发展及政策建议

为完成经济崛起并成为高收入国家，金砖国家正努力寻求实现经济基

---

[1] François Leclercq, et al., Maria Angélica B. Alves da Silva (tradutora da versão em português), BRICS-Construir a educação para o futuro: Propriedades para o desenvolvimento nacional e a cooperação internacional, Escritório da UNESCO em Brasília, 2014, p. 21.

[2] François Leclercq, et al., Maria Angélica B. Alves da Silva (tradutora da versão em português), BRICS-Construir a educação para o futuro: Propriedades para o desenvolvimento nacional e a cooperação internacional, Escritório da UNESCO em Brasília, 2014, p. 25.

[3] François Leclercq, et al., Maria Angélica B. Alves da Silva (tradutora da versão em português), BRICS-Construir a educação para o futuro: Propriedades para o desenvolvimento nacional e a cooperação internacional, Escritório da UNESCO em Brasília, 2014, p. 25.

础多元化的路径，减少对原材料出口的依赖，生产出更高附加值的产品，促进创造新型经济活动，鼓励创新，为实现经济稳步增长提供助力。如今，金砖国家政府面临的挑战主要在于如何向劳动力市场提供合格的技术人才。对此，报告书中指出，开展职业教育培训可解决青年失业问题，提升从业人员的工作能力，以提高生产力和竞争力。

尽管金砖国家经济增长迅速，但不可否认它们仍面临着贫富差距不断加大的问题，这将给金砖国家社会和政策的稳定带来挑战。而且，所有金砖国家政府都意识到，加强职业教育、培养技术人才对于平衡经济发展、维护社会稳定有着至关重要的作用。

报告书中表示，金砖国家的经济发展并没有满足就业市场的需求，男女工作比例不均、就业正规性不足都是亟待解决的问题。据所收集的数据显示，中国和俄罗斯的成人失业率与世界平均水平相差不大，尽管俄罗斯大多数就业都是正规的，但青年失业率仍较高；巴西的很多青年处于失业状态，且超过1/3的非农业工作是不正规的；在南非，不仅青少年，而且成年人的失业率也是很高的；在印度，除了几乎2/3的女性无工作外，还有超过80%的非农业工作是不正规的。[1]

面对人口的不断增长、老龄化的不断加剧和城镇化趋势的日益明朗，为维持经济发展与社会稳定，金砖国家都在制定计划及策略，为劳动力市场提供人才。一方面，通过基础技术培训、职业教育、高等教育、继续教育、进修等方式提升人才的技能水平；另一方面，制定资格框架，对从业人员的技能提出要求，使之更好地服务于劳动力市场。

报告书中指出，如何解决不同区域之间，如城市与农村、一线城市与二线城市、中部与西部之间资源分配不均衡的问题，也是金砖国家正在面临的挑战。对此，金砖国家需要加大资助力度，优化资助方案，鼓励并加强与私营部门的联系。

为加强金砖国家在提升职业教育水平、解决就业问题、实现经济转型

---

[1] François Leclercq, et al., Maria Angélica B. Alves da Silva (tradutora da versão em português), *BRICS-Construir a educação para o futuro: Propriedades para o desenvolvimento nacional e a cooperação internacional*, Escritório da UNESCO em Brasília, 2014, p. 32.

方面的合作，报告书提出以下政策建议：开发劳动力市场信息系统，对技能进行分析；建立国家资格框架与资格标准；加强职业教育公司与机构之间的联系，鼓励进修学习；满足女性与弱势群体的培训需求，鼓励其参与劳动力市场。[1]

(三) 金砖国家在教育与技能发展领域的合作

虽然金砖国家各自在教育、技能发展领域的侧重点有所不同，但仍具有以下共同点：注重与其他发展中国家的平等互惠关系，强调合作是由合作伙伴的需求和共同目标驱动的，不主张干涉其他国家的事务，不对援助附加政治条件；主要提供技术援助；不区分发展、贸易与投资领域的合作；关注与其有往来历史或战略伙伴关系的国家；把联合国发展合作论坛视为讨论发展合作的平台。[2]

报告书中关于金砖国家在教育与技能发展领域的不同合作方式有如下总结：[3]

1. 巴西以"南南合作"为平台开展合作，并鼓励教育局、高等教育机构、私立企业与社会组织参与教育发展合作。在教育发展方面，巴西优先考虑教育质量、教师培训、技术创新、职业教育与教育系统管理。

2. 中国一直以来致力于与其他国家的发展合作，并在商务部的管理下向其他发展中国家提供援助。在对外援助方面，中国将其援助重点放在与伙伴国之间的师生交流上。

3. 印度作为教育援助的主要接受者，在"南南合作"中扮演着重要角色。印度的重点不在项目资助上，而在共享技能与专业知识上。印度将教

---

[1] François Leclercq, et al., Maria Angélica B. Alves da Silva (tradutora da versão em português), BRICS-Construir a educação para o futuro: Propriedades para o desenvolvimento nacional e a cooperação internacional, Escritório da UNESCO em Brasília, 2014, p. 49.

[2] François Leclercq, et al., Maria Angélica B. Alves da Silva (tradutora da versão em português), BRICS-Construir a educação para o futuro: Propriedades para o desenvolvimento nacional e a cooperação internacional, Escritório da UNESCO em Brasília, 2014, pp. 53 - 54.

[3] François Leclercq, et al., Maria Angélica B. Alves da Silva (tradutora da versão em português), BRICS-Construir a educação para o futuro: Propriedades para o desenvolvimento nacional e a cooperação internacional, Escritório da UNESCO em Brasília, 2014, pp. 55 - 65.

育和培训视为发展合作的核心,并制定技术经济合作计划,以为伙伴国提供多领域的课程培训。与此同时,印度还与伙伴国开展项目合作。

4. 俄罗斯与周边国家开展合作,加强国际信誉,计划成立一个专门的发展机构。除此之外,其还为留学生提供奖学金,建立教育基金,并开展双边项目合作。

5. 南非在非洲国际关系中扮演着重要角色,并支持援助时效性议程与"南南合作"。南非公共机构与国有企业都参与国际合作,但缺乏有效的合作机制。对此,南非正计划成立一个南非发展伙伴机构,以对发展合作进行改革。在高等教育与培训方面,南非计划开展三角合作项目,并制定战略,用以指导未来在教育和技能发展领域的合作。

综上,虽然金砖国家的发展合作政策与实际做法各不相同,但都强调技术援助、支持非洲发展、提高金砖国家发展援助的质量,将这些共同关注的领域与各国发展的重点相结合,能为未来的合作建立基础。

(四) 未来合作的建议

依据金砖国家在教育领域的合作和发展现状,报告书提出以下建议:金砖国家可在改善教育机制、提升高等教育水平与促进技能发展上互帮互助——分享实现公立学校的平等性,提升学校的教育质量,制定并实施国家教育考试标准方面的经验;推动高等教育的普及,促进金砖国家之间学生与教学人员的流动;开发劳动力市场信息系统,以对劳动力市场做出分析与预测;建立并实施国家资格框架和技能标准;加强企业与职业教育培训机构之间的联系,鼓励从业人员进修;制定政策鼓励妇女和弱势群体参加工作,并满足妇女和弱势群体的培训需求。[1]

为实现金砖国家的合作带动全球教育的发展与进步的目标,报告书还提出以下建议:支持发展中国家的教育发展,建立关于教育发展合作的信息数据分享中心;制定支持非洲教育的联合方案或成立联合基金;承诺共

---

[1] François Leclercq, et al., Maria Angélica B. Alves da Silva (tradutora da versão em português), *BRICS-Construir a educação para o futuro: Propriedades para o desenvolvimento nacional e a cooperação internacional*, Escritório da UNESCO em Brasília, 2014, pp. 68 - 70.

同支持教育发展。此外，金砖国家还可根据已有经验和现状建立合作平台，以实现更多领域的合作。①

四、启示

综合国力与国际竞争力的提升需要知识水平的带动，而知识水平的高低主要取决于教育发展的好坏。换言之，教育是国家发展的基石，无论是对经济发展还是社会进步，均起着决定性作用。如何在全球化的背景下发展教育、如何提升教育质量、如何实现教育带动经济发展与社会进步的目标，均是当下需要思考的问题。

本报告书对金砖国家的教育机制与政策，技能发展计划与职业教育政策，以及在教育和技能发展领域的合作现状进行了客观、全面的介绍与分析。无论是对研究金砖国家的学术人员还是国家政策的研究人员来说，本报告书都具有很高的参考价值。报告书中的内容以极具说服力的数据信息为基础，总结出数据所反映出的现象与问题，并提出建议。其中提到的加强学生国际项目交流和人才培养交流，对社会发展具有重要意义。交流可以丰富知识、扩展视野，同时也可为本国文化走向国际舞台贡献力量。它不仅能加强国与国之间在学术、技术领域的交流，还能加深国与国之间的相互理解，促进共同发展，为实现民心相通奠定基础。

在此份报告书的启发下，我们可以发现，金砖国家虽然国情不同，但采取的政策之间具有互通性，面临的问题也具有共同点，而这些互通性和共同点也为金砖"人文交流"建造了桥梁。加强"人文交流"是提升国家软实力的必要手段，而教育合作是促进"人文交流"的重要途径。无论是加强教师、学生的出国交流，还是强化技能发展领域的共同合作，均能为拉紧人文纽带提供助力，亦能为提升国家综合竞争力贡献力量。

---

① François Leclercq, et al., Maria Angélica B. Alves da Silva (tradutora da versão em português), *BRICS-Construir a educação para o futuro: Propriedades para o desenvolvimento nacional e a cooperação internacional*, Escritório da UNESCO em Brasília, 2014, p. 71.

Theoretical Research

How to Promote People-to-people Exchanges between China and Other Countries

Jiang Shixue[*]

Abstract: Amity between people holds the key to sound relations between states. There are various ways to promote amity between people, among which the most effective is to promote people-to-people exchanges. Chinese and foreign people-to-people exchanges are conducive to telling good stories about China and well spreading China's voice, helping to improve China's national image, enhance China's soft power, facilitate the building of a community of shared future for mankind, eliminate the "trust deficit" between countries, and promote foreign economic and trade relations. In the process of further promoting Chinese and foreign people-to-people exchanges, the following measures should be taken: tell good stories of the Chinese Communist Party in governing China, correctly understand the ideological issues in Chinese and foreign people-to-people exchanges, pay more attention to the construction of

---

[*] Jiang Shixue, Distinguished Professor of Sichuan International Studies University.
① 特别说明：本书所有文章皆由李龙泉、李慧翻译，特此致谢！(Special Note: All articles in this book have been translated by Li Longquan and Li Hui. Thank them.)

discourse power, actively give full play to the scholars, vigorously respond to the "colored glasses" of the West and try to increase the non-government color. In promoting the BRICS people-to-people exchanges, the following three guidelines must be followed: correctly handle the relationship between people-to-people exchanges and other cooperation fields, highlight the color of multilateral cooperation, and abide by the principle of openness and inclusiveness.

Keywords: People-to-people Exchanges; Amity between People; Measures; Guidelines

Ⅰ. The Necessity and Importance of Promoting People-to-people Exchanges between China and Other Countries

Amity between people holds the key to sound relations between states. There are various ways to promote amity between people, among which the most effective is to promote people-to-people pxchanges.

People-to-people exchanges between China and other countries is an important part of the party and the country's work in the field of external relations, and an important way to consolidate the social and public opinion of Sino-foreign relations and improve the level of China's opening to the outside world. Since the 18th National Congress of the Communist Party of China, the Party Central Committee with Comrade Xi Jinping at the core has attached great importance to people-to-people exchanges. The Chinese and foreign cultural exchanges have been flourished and written to a new grand chapter, which has made important contributions to the promotion of China's opening up and has greatly promoted people-to-people exchanges and mutual learning between civilizations across the globe.[1]

---

① 中共中央办公厅、国务院办公厅印发:《关于加强和改进中外人文交流工作的若干意见》,新华网,2017 年 12 月 21 日, http://www.xinhuanet.com/2017-12/21/c_1122148432.htm。

People-to-people exchanges has a narrow and broad sense. Narrow people-to-people exchanges refer only to cultural exchanges, while broad cultural exchanges include personnel exchanges in the fields of culture, tourism, education, sports, science and technology, media, academia, health care, women affairs, trade unions, and religion. In this regard, the people-to-people exchanges covers everything in the national exchanges except the exchange of goods.

Participants in people-to-people exchanges can be either political parties and governments, or civilians; they can be either government organizations or non-governmental organizations; they can be either the "one track" of the diplomatic service or the "two tracks" of the non-diplomatic sector. It can be eitherthe academic circles or the business circles.

In contrast to people-to-people exchanges is public diplomacy. Public diplomacy faces all stratum of society, including bilateral and multilateral official and non-governmental dialogues and exchanges, covering fields of economy, education, humanities, media, science and technology, sports, and military.[1] It can be seen that public diplomacy does not directly engage in commodity exchange. Therefore, it should also be an important part of people-to-people exchanges to a certain extent.

Chinese leaders attach great importance to Chinese and foreign cultural exchanges. When visiting the world, there are often suggestions on how to further develop bilateral relations, one of which is to promote people-to-people exchanges. According to the "Vision and Action on Jointly Building the Silk Road Economic Belt and the 21st-Century Maritime Silk Road" jointly issued by the National Development and Reform Commission, the Ministry of Foreign Affairs and the Ministry of Commerce on March 28, 2015, the people-to-people bond is the social foundation of constructing the "Belt and Road" cooperation, and the purpose is to inherit and carry forward the spirit of friendship and

---

[1] 杨洁篪:《努力开拓中国特色公共外交新局面》,《求是》2011 年第 4 期, http: //www. qstheory. cn/zxdk/2011/201104/201102/t20110214_67907. htm。

cooperation on the Silk Roads, and extensively carry out cultural exchanges, academic exchanges, talent exchanges and cooperation, media cooperation, youth and women's exchanges, volunteer services, etc., to lay a solid foundation of public opinion for deepening bilateral and multilateral cooperation. In December 2017, the General Office of the State Council of the CPC Central Committee issued the "Several Opinions on Strengthening and Improving People-to-people exchanges between China and other countries", and put forward various principled requirements on how to strengthen and improve People-to-people exchanges between China and other countries.

The necessity and importance of promoting People-to-people exchangs between China and other countries are obvious.

(1) It is conducive to telling the story of China and spreading the voice of China. In May 2015, General Secretary of the CPC Central Committee, President of the State, and Chairman of the Central Military Commission Xi Jinping made important instructions on the 30th anniversary of the publication of the People's Daily overseas edition, demanding "telling good stories about China and spreading Chinese voices well". The report of the 19th National Congress of the Communist Party of China also pointed out: "Promoting international communication capacity building, telling good stories about China, showing real, three-dimensional and comprehensive China to improve the national cultural soft power."

There are many ways to tell stories, one of which is to promote people-to-people exchanges so that Chinese stories can be deeply rooted in the world.

(2) People-to-people exchanges between China and other countries help to improve China's national image. China's international status has been improved day by day, and its international influence is rising. What China does and says will have a big or small impact on the international community. Therefore, further improvement of China's national image will help strengthen China's international influence. In other words, China's national image and China's international influence are mutually influential and bring out the best in each

other.

However, with the development of China, "China threat theory" is spreading in the international world, sometimes even arrogant, posing a serious hazard to China's international image and international prestige.

The "China threat theory" and the "Yellow Peril theory" in history are of the same batch.[1] This ultra-nationalist theory holds that the yellow race poses a threat to white people, so whites should unite to deal with the yellow race.

An effective means of eliminating the "China threat theory" is to carry out people-to-people exchanges, show the effectiveness of China's economic development and its contribution to defending world peace and development, and eliminate misunderstandings and misjudgments of China's development.

(3) People-to-people exchanges between China and other countries help to enhance China's soft power. According to Joseph Nye's argument, hard power and soft power behave differently. Soft power is the ability of a country to achieve its purpose by relying on its own charm and attractiveness, rather than by means of military means or economic sanctions.[2] This means that a country can fully achieve the goal of pursuing its pursuit in international affairs by exploiting the advantages of soft power and getting the follow-up and support of other countries. China should pay equal attention to strengthening their hard power and soft power. One of the effective ways to improve soft power is to promote People-to-people exchangs between China and other countries, so that the outside world can more easily accept China's various ideas and words and deeds.

Moreover, People-to-people exchangs between China and other countries can contribute to the promotion of Chinese civilization. For example, although

---

[1] 欧洲人曾将13世纪蒙古人西征视为中世纪"最大的黄祸"。俄罗斯人巴枯宁的《国家制度和无政府状态》(1873年)和英国人皮尔逊的《民族生活与民族性》(1893年)使"黄祸论"进一步扩散。(见陈安:《中国特色话语:陈安论国际经济法学》,北京大学出版社2018年版,第163—164页)

[2] Joseph S. Nye Jr., Soft Power: The Means To Success In World Politics, Public Affairs, 2005.

the "four great inventions of ancient China" are well-known around the world, there are also a few countries that challenge this consensus from time to time. Scholars in these countries have used some plausible archaeological discoveries to deny that the "four major inventions" are China's major contributions to the development of human society. In the face of such challenges, we must increase the intensity of people-to-people exchanges and make those untrue words breakable.

(4) People-to-people exchanges is conducive to promoting the building of a community of shared future for mankind. Promoting the construction of a community of shared future for mankind is an important part of Xi Jinping's socialist ideology with Chinese characteristics in the new era, and is a banner established by China's diplomacy in the new era. When the 19th National Congress of the Communist Party of China revised the "Articles of Association of the Communist Party of China", "promoting the building of a community of shared future for mankind" has been written in the articles, making it one of the basic strategies for adhering to and developing socialism with Chinese characteristics in the new era. On March 11, 2018, the Third Plenary Session of the First Session of the 13th National People's Congress passed the Constitutional Amendment of the People's Republic of China. In the twelfth paragraph of the preamble of the Constitution, "developing diplomatic relations, economic and cultural exchanges with the countries" was revised to "developing diplomatic relations, economic and cultural exchanges with the countries, and promoting the building of a community of shared future for mankind". It can be seen that building a community of shared future for mankind has become China's national will.

However, little is known about the importance and necessity of promoting the building of a community of shared future for mankind. This requires us to promote China's diplomatic philosophy in a variety of ways, such as promoting people-to-people exchanges, so as to make this ambitious goal realized at an early date.

(5) People-to-people exchanges is conducive to eliminating the "trust deficit" between countries. Confucius said: "one can do nothing if he lose his credit or break his words." Trust is both a prerequisite for harmonious coexistence between people and a basis for peaceful coexistence between nations. In the history of mankind, there were countless examples that the lack of trust between nations resulted in their becoming dangerously explosive and appealing to arms. Therefore, President Xi Jinping regards trust as "the best adhesive in international relations". Indeed, diplomatic relations will be ended and scattered if based on forces and interests. Only amity between people can make the diplomatic relation last forever.

The world today isundergoing a great change in the past 100 years. In this change, although peace and development is still the theme of the times, the uncertainty of instability is more prominent. What's more, global problems are emerging and are unhealed with a long term of treatment. The common challenges facing humanity are becoming more and more serious. Therefore, when Chinese President Xi Jinping gave a speech at the UN headquarters in Geneva two years ago, he asked "what is the world, what can we do?"

The effectiveness of global governance is obvious. The signing of the Paris Climate Change Agreement, the breakthrough of the deadlock in the Doha Round negotiations, the rise of the anti-terrorist struggle, the containment of cybercrime and the disappearance of the Ebola epidemic are all strong evidence. However, compared with the seriousness of global problems, especially the expectations of people of all countries, the effectiveness of global governance is less satisfactory.

The poor performance of global governance is related to a variety of factors, the most important of which is the lack of trust between countries. Chinese President Xi Jinping called it "trust deficit".

One of the effective means of eliminating the "trust deficit" is to expand people-to-people exchanges to make the country's foreign policy objectives known and understood by the outside world, so that countries around the world can assume common and differentiated responsibilities in promoting global governance.

(6) People-to-people exchanges between China and other countries are conducive to promoting foreign economic and trade relations. Economic and trade relations are not just simplistic commodity trading, but a bilateral relationship containing political, diplomatic and humanistic content. Therefore, the development of economic and trade relations have enhanced the necessity of people-to-people exchanges. people-to-people exchanges can improve economic and trade relations, enable market information between trading partners to circulate in a smoother channel, and also enhance each other's cognition of the market environment and investment climate. It is hard to imagine that economic and trade relations can take place between countries that lack people-to-people exchanges.

Ⅱ. Ways and Means to Promote People-to-people Exchanges between China and Other Countries

In the process of further promoting people-to-people exchanges between China and other countries, the following measures should be taken:

(1) Telling good stories of the Chinese Communist Party in governing China. The Communist Party of China is the ruling party. Therefore, when telling the Chinese story to the outside world, we must first tell good stories of the Chinese Communist Party in governing China. In this regard, Xi Jinping sets an example by personally taking partin and uses every opportunity to tell stories. He is good at translating profound thoughts and abstracting theories into easy-to-understand stories. Therefore, in a certain sense, Xi Jinping is a great story teller.

It should be pointed out that telling the good stories of the Chinese Communist Party in governing China is not to export the so-called "Chinese model", nor to strengthen the fictitious "sharp strength", but to let the outside world understand what and how the Chinese Communist Party has been doing for the Chinese people and contributing to the maintenance of peace and development in the world.

Governing a state and promoting economic growth is a broad concept covering a wide range of content. Therefore, a multi-faceted, three-dimensional perspective should be adopted in telling the good stories of the Chinese Communist Party in governing China. In other words, this perspective should care for both historical accumulation and today's reality; it should focus on the Communist Party of China as a whole, and should also focus on every party member who constitutes this party; it should include both spiritual civilization and material civilization; it should not only talk about China's internal affairs, but also publicize China's diplomacy; it should interpret the concept of human destiny and the "Belt and Road" initiative, and should also introduce the work and life of ordinary Chinese.

(2) Correctly understanding the ideological issues in people-to-people exchanges between China and other countries. Different countries in the world have different political systems, social systems and cultural traditions, as well as different values. Therefore, people-to-people exchanges between different countries can be ideological. In fact, when the western developed countries implement their people-to-people exchanges, they also do not despise the role of ideology or never forget to promote their values. Therefore, we must not be afraid of ideology when promoting people-to-people exchanges between China and other countries. For example, China's reform and opening up is a great project led by the Communist Party of China to realize the "Chinese Dream" and its achievements are well-known. In promoting Chinese and foreign people-to-people exchanges, the promotion of China's achievements in reform and opening up is actually promoting the wise leadership of the Chinese Communist Party. Moreover, the political system of China with the population more than 1.3 billion must be unique and cannot follow the so-called democratic political

system of the West. When promoting people-to-people exchanges between China and other countries, introducing China's populous national conditions is actually introducing China's political system in line with its own national conditions. This shows that it is difficult for people-to-people exchanges to rise above ideological differences.

Of course, we should abandon the political slogan language of the "Cultural Revolution" era, but maximize the use of words and expressions that are consistent with international style and are easy to accept and understand. Practices such as the Cairo Declaration movie posters can only be counterproductive.

It should also be pointed out that the purpose of people-to-people exchanges between China and other countries should not be to achieve "de-Westernization" in developing regions such as Asia, Africa and Latin America. This is related to the following factors: First, "de-Westernization" is contrary to China's assertion of civilized pluralism and civilized family. Second, China is still unable to "de-Westernize"; third, there are a lot of essences in the western culture, and there is no need to "throw the baby out with the bathwater".

(3) Paying more attention to the construction of discourse power. One of the important forms of people-to-people exchanges is international communication. It is gratifying that China already has a huge international communication system including TV, radio, books, newspapers, periodicals and the Internet.

The pillar of international communication is the discourse system. The discourse system includes right of speech and discourse power, which are not the same. The right of speech is the right and qualification to "speak", so any country in the world has the right to speak. Discourse power is the penetrating power of "speech", which is the effect of international communication.

Improving the discourse power should keep to the following: first, the principle of seeking truth from facts must be abided by, and falsehoods, big words, and empty talks should be avoided, also, and the pattern "reporting only what is good while concealing what is unpleasant to domestic audiences" the media often uses should be tried to avoid. Second, the language expression that foreign audiences can accept should be adopted, and the quality of translation should be improved. Third, the advantages of modern media technology should be made full use of to make our promotion touch more people visually, acoustically and spiritually in the international arena. Fourth, the situation of lacking talents in professional international communication field should be improved as soon as possible. Fifth, the coverage of the Chinese media should be expanded on a global scale.

The first and second volumes of *Xi Jinping the Governance of China* have been published in more than 20 languages in the world since its publication in September 2014, covering more than 160 countries and regions. Its popularity abroad is unprecedented. The reasons for the book to achieve the great success in international communication are many, one of which is the book's strong discourse power. The book is not the Chinese leader's external preaching, but uses facts to talk about China's development path; instead of repeating the Chinese position already known to outsiders, it proposes a series of new concepts, new ideas and new strategies with groundbreaking significance; instead of using rigid, embarrassing, and incomprehensible words, it is based on historical allusions in traditional Chinese culture, and expounds the CCP's ruling strategy in plain, easy-to-understand language.

(4) Activelygiving full play to the scholars. In many countries, scholars can make an important contribution to the strengthening of their international right of speech because they have expertise in a particular profession or field. On the one hand, the international right of speech requires scholars to provide academic support; on the other hand, in the minds of the public, politicians' remarks serve political interests or government interests completely, while scholars' speeches are considered to have more impartiality and reasonableness. Therefore, in order to strengthen China's international right of speech, it is necessary to take the following measures: first, encouraging scholars to publish

their research results in international academic journals or international media; second, reducing restrictions on retirement scholars to participate in academic activities abroad; third, translating more scientific research results into English or other major foreign languages; fourth, requiring all academic institutions to open foreign language websites to introduce the main scientific research results of their scholars; fifth, creating more foreign language periodicals; sixth, offering more space and convenience for scholars' innovation in the field of the right of speech.

As China's international status rises, more and more foreign universities offer courses related to China's political, economic, diplomatic, cultural and social fields. They recruit professors in an open manner, and the candidates are mainly from countries and regions outside China. These professors are superficial in understanding and cognition of China, and they are also very one-sided. In addition, they rarely use Chinese published textbooks. It is conceivable that such courses are helpless to cultivate students who are friendly to China, and are not conducive to the improvement of the China's right of speech.

In order to change this situation, the relevant departments should encourage Chinese professors to apply for job applications to foreign universities, and reduce their worries in terms of personnel relations, salary and promotion of titles. In addition, textbooks written by Chinese scholars should be promoted to foreign universities in order to change the situation that foreign professors use foreign textbooks to open courses on Chinese in foreign universities as soon as possible, which is not conducive to strengthening China's right of speech.

（5）It is necessary to vigorously respond to the "colored glasses" of the West. As mentioned above, one of the purposes of promoting people-to-people exchanges between China and other countries is to eliminate foreign misconceptions about China and to improve China's national image. In order to achieve this goal, China has done its best and done everything for a long time, so that it is difficult for Chinese scholars to propose more and better policy recommendations.

Undoubtedly, one of the reasons why there are still a lot of prejudice and misunderstanding of China in the world is that it is difficult to eliminate "colored glasses". This means that no matter how China promotes and introduces itself, China's image in their mind is always negative.

In the international world, there are many people who observe China through "colored glasses". Under the prejudice, they believe that the socialist system under the leadership of the Communist Party is full of such shortcomings, or that the socialist system will collapse or be full of "threats". In their eyes, China's behavior in the international world is to satisfy its own interests. What is even more surprising is that China's act of safeguarding national sovereignty and territorial integrity is seen as "showing muscles".

Unquestionably, Chinese and foreign people-to-people exchanges help to eliminate "colored glasses", while "colored glasses" also constitute a huge obstacle to people-to-people exchanges. This means that, on the one hand, we must continue to do a good job in publicity, so that more foreigners can hear our voices; on the other hand, we should continue to do "homework" and make "colored glasses" fall to the ground without being attacked.

(6) Trying to increase the non-government color. The government has sufficient economic resources and diplomatic resources to promote people-to-people exchanges at the national level. However, the role of the government in people-to-people exchanges is not omnipotent. Moreover, many Westerners are quite vocal about the Chinese government's direct participation in people-to-people exchanges. For example, Steven W. Mosher, director of the US Think-tank Population Research Institute, said at the US Congressional hearing that the Confucius Institute is a "Trojan horse with Chinese characteristics" and is far from with the French "Alliance Française" and Germany "Goethe-Institut". He believes that the Confucius Institute led by the United Front Department and the

Ministry of Education has a politicized mission overseas.[①]

Such comments are biased and even absurd, and we must maximize the role of non-governmental organizations, private enterprises and other civil forces in promoting Chinese and foreign people-to-people exchanges.

Cases such as China Wanda Group having acquired the Legendary Pictures, one of Hollywood's famous film, television production companies, Alibaba Group Holdings Co., Ltd. having acquired the *South China Morning Post*, etc., show that private enterprises have the ability to enter the foreign media, publishing and entertainment industries. Of course, this pace will not be smooth. Southern Newspaper Group and Chengdu B-Ray Communications have tried to acquire US Newsweek, but were foiled by the so-called "nationality" issue of bidders.

Ⅲ. How to Promote BRICS People-to-people Exchanges

The importance of strengthening the BRICS people-to-people exchanges is self-evident. In the past decade, the BRICS have achieved remarkable results in strengthening solidarity and cooperation, developing economic and trade relations, and participating in global governance. This is inseparable from the wonderful BRICS people-to-people exchanges. It should be pointed out that in order to implement the consensus reached by the leaders of the five countries and achieve greater achievements in the BRICS future cooperation, it is necessary to increase the intensity of people-to-people exchanges.

Ufa Declaration announced on the 7th BRICS Summit on July 9, 2015 stated: "Considering UNESCO Declaration of International Cultural Cooperation

---

① Steven W. Mosher, "Confucius Institutes: Trojan Horses with Chinese Characteristics", Testimony Presented to the Subcommittee on Oversight and Investigations House Committee on Foreign Affairs, March 28, 2012. https://www. pop. org/content/confucius-institutes-trojan-horses-chinese-characteristics.

Principles in 1966 and the Declaration on Cultural Diversity in 2001, we recognize that cultural diversity is the source of development and believe that people-to-people exchanges and cooperation will promote mutual understanding. We reassert the importance of BRICS cooperation in the field of culture. To strengthen the friendly relations between the countries and the people, we will continue to encourage BRICS direct exchanges in culture field in various ways. We welcome the BRICS to sign intergovernmental cultural cooperation agreements, which will play an important role in expanding and deepening cultural and artistic cooperation and promoting cultural dialogue, and will be helpful for bringing the BRICS culture closer and narrowing the distance between people."

On September 3, 2017, President Xi Jinping emphasized at the opening ceremony of the Xiamen BRICS Business Forum, "We should play the role of people-to-people exchanges and bring people from all walks of life to the BRICS cooperation course to create more activities bounded up with the mass and benefiting the well-being of people, such as cultural festivals, film festivals and the sports meeting, and let the BRICS stories spread all over the streets, the exchanges and friendship of the five peoples merge into the ever-flowing rivers, and inject momentum into the BRICS cooperation."[①]

Indeed, promoting BRICS people-to-people exchanges is conducive to strengthening exchanges between the five countries and understanding among the people, helping to enhance mutual feelings, and laying the foundation for promoting BRICS cooperation in global governance and other fields.

In promoting the BRICS people-to-people exchanges, the following three guidelines must be followed:

The first is to correctly handle the relationship between people-to-people

---

① 习近平:《共同开创金砖合作第二个"金色十年"——在金砖国家工商论坛开幕式上的讲话》，人民网，2017年9月3日，http://cpc.people.com.cn/n1/2017/0904/c64094-29512050.html。

exchanges and other cooperation fields. Although people-to-people exchanges is very important, the main purpose of cooperation among the five emerging economies within the BRICS framework should not be only people-to-people exchanges, but how to play an important role in the international arena (especially in the process of promoting global governance). In other words, the evaluation criterion of the achievements of the BRICS cooperation cannot be limited to the number of cultural festivals, film festivals or sports events, but their actions on the international stage.

The second is to highlight the color of multilateral cooperation. As everyone knows, China and other countries of BRICS have already carried out various forms of people-to-people exchanges, and the results have been remarkable. Other countries of BRICS also conduct people-to-people exchanges of different forms and sizes with different BRICS countries. Therefore, the BRICS people-to-people exchanges are not a simplistic superposition of bilateral exchanges, but holistic exchanges at the multilateral level with the BRICS as a whole. In other words, people-to-people exchanges at the multilateral level of all BRICS countries cannot be replaced by the existing bilateral people-to-people exchanges.

The third is to abide by the principle of openness andinclusiveness. The purpose of BRICS people-to-people exchanges is not to "de-Westernization" but to promote mutual understanding between the BRICS countries and to consolidate the foundation of public opinion. Therefore, the so-called "BRICS Culture" proposed by some scholars may be counterproductive and violate the principle of openness and inclusiveness.

In fact, the unconventional concept of "BRICS Culture" is unscientific in theory and practice. The cultures of the BRICS countries have their own characteristics and are self-contained. It is difficult to develop into a new culture, and should not be integrated into a "hodgepodge".

In order to further promote the BRICS people-to-people exchanges, it is necessary to take the following measures:

(1) Giving full play to the public diplomacy. Public diplomacy faces all stratum of society, including official and non-governmental dialogues, covering fields of economy, education, humanities, media, science and technology, sports, and military. It can be seen that although public diplomacy does not directly engage in commodity exchange, its status in international exchanges cannot be underestimated. Public diplomacy should be in the supremacy in BRICS people-to-people exchanges and its important role should be maximized.

(2) Establishing BRICS study abroad fund. At present, each member of BRICS has its own study abroad funds of different sizes, providing scholarships for international students from all over the world. In order to expand the scale of exchanges of international students at the BRICS level, it is necessary to establish a study abroad fund specifically for BRICS. It is not a fund funded by a single BRICS country, but a fund jointly funded and jointly managed by the five countries.

International students who enjoy this scholarship can only study in the BRICS countries. In addition, the number of international students who enjoy this scholarship is matched with the ratio of national funding, that is, the amount of capital contribution is proportional to the number of scholarships. In the first few years, the total number of scholarships for international students can be controlled at around 1,000 per year, with an average of 200 ones per member of BRICS.

(3) Establishing a cooperation mechanism for cultural industries. The BRICS cultural traditions are broad and profound and each has its own characteristics. This has laid a solid foundation for their cooperation in the cultural industry. The government departments of the five countries should follow the "Internet +" development trend and support the business, academic, media, think tanks, literary and art circles and other industries, with cultural tourism, entertainment, arts and crafts, animation games, creative design and digital culture as breakthroughs to establish a mutually beneficial and win-win cooperation mechanism in the cultural industry.

(4) Increasing the academic research. As the name implies, people-to-people exchange is bidirectional, not one-way. This means that in the process of promoting BRICS people-to-people exchanges, each member should let the other party understand their own demands and understand each other's appeals. There is no doubt that only by better understanding each other can we promote the people-to-people exchange in a manner of getting twofold results with half the effort.

Academic research plays a pivotal role in promoting people-to-people exchange. Chinese scholars have become more and more aware of other BRICS countries, but it is hard to say that they have reached the point of knowing them very well; other BRICS countries are more superficial in their perceptions of China. If such a situation cannot be changed as soon as possible, it will certainly weaken the effectiveness of Chinese and foreign people-to-people exchanges. Therefore, BRICS scholars should be encouraged to increase their research on BRICS cooperation and basic national conditions. When conditions permit, a BRICS scholar-visiting program can be established to increase exchanges between scholars.

(5) Giving free rein to the special advantages of the embassy and the consulate. The BRICS embassies and consulates know the country conditions of residence very well, and they all shoulder the important responsibility of promoting their country. Therefore, it is necessary to give free rein to the special advantages of these diplomatic institutions in promoting BRICS people-to-people exchanges.

(6) Adopting the form that the public loves to see and hear. people-to-people exchanges are spiritual exchanges, so such exchanges must be materialized into forms that people like to see, such as cultural festivals, film festivals, book exhibitions, cultural relics exhibitions, and sports games. In addition, the BRICS should encourage domestic tourists to travel to other countries of BRICS or attract tourists from other BRICS countries to travel to their country by means of holding a year of tourism and relaxing visa

restrictions, etc.

Ⅳ. Conclusion

People-to-people exchanges between China and other countries is an important part of the party and the country's work in the field of external relations, as well as an important way to consolidate the social and public opinion of Sino-foreign relations and improve the level of China's opening to the outside world.

People-to-people exchanges between China and other countries are conducive to telling good stories about China and spreading China's voice well, improving China's national image, enhancing China's soft power, facilitating the building of a community of shared future for mankind, eliminating the "trust deficit" between countries, and promoting foreign economic and trade relations."

In order to effectively advance People-to-people exchanges between China and other countries, efforts should be channeled into telling good stories of the Chinese Communist Party in governing China, correctly understanding the ideological issues in Chinese and foreign people-to-people exchanges, paying more attention to the construction of discourse power, actively giving full play to the scholars, vigorously responding to the "colored glasses" of the West and increasing the non-government color.

On New Year's Day of 2017, President Xi Jinping at the official BRICS presidency, gave a letter to Russian President Putin, South African President Zuma, Brazilian President Temer and Indian Prime Minister Modi, and briefed the leaders of the four countries on the ideas of advancing BRICS cooperation process during the presidency.

He hoped that the Xiamen Summit would focus on the following aspects: the first is to deepen pragmatic cooperation and promote common development;

the second is to strengthen global governance and jointly meet challenges; the third is to carry out people-to-people exchanges and consolidate the foundation of public opinion; the fourth is to promote mechanism construction and build wider partnerships. It can be seen that people-to-people exchange has become one of the important fields of BRICS cooperation.

Promoting the BRICS people-to-people exchanges is conducive to strengthening exchanges between the five countries and understanding among the peoples, enhancing mutual feelings, and laying the foundation for promoting BRICS cooperation in global governance and other fields.

How to Make People-to-people Exchanges Possible?

——Based on the Discussion of the Cultural "Self" and "Other" Identities

Zhang Qing*   Cui Yige**   Yang Sheng***

Abstract: Grasping the "self" and "other" identities of culture provides a way to deeply understand the possibility of people-to-people exchange. Based on the paradox of modernity in people-to-people exchange and the group consciousness of "self", cultural communication is mainly confronted with two kinds of situations: confrontation and harmonious equality. By observing the misunderstanding of cultural diversity, we can draw a unified path of cultural diversity, which may be achieved in terms of cultural adaptability, commonality of thinking, cross-cultural communication ability and the promotion of media technology.

Keywords: People-to-people Exchange; "Self"; "Other"; Identity

---

* Zhang Qing, Associate Professor, School of International Relations, Sichuan International Studies University, Director of Center for People-to-people Exchange Studies, Institute of BRICS Studies, Sichuan International Studies University.
** Cui Yige, Master Degree Candidte of Sichuan International Studies University.
*** Yang Sheng, Master Degree Candidate of Sichuan International Studies University.

I. Introduction

With the enhancement of China's comprehensive national strength and the improvement of its international status, people-to-people exchange has become the third pillar of Chinese and foreign cooperation after political security and economic finance. In recent years, the discussion on people-to-people exchanges has been endless, but most of them are based on the discussion of necessity and realization approach, and the ontological thinking about its possibility is rare. Based on the cultural "self" and "other" perspectives, it is more helpful to understand the essence of culture and communication, form cultural intersubjectivity, and thus respond to cultural differences with a more peaceful attitude and enhance the effect of people-to-people exchanges.

II. The Paradox of Modernity in People-to-people Exchanges

Judging from common sense, as long as two heterogeneous cultural groups have the willingness to communicate with each other and the means of communication, people-to-people exchange is well-reasoned. But reality is often not the case. The modern industrialization and commercialization process has provided us with more convenient channels for information spreading than before, such as radio, film, television, internet, etc., but people do not seem to find an effective way to break through the barriers of cultural barriers and understanding. "When we walk into the world of communication mythology created by communication technology, we fall into the abyss of communication, which results in that we have to solve the cultural conflicts between each other with efforts several times that for the wars and violence before."[1]

Charles Dickens pointed out in the opening of *Tale of Two Cities*: "It was

---

[1] 单波:《跨文化传播的问题与可能性》,武汉大学出版社2010年版,第2页。

the best of times, it was the worst of times, it was the age of wisdom, it was the age of foolishness, it was the epoch of belief, it was the epoch of incredulity, it was the season of Light, it was the season of Darkness, it was the spring of hope, it was the winter of despair".[1] Such a description is equally applicable to modernity. Modernity promotes the development and progress of society, but it also spawns some paradoxes arising from the division of instrumental rationality and value rationality, such as the crisis of nature, the lack of value, the loss of morality, the abstraction of the world, the loss of freedom, etc. As a classic theorist on modernity, Max Weber reflected on the paradox of modernity and its roots through "rationalization", and put forward the rational "paradox". Weber believed that modernity was the "rationalization" process of society and culture. A core feature of modern society is that people are used to thinking with reason. For this reason, grasping rationality is the key to understanding modern society. "The development of the spirit of capitalism can be understood as part of the overall development of rationalism, and it can be deduced from the fundamental position of rationalism on basic issues of life."[2]

Although modernity has greatly advanced human progress, economic prosperity and social development, but beyond the expectations of enlightenment thinkers, instead of helping human society to overcome the obstacles in the historical process and step out of the cage of slavery to get liberated and free, modernity has strengthened the bondage and non-freedom of people. As Isaiah Berlin has mentioned, rationality is the basis for building social models and its original intention is to liberate human beings from mistakes, confusion, and from the unrecognizable but recognizable world with the application of some patterns. But, without exception, these patterns re-enslave the liberated human beings and cannot explain all experience of human beings. Thus, the original

---

[1] [英]查尔斯·狄更斯，石永礼等：《双城记》，人民文学出版社2004年版，第1页。
[2] [德]马克斯·韦伯，于晓等译：《新教伦理与资本主义精神》，三联书店1987年版，第56页。

liberator eventually becomes the dictator in another sense."①

Modernity breeds people's desires while meeting people's needs. According to John Durham Peters, "communication" is a registry of modern longings. This term evokes a utopia where nothing is misunderstood, hearts are open, and expressions are uninhibited. Desire is the most intense when object is absent."② From another perspective, we are eager to communicate because we feel the lack of social relations. On the one hand, Peters acknowledged the urgency of communication. "Communication is a rich tangle of intellectual and cultural strands that encodes our time's confrontation with itself. To understand communication is to understand much more. We can obtain an apparent answer to the painful divisions between self and other, private and the public, and inner thoughts and outer words."③ On the other hand, there is a lack of confidence in realizing real communication between people. "The notion of 'communication' illustrates our strange lives at this point in history. It is a sink into which most of our hopes and fears seem to be poured."④

In Peters' view, as a bridge of communication, exchange is a blurring attempt constructed by symbol, which only has appearance in form and lacks content support. There are no certain signs in the exchange, only hints and conjectures. Our interaction cannot be the blending of thoughts, but at most the dance of thoughts; in the dance process, we can sometimes touch each other.⑤ "Communication is an unsecured adventure. Any attempt to establish a

---

① [英] 以赛亚·柏林, 吕梁等译:《浪漫主义的根源》, 译林出版社2008年版, 第11页。
② [美] 约翰·彼得斯, 何道宽译:《交流的无奈: 传播思想史》, 华夏出版社2003年版, 第2页。
③ [美] 约翰·彼得斯, 何道宽译:《交流的无奈: 传播思想史》, 华夏出版社2003年版, 第2页。
④ [美] 约翰·彼得斯, 何道宽译:《交流的无奈: 传播思想史》, 华夏出版社2003年版, 第2页。
⑤ [美] 约翰·彼得斯, 何道宽译:《交流的无奈: 传播思想史》, 华夏出版社2003年版, 第252页。

connection with a symbol is a gamble, whether its size is large or small."[1] Pierce was also full of distrust of the symbolic meaning system: "the symbol has only a general meaning objectively with uncertain effective interpretation. It leaves the right to complete the meaning to the interpreter."[2]

In addition, communication is always combined with power, and "pure" and "de-powered" communication is extremely difficult to realize. If we want to seek a certain spirit of fulfillment or satisfaction in communication, our efforts will be in vain. Since we are mortal, communication is always a question of power, ethics and art."[3] For this, Li Jinquan believes that the obstacle to communication in modern society is that we pay too much more attention to "intercultural communication" rather than "international exchanges". We must see that the modern world order is still based on the nation-state.[4] The influence of state power on cross-cultural communication cannot be ignored. However, the paradox is that the exchanges between different countries and nations have to necessarily safeguard the state power while obscuring the boundaries of the state, because it is the state that has an effective means to fight global financial and information storms.[5]

The way of communication directly affects the effect of communication. Thinking and speaking with the fragments of dialogue has become the main way of communicating. Raymond Williams said: "that 'I heard', 'as if the first time I heard that', according to the habit, it is still called as the so-called dramatic language, even as dialogue: first, listening to the words of Chekhov, I noticed a chronic strangeness: people no longer communicate with others, and

---

[1] [美] 约翰·彼得斯, 何道宽译:《交流的无奈:传播思想史》, 华夏出版社 2003 年版, 第 251 页。

[2] Buchler, J. Philosophical Writings of Peirce, New York: Dover, 1955: 295.

[3] [美] 约翰·彼得斯, 何道宽译:《交流的无奈:传播思想史》, 华夏出版社 2003 年版, 第 252 页。

[4] Lee, Chin-Chuan. Internationalizing "International Communication", Ann Arbor: University of Michigan Press, 2015: 1.

[5] Touraine, A. What is democracy?, Boulder: Westview Press, 1997.

there is no longer any coming and going; people's conversations may be self-talking in front of others…no one can say what he started to say; instead, people chip in others' conversation in a random and absent-minded manner and others' words go to die."[1] In the context of modernity, the essence, content, approach, and power of communication are telling us that "pure" and "effective" communication is hard to occur. "We have to admit that communication as a bridge is a real illusion, and communication as a gully is a cruel reality."[2] This is especially true for heterogeneous cultural groups which either are subject to the binary opposition between the "self" and the "other" and have difficulties in breaking through the barriers of the mindset, or are kidnapped by state power to form the so-called cultural power domination.

In view of this, Peters simply gave up the discussion about the possibility of people's communication, and instead of asking "Can we love each other and be able to treat each other fairly and generously?"[3]

Ⅲ. Who am I: the "Self" Group Identity

In the interpersonal communication, it is required to scientifically judge the identity of the "self". From the perspective of sociology, society consists of different "selves". Each individual must abandon some individuality in the social environment and keep consistent with the public value and thinking of the group. At this time, "I" with specialty has been replaced by "me" with the universals and "me" in the concept sense. The real "I" has been obscured by "us", that is, the individual is obscured by the group.[4] From a psychological

---

[1] O'Connor, A. Raymond Williams on Television: Selected Writings, London: Routledge, 1989: 12.

[2] 单波：《跨文化传播的问题与可能性》，武汉大学出版社2010年版，第3—4页。

[3] [美] 约翰·彼得斯，何道宽译：《交流的无奈：传播思想史》，华夏出版社2003年版，第252页。

[4] 单波：《跨文化传播的问题与可能性》，武汉大学出版社2010年版，第9页。

point of view, the social nature of "self" is closely related to group identity. Once a person becomes a social person, he is given a significant group identity. People who are connected to each other by social ties have similar emotions and ways of thinking and will exhibit new characteristics that are different from each individual. With the fading of personality, a "collective psychology" or "psychological group" gradually formed. "The most striking features of a psychological group are as follows. The fact is that for the individuals who make up this group, regardless of their alike or different lifestyle, occupation, personality or intelligence, they have become a group, which enable them to get a collective psychology that makes their feelings, thoughts, and behaviors quite different from their feelings, thoughts, and behaviors when they are alone. Some thoughts or feelings will not be produced in the individual, or impossible to be turned into action if the individuals do not form a group. A psychological group is a temporary phenomenon composed of heterogeneous components. When they are combined, they will have some characteristics like cells forming a living body. They are very different from the characteristics of a single cell."[1] In the interaction with others, everyone's speech and behavior will consciously and unconsciously have a strong group color, thus having the distinction between "self" and "other". "We are Chinese, while they are foreigners; we are civil servants, while they are self-employed; we are notable family and great clan, while they are impoverished family ……" We are constantly using this "labeling" way to strengthen the group identity sense. Expressing "who am I" is used to distinct themselves from other people who do not have the essential attributes of the group. It should be said that this division is a "double-edged sword". On the one hand, it helps to simplify the understanding of one's social status and enhance the understanding of social composition. On the one hand, it increases group bias such as ethnic and racism and political conflicts.

---

[1] [法] 古斯塔夫·勒庞，冯克利译：《乌合之众：大众心理研究》，中央编译出版社2014年版，第7页。

Furthermore, under the influence of "collective psychology", independent individuals will undergo an essential change in their psychology. The existence space of self-consciousness is constantly being compressed, and the development of personality is constantly being suppressed. Over time, collective psychology will be regarded as self-psychology, whose outstanding performance is simple thinking and herd mentality.[①] Specifically, in a highly socialized atmosphere, individual thinking is highly susceptible to the general evaluation and internal expectation of a member's identity based on identity. Former Soviet psychologist A. A. Bodalev had done a very interesting experiment. He took a photo and said to a group of college students: "I will show you a photo of a big scientist. Please talk about the facial features of this scientist." The unanimous opinion of the students after reading the photos was: the deep eyes of the scientist showed the depth of his thoughts; his prominent chin showed his determination to overcome difficulties on the road of scientific research. A. A. Bodalev then took this photo to another group of college students. He repeatedly said to them: "I will show you a photo of a big criminal. Please talk about what the facial features of this criminal are." The unanimous opinion of this group of college students after reading the photos was that the criminal's eyes were deep and his hatred was revealed in his heart; his prominent chin indicated his determination to die without repentance. The two groups of college students had observed the same photo. Why did they have such a big difference? The reason is obviously not their different ways of thinking, values or aesthetics, but from the different introduction to the identity of the character in the photo provided by the psychologist A. A. Bodalev. In the long-term social interaction, the basic characteristics of different identities have a fixed meaning and pattern in people's minds. People often make basic judgments on his personality traits, behaviors and behavioral expectations according to one's identity.[②]

---

① 单波:《跨文化传播的问题与可能性》,武汉大学出版社2010年版,第10页。
② 夏建平:《认同与国际合作》,世界知识出版社2006年版,第48页。

IV. Confrontation and Harmonious Equality: Two Pose of Cultural Communication

The conflicts and obstacles between cultureshave been existing since ancient time. Antonio Gramsci believes that the East and the West have never stopped discussing about "objective reality". Even in research, "objective reality" is only taken as a historical or traditional construction at most." Obviously, the concepts of the East and the West are arbitrary and traditional, because every place on the planet can be considered as the East and the West. For Europeans, Californians, and even some Japanese, Japan may count as the Far East. ……"① Especially when the same event or text can deliver different meanings, it is easy to cause potential resistance in the construction process of meaning. V. N. Volosinov noticed the problem of the "social multi-accentuality of the ideological sign". He pointed out that the multiple meanings of a symbol can be presented in different pronunciations and in different situations, can play different roles, and refer to different things. Therefore, a symbol often represents the aggregation point of "the tendency of different social interests", which is equivalent to an independent "resistance field".②

The conflict between cultures is manifested in the mindset of cultural hegemonism and cultural imperialism. The "regular" action of cultural hegemonism is to singularize the meaning of symbols and forcibly unite various cultural symbols that are originally meaningful in a specific way.③ Lenin explained "what is imperialism" in his article *Imperialism is the highest stage*

---

① Gramsci, A. Prison Notebooks, edited and translated by Joseph A. Buttigieg. New York: Columbia University Press, 1975: 176.
② Vlolsinov, V N. Marxism and the Philosophy of Language, New York: Seminar Press, 1973: 23.
③ 单波、肖珺、刘学:《全球媒介的跨文化传播幻想》,上海交通大学出版社2015年版,第46页。

of capitalism; "If it is necessary to give imperialism a definition as short as possible, then it should be said that imperialism is the monopoly stage of capitalism. Such a definition can include the most important point, because on the one hand, financial capital is the bank capital of the few monopolistic largest banks integrated with the capital of the industrialist monopoly alliance; on the other hand, carving up is transitioning from a colonial policy of unimpeded colonization of areas not occupied by any of the great capitalist powers to the colonial policy carving up the occupied territories of the world."[1] According to research, the concept of cultural imperialism was first usedand interpreted by the American University of Communications research professor Herbert Schiller in the book *Communication and Cultural Domination* in 1976. After the Second World War, many nation-states were separated from Western colonial rule, but most of them still rely heavily on a few capitalist countries economically and culturally. In terms of communication and culture, several large-scale news agencies in the West have dominated the circulation and interpretation of global information. The exchange of international culture has been seriously unbalanced, and the cultural development space of emerging countries has been severely squeezed. In his view, the presentation of cultural information is "determined by the same market dynamics that control the production of goods and services throughout the system."[2]

In the process of communication between different cultural groups, confrontation is only a means, not a purpose of communication. Through cultural communication and exchange, people will eventually achieve a harmonious state. In this sense, conflict is not wise, because the parties trapped in the conflict will always stick to their respective cultural sites by delineating the interests of the self and the self-group, and thus it is difficult to have transcendent performance.

---

[1] 孙晶:《哲学系列:文化霸权理论研究》,社会科学文献出版社2004年版,第61页。
[2] Schiller, H I. Communication and Cultural Domination, New York: International Arts and Sciences Press, 1976: 6.

In the process, each of us is likely to become a cultural fundamentalist, constantly strengthening the distinction between "self" and "other". Harmony is wisdom. It can not only help to distinguish who I am, who they are, but also help to exceedingly reflect on questions of how can we restore the freedom of living across groups? What can we do in cooperation? To answer these questions needs to deal with the relationship between "me, us and them". First, it needs to recognize that everyone has the freedom to choose and identify different cultures when realizing cultural differences; second, efforts should be channeled into constructing the equal status of different cultural groups in the process of communication; and third, attempts should be made to ease the tension in communication and the negative consequences brought about by cultural differences; fourth, efforts should be put into weakening the power domination system of inter-group communication at the institutional level, thus ensuring the free existing space of cultural groups.[①]

V. Misunderstanding of Cultural Diversity

As early as thousands of years ago, people used the term "Babel" to refer to the difficulty of communication. According to the *Old Testament. Genesis*, after the Great Flood, the Noah descendant who walked out of the Ark said a common language and founded many countries. These people living in the two river basins decided to build the tower of Babel in order to spread their reputation. These people worked together and really built the tower of Babel on the fertile plain. Seeing the tremendous power of people uniting, God was alarmed, so he disrupted the human language and made them impossible to communicate, so that they could no longer work together to build the tower. On the one hand, the story of "the tower of Babel" illustrates people's yearning for

---

① 单波:《跨文化传播的问题与可能性》,武汉大学出版社2010年版,第14—15页。

"unity" of language. On the other hand, God disrupting human language is not only a punishment for human delusions and lies, but also one type of restoring the diversity of human language, that is, the diverse languages correspond to the diverse human species.[①]

After continuous exploration, people have gradually formed a consensus on cultural diversity. The soaring industrialization and colonization in the 19th century made sociologists begin to recognize the issue of cultural equality between different groups. In the second half of the 20th century, as the critique of modernity deepened, ethnic minorities, especially national minorities and immigrant ethnic groups, increasingly demanded to retain their unique social formation and use various forms of autonomy or independent governance to ensure the social formation as the existence of a unique cultural carrier.[②] Since 1990s, UNESCO has incorporated cultural diversity into its organizational principles. According to the report *Our Cultural Diversity* published by UNESCO in 1995, "Cultural diversity, such as the existence of ecological diversity, indicates the infinite extension of human creativity. Its aesthetic value is reflected in many ways and will inspire new creations." In 2001, UNESCO adopted the "Cultural Diversity Declaration", emphasizing the importance of respecting and maintaining cultural diversity for the survival and development of all mankind in the process of economic globalization.[③]

It should be said that the analogy of cultural diversity to ecological diversity is of positive significance. As the German zoologist Ernst Haeckel in the 19th century said, diversity means "the interaction of the various elements of the natural environment and how this interaction leads to a balanced and

---

① Postman, N. The Humanism of Media Ecology, Proceedings of the Media Ecology Association, 2000 (1): 10-16.
② [加] 威尔·金里卡,杨立峰译:《多元文化公民权:一种有关少数民族群权利的自由主义理论》,上海译文出版社2009年版,第12—13页。
③ 郑育林:《唤醒遗迹:城市化背景下的大遗址保护与利用问题》,文物出版社2014年版,第209页。

healthy environment."[1] At the same time, we should pay more attention to this ecological analogy thinking trap. In the ecosystem, various organisms occupy different positions in the biological chain and the food chain, presenting different forces and exerting different influences. That the fittest survives in natural selection is the only rule of survival based on the system of power domination. Once the power domination system is introduced into the category of cultural diversity, we have the impulse to seek a dominant cultural force. "We will mistake the melting pot of the American culture that seeks to assimilate as diversity, the segregation based on the absolute nature of racial and cultural differences as diversity, the mainstream and edge framework of culture as diversity."[2] Another challenge in understanding cultural diversity is how to unify. The judgment of UNESCO is that "the development has a characteristic that is essential to the future of mankind, that is, the balance between unity and diversity. This balance is essential for all forms of development and evolution. The same is true in nature and history. Once getting away from a certain degree of unity or diversity, nothing can grow and develop... Without diversity, each part cannot form an entity that can grow, develop, breed and create. Without integration, different components cannot be combined into a single dynamic structure."[3] This passage describes a perfect state of cultural diversity to us, that is, the harmony and balance between the two. The real question is: where is the path to such a harmonious balance? In other words, based on the logic of power discourse, who should dominate the unity of cultural diversity, and who will dominate it? In the wave of economic globalization, the influence power of capital in the cultural communication of various countries should not be ignored. In contemporary society, it is difficult for a poor and backward nation to win an

---

[1] Postman, N. The Humanism of Media Ecology, Proceedings of the Media Ecology Association, 2000 (1): 10 - 16.

[2] 单波:《跨文化传播的问题与可能性》,武汉大学出版社2010年版,第16页。

[3] [意] 欧文·拉兹洛,戴侃等译:《多种文化的星球:联合国教科文组织国际专家小组的报告》,社会科学文献出版社2001年版,第11页。

opportunity in an equal cultural dialogue to influence or assimilate another nation with developed economy, science and technology and balanced cultural development.[①] In addition, the global expansion of capital is also eroding the foundation of national culture. The modernization process, either explicit or implicit, has allowed the national culture that does not conform to modernity to die out, thus moving towards global cultural homogenization. This mode of modernization is a "gentle way" to enforce national assimilation more than the promotion of national development.[②] What is more, according to the logic of the power domination system, the process of unifying multiple cultures eliminates the need for cross-cultural communication. If people are only prisoners of thought, and follow the ideology in communication, understanding, or language practice, and these puppets of ideology have no requirement for cross-culture communication, but are conquered by and obey some ideology. Perhaps, cross-cultural communication will become completely impossible because of ideological hegemony, and will eventually become a false proposition.[③]

Ⅵ. The Path of Unifying Cultural Diversity

According to the foregoing, it seems that cultural diversity is an ironclad fact in front of us, and cultural unity is water without source and a tree without roots. We cannot make such judgments categorically. After all, multiculturalism has its own developing logic and cannot be completely controlled by the system of power domination. According to this, Stuart Hall proposed the famous "articulation" theory, which believes that the connection can unify different

---

① 李炎:《西部文化产业理论与实践》,云南大学出版社2015年版,第3—4页。
② 金星华、张晓明、兰智奇:《中国少数民族文化发展报告(2008)》,民族出版社2009年版,第168页。
③ 单波:《跨文化传播的问题与可能性》,武汉大学出版社2010年版,第18页。

elements under certain conditions. This association is not necessary, definite, absolute or essential at all times. The so-called "unity" is essentially the connection of different elements. It should be noted that these elements do not have an inevitable "belonging", so they can be reconnected in different ways.[1] In interpersonal communication, the information exchanged between each other conveys a very different meaning in different contexts. Hall believed that through cultural and political practice, meaning operates within its possible scope, links to different social positions, and constructs and recreates social subjects to the extent possible.[2] That is to say, only "information" exists in real life, and the meaning is constructed, ambiguous, and contextualized. The meaning emphasizes more on the process than the result.

The "connection" between things provides the following possibilities for the exchange and unity of diverse cultures.

First of all, the adaptability of culture provides the premise and foundation for cultural exchanges. The relationship between the social structure, stratum and culture is neither a one-to-one correspondence nor an inconsistent relationship, but is constructed. It is not necessarily existent but is resulted from the constant struggle and the collision between social groups.[3] In the interaction between "self" and "other", "self" affects "other" and also is shaped by "other". Both parties need to express their opinions, understand each other, correct strategies, and ultimately achieve the purpose of communication in continuous contact and collision.

Secondly, the commonality of thoughts should be built by reflecting on the differences of language. Although different ethnic groups have different cultural forms, diverse contents, and diverse expressions, they share the value orientation

---

[1] Morley, D., Chen, K. Stuart Hall: Critical Dialogues in Cultural Studies, London: Routledge, 1996: 141.

[2] Dervin, B., Grossberg, L., O'Keefe, B J., and Wartella, E. Rethinking Communication, California: Sage Publications, 1989: 45.

[3] 林立树:《现代思潮: 西方文化研究之通路》, 中央编译出版社2014年版, 第161页。

shared by all mankind—seeking the true, the good, and the beautiful. Different cultures themselves have value convergence, which is also the "the greatest common divisor" between heterogeneous cultures.[1] As a code and carrier of culture, the difference in language is mostly in form. Ethnic groups with different language backgrounds can understand and communicate with each other through translation.[2] People study the logic behind the philosophical and linguistic formation of language, trying to cross the barriers of language and seek the commonality of thoughts to continue the miracle of "Babel".

Third, emphasis should be put on the main factors of cultural exchange to enhance people's ability to communicate across cultures. On the one hand, we should constantly correct the cultural concept and cognitive ability of the "self" subject; on the other hand, we should raise the awareness of empathy, that is putting ourselves into others shoes to make the language and behavior of "self" conform to "cultural habits and mental models" of the "other".

Fourth, modern media technologies in promoting people-to-people exchanges should be explored. The rapid development of modern media technologies not only helps to effectively overcome the spatial barriers of cultural exchange, but also helps to expand the scope of influence of various cultures, increase the speed of communication, and improve cultural cognition. This magnificent technological revolution reconstructs the relationship between cultural nationality and cultural cosmopolitan, and also changes the stability, conservativeness, exclusivity and gradual change of culture itself.[3] In this context, we should reflect on the comprehensive influence of cultural media on the basis of exploring the essence of modern media technologies, for example, how to overcome the technical rationality that it constantly demonstrates; how to combine modern media technology with excellent narrative methods to enhance

---

[1] 胡惠林、陈昕：《中国文化产业评论（第24卷）》，上海人民出版社2017年版，第253页。
[2] 单波：《跨文化传播的问题与可能性》，武汉大学出版社2010年版，第20页。
[3] 李炎：《西部文化产业理论与实践》，云南大学出版社2015年版，第4页。

the expressiveness of cultural communication and so on.[1]

Ⅶ. Conclusion

In general, people-to-people exchange is not aimed at eliminating the differences between different cultural groups, nor is it to strengthen the uniqueness of the "self" identity, but to strive to achieve a cultural mentality and awareness of mutual listening, understanding and inclusiveness between people. To achieve this needs people to stand on "others'" position and form a cultural intersubjectivity to respect each other. From this point, the ultimate expression form of people-to-people exchanges is cultural integration. Like all things in nature, culture is not an unchangeable static performance, but a dynamic process of development and decline. people-to-people exchanges inject the genes of new ideas into the motherland of their respective traditional culture through equal dialogue among people to promote the gestation and development of a new culture, and thus advance the overall development of human culture to a higher stage.

---

[1] 胡惠林、陈昕:《中国文化产业评论(第24卷)》,上海人民出版社2017年版,第255页。

Diplomacy Through Narratives: the Interaction between the Head of the State and the Public

Chen Huaqiao[*]

Abstract: The public from various countries encounter differences in information and cognition in people-to-people exchange among countries, and the information closure should be broken in time. Different countries can promote people-to-people exchange through the form of story diplomacy: the stories experienced by the public will become the material of the public speech in the foreign affairs and visits of the head after being explored by the media. The storytelling of the leaders and the media reports will strengthen the communicating effect of the story. The story of the mother and son from Wanzhou, Chongqing guarding Soviet Red Army's Kulishenko tomb for more than half a century has become the material for the speech of the head of China at the Moscow Institute of International Relations during his first state visit after extensive media coverage. After the story sharing of the leaders, the news media conducted a series of follow-up reports, and the relevant units subsequently

---

[*] Chen Huaqiao, Associate Professor of Chongqing College of Multi-languages, Sichuan International Studies University.

filmed the story, which was further spread between the two countries and brought the Chinese and Russian people closer.

Keywords: Story; Diplomacy; Amity between People

In the diplomatic discourse, some vivid stories help to arousepeople's perceptual cognition and positive sense of identity. As a form of diplomacy with strong personal qualities, the summit diplomacy has the characteristics of being prominent compared with other forms of diplomacy because of the personal involvement of the top leaders. The speeches of state leaders during the foreign visits are likely to attract widespread attention from people at home and abroad, and the stories involved in the speech may have far-reaching effects. This article focuses on the stories told in the public speech section of the summit diplomacy. After initially defining the concept of story diplomacy, it attempts to extract the general generation logic of story diplomacy, verify the existence of such logic through typical cases and propose beneficial measures to promote story diplomacy.

I. Definition of Story Diplomacy

Through the Chinese and foreign classic etymology search, the concept and its connotation of the story are accordingly determined. Subsequently, the results of diplomatic studies help to determine the concept and function of the summit diplomacy. Finally, by virtue of the existing concept and the relationship between logical attributes and species differences, story diplomacy is constructed, and its connotation and characteristics are clarified to jointly lay the foundation for academic discussion for subsequent research.

(1) Definition of the Story

In *Ci Hai* (a full-length dictionary of words and expression), when used as a noun, the story is defined as "old matters"; as a means, the word "story" is defined as "a kind of literary genre, focusing on describing the event process, emphasizing the vividness and coherence of the event and being applicable to oral presentation, popular and easy to understand."[1]

In the *Modern Chinese Dictionary*, the word "story" is a noun that means "real or fictional things that are told, which is coherent and attractive".[2] The *Collins High-Level English-Chinese Dictionary* defines story as "a description of an event or something that happened to someone, especially a spoken description of it". Meanwhile, it can also be understood as "news reports in newspapers or news programs".[3] In the *Longman Dictionary of Contemporary English*, as a noun, the word "story" is defined as a "real or fictional event", or an article in a media such as a news or magazine.[4]

From the above-mentioned Chinese and English etymology, theword "story" has at least the following meanings: when used as a noun, the story is a real or fictional thing that is spoken orally; also as a noun, the story also refers to a news report in a newspaper or news program; as an expression, the story is an oral description of the event process. In a nutshell, as an objective existence, the story is something that is spoken orally; as a relationship existence with the media, the story is a report in the media such as newspapers and news; as for expressing an object, the story is the subject's oral account of the event process.

---

[1] 辞海编辑委员会:《辞海》,上海辞书出版社1999年版,第4172—4173页。
[2] 中国社会科学院语言研究所词典编辑室编:《现代汉语词典(第5版)》,商务印书馆2005年版,第493页。
[3] 英国柯林斯公司编,姚乃强等审译:《柯林斯高阶英汉双解词典》,商务印书馆2008年版,第1575页。
[4] 朱原等译:《朗文当代高级英语辞典》,商务印书馆1998年版,第1522页。

(2) Definition of the Summit Diplomacy

Generally speaking, diplomacy refers to that "the actions and processes of a sovereign state (and a consortium of states) addressing international relations and international affairs with an aim to achieve its foreign policy objectives in a peaceful manner through communications, visits, talks, negotiations, and agreements based on international law and related practices via the official representation of the country's top leaders and the central government department with the full-time diplomatic service as the core, or other semi-official and non-official institutions, social groups, and individuals under their leadership". The summit diplomacy is "a diplomatic activity carried out by the top leaders of the state and international organizations so as to realize their foreign policy".①

Compared with the general form of diplomacy, the summit diplomacy is a highly unified diplomatic activity between the diplomatic subject and the diplomatic executor. Its distinctive feature is that the top leaders personally participate in it, and therank of diplomatic subjects is high, and is of leading and demonstrative significance. Since the Second World War, with the emergence of new media brought about by the technological revolution, the summit diplomacy has shined. The diplomatic activities of the highest leaders of the states have been reported by the media, so that more people can know the contents of high-level diplomatic activities in a timely manner. The summit diplomacy also has a communication function for this purpose and is one of the effective ways to communicate between the top leaders of the states and the general public.

(3) Definition of Story Diplomacy

The summit diplomacy mainly includes the forms of communication and talks between the leaders, the special envoys of the summit, the summit

---

① 陈志敏、肖佳灵、赵可金著:《当代外交学》, 北京大学出版社 2008 年版, 第 5—6, 195 页。

declarations, summit visits, and the summit meetings. Depending on the importance of the summit visit, the visits can be divided into state visits, official visits, informal visits, friendly visits, courtesy visits, and "state affairs stays". The state visit is the highest form of the summit visit. It generally refers to the visit of the head of state to the official invitation of the head of another state, including the official welcoming ceremony, reviewing the guard of honor, singing and salute, public speech, parliamentary speech, press conference and so on.[1] In general, the main activities of state visits are broadcast live through a variety of media, and are played again in prime time, often becoming a hot spot in the national media reports during the visit, causing widespread concern of the general public.

According to the logistics, "the definition of per genus et differentiam" is used to explain the conventional connotation of a term, which has wider applicability than any other method. Classes that are sub-classed are "genus", and various subclasses are "species". A genus can be divided into multiple species, and the nature of the different species within a genus is the "species difference".[2]

According to the general applicability principle of logistics research results, we define story diplomacy as an important form of public speech in the summit diplomatic visit. According to the "the definition of per genus et differentiam" method, story diplomacy has the genus of summit diplomacy and has the same species of public speech. To this end, this article defines story diplomacy as that a head of state tell the story which is widely reported in the public speech and reflects the real and touching things between ordinary people during the state visit in different countries.

Story diplomacy has been given the communication function of the summit

---

[1] 陈志敏、肖佳灵、赵可金著:《当代外交学》, 北京大学出版社2008年版, 第205页。
[2] [美] 欧文·M. 柯匹、卡尔·科恩著, 张建军等译:《逻辑学导论（第11版）》, 中国人民大学出版社2007年版, 第142—143页。

diplomacy because of its genus of summit diplomacy. That the head of the state tells the real story realizes the direct communication between the leader of the country and the public in the host country, and narrow the distance between the leader and the ordinary people. If this public speaking process is broadcast live by the media and played again, it will help to strengthen the spread of real stories among ordinary people.

Ⅱ. The Generating Logic of Story Diplomacy

According to the definition, the whole process of story diplomacy involves three mainbehavioral agents, namely the public, the media and the head. According to the chronological development sequence of the event, the story diplomacy needs to go through three stages: the people's personal experience, the media mining cases, and the head storytelling. The main behavioral agents in each stage must take clear actions and point to clear targets and generate certain results. Such behavioral agents at different stages take different actions according to certain time series and bring forth a specific result, and ultimately develop a more stable mechanism,[1] which is the generating logic of story diplomacy.

(1) **People's Personal Experiencing Events**

With the further development of science and technologyand the increasingly improved transportation, the time of long-distance commuting is constantly compressed, and the scope of activities of ordinary people has been gradually broadened and the traditional category of a country's borders has been broken through. The public has move freely and more frequently around the world. According to statistics from some ICAO annual statistics, the number of

---

[1] 关于机制的一般性解释, 参见 Mario Bunge, "Mechanism and Explanation," Philosophy of the Social Sciences, Vol. 27, No. 4, 1997, pp. 410 - 465。

passengers on international flights increased from 808 million in 2006 to 1.436 billion in 2015, and the air mileage increased from 2.5 trillion km to 4.1 trillion km.[①]

With the increase of cross-border movements of people around the world, the interaction between residents of a country and foreign residents has become more frequent, and the exchanges between ordinary people in different countries have become increasingly close, and the various experienced events are likely to increase substantially. Some of these typical events may be recorded and preserved in a variety of ways, and become an important historical testimony of the relationship between countries. More personal experiencing events may be left between ordinary people in the form of an anecdote.

The increase in people's personal experiencing events is the inevitable result of the population's cross-border movement. With the development of the scientific and technological revolution, the process of global integration has further accelerated, and the transnational flow of population will inevitably accelerate. What can be expected is that people's personal experiencing events will increase due to the cross-border movement of the population.

(2) **Media Mining Cases**

The events experienced by ordinary people in foreign exchanges are most likely unconscious events. As time goes by, these personal events of foreign exchanges may disappearfrom the public and become a dust of history. Because of keen professional sense of smell, journalists are likely to find such a subject in their daily life or work. With the continuous development of the media industry, the competition among journalists is becoming increasingly fierce. Journalists need to be able to grasp the ability of deeply digging the story behind news reports, and re-report these dusty events for the public to know.

---

① 详细数据参见国际民航组织官方网站年度报告，https://www.icao.int/sustainability/Pages/FactsFigures.aspx，2019 年 5 月 6 日登陆。

That the media deeply explores the case behind the news is not only an inevitable requirement for the survival of the media in the all-media era, but also the basic ability requirement for journalists. Driven by the internal and external factors of the industry environment and personal qualities, the media and its practitioners are very likely to dig out more typical cases from the general events.

(3) **The Head Telling the Story**

In the foreign affairs activities of the summit, especially during state visits, they often accept joint media interviews before the visit. The leaders often choose to publish the signed articles in the main media of the host country. During the visit, they will make important announcements during the welcome banquet or the speech of the congress. In these signed articles and important speeches for the general public in the home country and the host country, the articles or speeches of the leaders often involve touching stories about the people's exchanges between the two countries.

Such stories have been personally elaborated by the leaders during the foreign affairsand visits, and have been disseminated on a larger scale through media reports, realizing the communication between the leaders and more ordinary people, and causing resonation with ordinary people. Not only that, such stories can be widely spread among the ordinary people of the two countries through extensive coverage by the media in both countries.

In summary, the story diplomacy has gone through three stages: people's personal story, the media mining case, and the head storytelling. The story diplomacy gradually develops from the story of ordinary people, is mined and covered by the media and then rise to be part of the summit diplomacy after the storytelling by the head of the state during the state visit, and finally becomes a component of international relations.

Judging from the generating logic of story diplomacy, because of the frequent foreign exchanges, the amount of people's personal story is

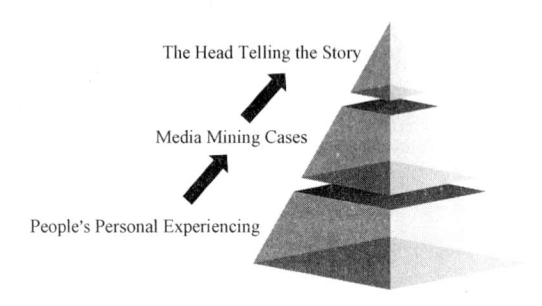

Figure 1: The Generating Logic of Story Diplomacy
Source: Made by the Author.

considerable. Due to the difference in the nature of work, the focus of media is limited, and the cases that can be mined deeper are only a part of the typical events. The story in the people's exchanges told by the heads during the state visits may be the story that the media have explored and reported and that can best reflect the exchange between two common peoples from two countries. The focuses of different behavioral agents are various, and the development process of story diplomacy is actually a re-screening process for people's personal events, thus, the number of the stories will decrease.

Ⅲ. Typical Cases of Story Diplomacy

According to the author's incomplete statistics, Chinese President Xi Jinping's important speeches during the state visits involved real stories in the exchanges between the two peoples.① In the typical case section, we choose the story diplomacy of President Xi Jinping's first state visit, and look forward to concluding the logic of story diplomacy through this typical case.

---

① 统计的范围主要是根据国事访问过程中人民日报和新华社的文字稿为准。

(1) The Prototype of Kulishenko

Grigori Akimovich Kulishenko was an Ukrainian, also the former Soviet air squadron commander. After the outbreak of the World Anti-Fascist War, he and Kazlov were dispatched by the Soviet government. In 1939, they led two Dasha-style bomber squadrons to China to aid the War of Resistance against Japan and stationed at the Taipingsi Airport in the southern suburbs of Chengdu. On October 14, 1939, Kulishenko received a task of operation and led the squad to attack the Japanese military base. When the aircraft flew over Wuhan, it was intercepted by Japanese enemy planes. In the fierce battle, the air squadron led by Kulishenko bombed out 103 enemy planes and shot down 6 planes. However, the aircraft he was driving was hit hard by Japanese aircraft, and returned to the upstream station along the Yangtze River with only one engine. When the plane flew above Wanxian (Wanzhou District, Chongqing), the fuselage lost its balance. In order to protect the buildings on the land, the plane finally landed in the Yangtze River in Wanxian. The bombers and shooters on the plane jumped in the water and swam to the shore, but Kulishenko was unable to jump out of the cabin because of great consumption of physical strength in a long fierce battle, and was swallowed up by the ruthless river.

After the death ofKulishenko, the body of the Kulishenko Martyrs was buried in Wanxian and the Wanxian government and people had held a grand memorial meeting for Kulishenko. After the founding of the People's Republic of China, in July 1958, the Wanxian Municipal People's Government built a martyrs cemetery for the Kulishenko in the scenic Xishan Park along the Yangtze River, and held a graveyard-moving ceremony. After that, the hero slept in Xishan Park in Wanzhou District, Chongqing along the Yangtze River. Tan Zhonghui has also been keeping the tomb for Kulishenko since 1958.[①] When she gets on in years, his son Wei Yingxiang begins to keep the tomb like his

---

① 库里申科牺牲过程的详细记录参见魏拥锋:《一曲中苏友谊之歌: 纪念库里申科诞辰110周年》,《中国档案》2013 年第 6 期, 第 78—79 页。

mother. The two generations of mother and son have been guarding the tomb for more than half a century, and have touched thousands of people and witnessed the profound friendship between the two countries.

(2) The Case was jointly reported by Chinese and Russian media

After the sacrifice of Kulishenko, his deeds were widely reported in the media in China, which had great social influence at that time, but there was no response in his native country Soviet Union. This is because the whereabouts of volunteers at the time were confidential. In his letter for his wife, Kulishenko only wrote that he was transferred to work in an area of the East, and people here were very nice to him, and it felt like living in his hometown. At that time, the family of Kulishenko did not know his sacrifice, or the place of burial. The official notice only wrote about the sacrifice in operating the government mission, and the family wanted to know where, when and why he sacrificed himself.[①]

Until 1954, Chinese student Zhu Yuli, who was studying in the Soviet Union, found that the leader of the school class was named Ina Kulishenko, which inevitably reminded him of the Soviet Union, Grigori Akimovich Kulishenko, his worshipped hero at the age of nine. Thus, Zhu Yuli asked the leader whether he knew the hero. It happened that this classmate was the daughter of the hero Kulishenko and thus uncovered the dusty past event. After the family learned that Kulishenko had died in Wanzhou, they found the burial place of their loved one according to Zhu Yuli's song and went to worship Kulishenko many times. On the eve of the National Day of 1958, when Inna Kulishenko and her mother visited China, they were cordially received by Premier Zhou Enlai.

On December 18, 2010, CCTV and Russian National Television recorded

---

① 库里申科牺牲过程的详细记录参见魏拥锋:《一曲中苏友谊之歌: 纪念库里申科诞辰110周年》,《中国档案》2013年第6期, 第79页。

and broadcasted the Sino-Russian large-scale multinational public welfare program *Waiting for Me*. The first issue of the show told the story of Zhu Yuli's interaction with the Soviet classmate Ina Kulishenko, and found the story of the heroic family, and brought this touching story to the screen. Through this column, Zhu Yuli wanted to search for the Soviet classmate Ina Kulishenko many years ago and happened to meet the Russian column director Sergei, who was the son of Ina Kulishenko and got in contact with his Soviet classmate.

(3) **President Xi told the story of keeping the tomb**

On March 23, 2013, during the first state visit, President Xi Jinping delivered a keynote speech at the Moscow Institute of International Relations, "Conforming to the Trend of the Times and Promoting Peaceful Development in the World". During the speech, President Xi mentioned three typical examples of mutual support and help between the two peoples when they talked about unswervingly developing the friendly relations between the two peoples. The first case was the touching story of Chongqing Wanzhou mother and child keeping the tomb for the Soviet Air Force for half a century: "In the period of the War of Resistance Against Japanese Aggression, the Soviet air squadron commander Kulishenko came to China to fight alongside the Chinese people and ever said emotionally: 'Like experiencing the disaster of my country, I experienced the disaster that the working people of China are suffering'. He heroically sacrificed on the land of China. The Chinese people have not forgotten this hero, and a pair of ordinary Chinese mother and son has been guarding him for more than half a century."[①]

Not only that, during the speech, President Xi also described two other stories witnessed by the Chinese and Russian people, namely, after the Beslan hostage incident and the Wenchuan earthquake, China and Russia have

---

① 习近平:《顺应时代前进潮流, 促进世界和平发展》, 中国共产党新闻网, http://theory.people.com.cn/n/2013/0323/c49150 - 20892222.html, 2019 年 5 月 12 日登陆。

rehabilitated the victimized children.

"After the Beslan hostage incident in Russia in 2004, China invited some injured children to China for rehabilitation. These children were taken care of in China. The Russian doctor Alan said: 'your doctors have given such great help to the children and our children will always remember you.'"

"After the 2008 Wenchuan earthquake in China, Russia gave an aid to China in the first time, and invited children from the disaster area to go to the Russian Far East to rehabilitate. Three years ago, I was in Russian Ocean Children's Center in Vladivostok and witnessed the warm care of the Chinese children given by the Russian teachers. The Chinese children personally experienced the friendship and kindness of the Russian people, which fulfilled the saying "love is boundless" that the Chinese people often say.[①]

(4) The Follow-up Progress of Story Diplomacy

After President Xi Jinping delivered a speech at the Moscow Institute of International Relations, various units continued to follow up the story. On the second day of the speech, on March 24th, 2013, in the *News Live Room* column of CCTV, *Kulishenko Martyrs Cemetery: Witness of Friendship*, *Kulishenko: the Hero of the Soviet Union Sacrificed for the War of Resistance Against Japan*, *Kulishenko Cemetery: Flowers for Martyrs and Friendship in Hearts*, *Kulishenko Cemetery was Guarded by Two Generations*, the Sino-Russian large-scale multinational public welfare program *Waiting for Me* and other short films have made intensive special reports on the deeds of Kulishenko and the story of Wei Yingxiang and his mother. On the eve of 2014, three reporters from the CCTV News Channel went to the Wanzhou District Archives Bureau to interview the heroic deeds of Kulishenko. On September 4, 2015, CCTV went to Moscow to interview Ina Kulishenko and broadcasted the

---

① 习近平:《顺应时代前进潮流, 促进世界和平发展》, 中国共产党新闻网, http://theory.people.com.cn/n/2013/0323/c49150-20892222.html, 2019年5月12日登陆。

interview in the *Morning News* in the name of *Kulishenko in the eyes of daughter*. On the eve of the 70th anniversary of the victory of the anti-fascist victory, on May 10, 2015, the *Morning News* column of CCTV re-reported the story of Kulishenko with the name *Kulishenko: Defending the Chinese People with Life*.

In recent years, the Wanzhou District Archives Bureau has attached great importance to the rescue, protection and utilization of the precious archives of Kulishenko. On the one hand, the bureau strengthens the daily management and jointly with, the bureau and the district museum have jointly carried out a special photo exhibition event *Sincerely Cherishing the Memory of Kulishenko Centurial Guarding of the Cemetery* to commemorate the 110th anniversary of the birth of the Kulishenko martyrs.

On December 24th, 2014, based on the real story of Kulishenko, the launching ceremony of the film *Accompanying Kulishenko* jointly produced by Bayi Film Studio and the Propaganda Department of the CPC Chongqing Municipal Committee was held in Shenko Memorial Park, Wanzhou District, Chongqing. The film was officially released on the occasion of the 70th anniversary of the victory of the Anti-Japanese War in 2015.

Ⅳ. Measures for Promoting Story Diplomacy

As can be seen from the typical case of the above-mentioned story diplomacy, the events experienced by a large number of ordinary people may notbe remembered by the general public as time goes on. If the touching events are aimed to last for a long time and become the focus of media reports and a typical story told by the top leaders of the state during the foreign affairs and visits, the following measures can be taken to promote the development of story diplomacy, and advance it to play a greater role of connecting two peoples.

(1) **Using the Internet platform to build a people-to-people exchange story library**

As the activities of ordinary people break through the borders of a country and foreign exchanges become more frequent, the number of people-to-people exchange stories between the people of various countries is increasing. Over time, it is expected to form massive information. Therefore, it is necessary to use modern information technology to establish an online story collection platform, and gradually develop it into a people-to-people exchange story library to provide a large and diverse data platform for story diplomacy.

(2) **All kinds of media should be good at discovering people-to-people exchange stories with the moral of international relations.**

The people-to-people exchange stories among the people of different countries still exist in various specific time and space because of the differences in type attributes. A large number of touching stories are still unknown to the world. Because of their professional attributes, all kinds of media are easy to find such stories, and report to the outside world through different media channels, so that the world knows the touching stories in the history. To this end, the relevant media should strengthen the case awareness, dig deeply into the stories behind the news, and enrich the story dimension of people-to-people exchange between countries.

(3) **Giving full play to the exemplary role of the summit diplomacy and expanding the appeal of people-to-people exchange stories**

Because of the personal involvement of the top leaders of the country, the summit diplomacy often plays a leading role in developing international relations. During the foreign affairs and visits of the heads of state, the media of various countries generally conduct a wide range of follow-up reports on relevant activities, and the public is easy to know the contents of the speech of the summit. people-to-people exchange stories are easily spread to the outside world through multiple types of media at such special moments and are spread across a wider range.

V. Enlightenment

In recent years, it is the innovative turn of cross-cultural communication in Chinato use "story" instead of "slogan", try to dissolve the alienation between cultures in a vivid and three-dimensional narrative form and "telling good Chinese stories".[①] China's external communication is showing a new trend. By virtue of a kind of more natural interpersonal communication, China has used a more grounded discourse style to tell foreigners about the interpersonal stories between China and the host country.

The importance of the anecdotes that carry the history of the exchanges between the two peoples in diplomacy has gradually become prominent, and the people who are the protagonistsof the anecdotes have gradually returned to diplomatic practice. The anecdote of interpersonal communication has become an important witness of international relations through media reports and pro-reports of leaders in state visits, and transformed the interpersonal relationship to international relations, thus forming a humanistic return path of international relations.

The anecdote between the peoples of different countries is a valuable historical legacy between their countries, and is an international social capital with spiritual values. The anecdotes of people from various countries will continue to gather and increase with the accumulation of time, and the contemporary value will gradually emerge through the development of individual and collective practitioners such as the media and the government. Under the influence of the leaders, the international social capital generated by the

---

① 徐明华、李丹妮:《情感畛域的消解与融通:"中国故事"跨文化传播的沟通介质和认同路径》,《现代传播》2019 年第 3 期,第 38—42 页。

anecdote will be optimally allocated and its value will be maximized.

We are soberly aware that the research in this paper needs to be further expanded. The public personal experiencing events studied in this paper are still limited and should include a wider range of anecdotes. Not only that, it is also needed to further dig out the subject and object content of story diplomacy, explore the function mechanism of story diplomacy from the perspective of system, analyze the ways and steps through which anecdotes are gradually transformed from non-material capital to international materiality social capital, as well as approaches to optimizing resource allocation to achieve its maximum value. Such exploration is conducive to further enriching the mechanism of people-to-people exchange in international relations and clarifying the theoretical and practical value of people-to-people exchange in international relations.

Applied Research

Experience and Improvement of BRICS People-to-people Exchanges Mechanism

Wang Wei* Wang Junliang**

Abstract: On July 25-27, 2018, the 10th BRICS Summit was successfully held in Johannesburg, South Africa, and the Johannesburg Declaration was issued. The BRICS Summit has gone through 10 years of history and has entered a new golden decade. In the current complex and volatile international environment, the BRICS, as representatives of emerging market countries, can maintain and continuously strengthen this multilateral cooperation mechanism, which is very important for maintaining the multi-polarization and multilateralism of the world. After ten years of development, the BRICS cooperation has been gradually expanded and deepened from the initial economic field with the three pillars of political security, economic finance and people-to-people exchanges having been formed. Although the people-to-people

---

* Wang Wei, Professor, Doctoral Supervisor, Doctor of Laws in International Relations, Deputy Director of the Management Committee of China-Shanghai Cooperation Organization International Judicial Exchange and Cooperation Training Base, and Dean of the "Belt and Road" Safety Research Institute of Shanghai University of Political Science and Law.

** Wang Junliang, LL. M., teacher of Sanda University.

exchange started late, it has developed rapidly: the proportion of people-to-people exchanges content in the summit declaration has been increasing; the convening of ministerial conferences in related fields has become a practice. The characteristics of BRICS people-to-people exchanges are also becoming increasingly clear: basic value identification is the basis of humanistic exchange; the coverage of humanities communication is expanding; the form of exchange is gradually becoming a system. While achieving development results, it should also be noted that there are still shortcomings in the BRICS people-to-people exchanges: the participation degree of member states in people-to-people exchanges is not balanced enough; the role of nongovernmental forces in people-to-people exchanges is not outstanding. To this end, BRICS should continue to attach importance to and play the role of people-to-people exchange, highlight the key points of people-to-people exchanges and form a brand, use the advantages of Internet technology to enrich the forms of people-to-people exchanges, continue to consolidate the language and national conditions of people-to-people exchanges, and improve safeguard mechanism people-to-people exchanges. All the above efforts will enable people-to-people exchanges to play a more important role in the next golden decade of BRICS cooperation.

Keywords: BRICS; People-to-people Exchanges Mechanism; Experience

I. People-to-people Exchanges has Become One of the Pillars of BRICS Cooperation

On July 25-27, 2018, the 10th BRICS Summit was held in South Africa to start a new golden decade. The "BRICS", the earliest concept used to specifically refer to the emerging markets of the world, has become an important international mechanism for communication, exchanges and cooperation among emerging market countries after 10 years of development. The partners have also increased from the first four countries to five countries; their communication, exchanges and cooperation have gradually expanded from the economic and trade fields to political security and people-to-people exchanges, which have increased the number of issues for BRICS to cooperate and exchange. The scope of cooperation and exchange has become more extensive, and the cooperation and exchange has been deepened in depth. In the continuous development and practice, the BRICS have formed three pillars of cooperation in political security, economic finance and people-to-people exchanges.

Compared with cooperation and exchangesin the fields of political security and economic finance, the field of people-to-people exchange is in the post-development position in the BRICS cooperation and exchange mechanism. On the one hand, the latter means a short board, which needs the five countries to work together to make up. Scholars have summed up the two major manifestations of the "short board": First, there are "deficits" in the understanding of the cultures of other countries; second, the culture "soft power" of the five countries is not strong in the international arena, and does not match their "hard power", the economic power in their position in the world. On the other hand, late-mover means there are more conditions and possibilities for accelerating development and "corner-overtaking". It should be clearly recognized that the late-mover position of the BRICS people-to-people exchanges is of certain rationality: one is related to the purpose of establishing the mechanism at the beginning and the main problems solved at that time. As mentioned above, "BRICS" was originally an economic concept. After developing into a platform for international cooperation, it was mainly to solve the economic, financial and security problems faced by the emerging market countries. In addition, the first summit in 2009 was held under the background of the international financial crisis, which has made exchanges and cooperation in the economic field inevitably become a major issue. Second, it is in line with the interactive relationship between economic exchanges and people-to-people exchanges in international cooperation: the results of economic and trade exchanges and cooperation are the basis and cornerstone of people-to-people exchanges and cooperation, and people-to-people exchanges and cooperation can magnify the results of economic and trade exchanges and cooperation.

In fact, as early as 2009, when participating in the first BRICS Summit in Yekaterinburg, China has clearly proposed to promote people-to-peoples exchanges as an important topic for the next cooperation of the BRICS. At the time of the summit, Hu Jintao pointed out: "The four countries have a long history and culture, profound humanistic connotation and friendship of long standing. We should actively expand exchanges and cooperation in the fields of culture, education, health, tourism and sports to promote mutual understanding, advance all walks of life to become good friends and good partners, and lay a solid social foundation for deepening all-round cooperation."[①] With the full spread and deepening of BRICS cooperation and the intertwining of economic, political, social and cultural fields, various initiatives and plans on people-to-people exchanges have become an important part of BRICS cooperation and have achieved great results. The results can be reflected in the declaration documents of the BRICS summits and the convening of the ministerial meetings in in the BRICS people-to-people exchanges (see Tables 1 and 2 for details).

Table 1: People-to-people Exchanges Fields Involved in the
Declaration Documents of the BRICS Summits

Year	Declaration Documents	The Involved People-to-People Exchanges Fields (The number in the brackets is the serial number in the declaration document)
2009	Joint Statement of the BRIC Summit in Yekaterinburg, Russia	science and technology and education (11)

---

① 胡锦涛:《在"金砖四国"领导人会晤时的讲话（2009 年 6 月 16 日，俄罗斯叶卡捷琳堡）》，中国新闻网：http://www.chinanews.com/gn/news/2009/06 - 17/1736908. shtml, 2018 年 8 月 4 日最后访问。

Continued Table

Year	Declaration	Topics
2010	Joint Statement of the BRICS Summit in 2010	think tank, science and technology, culture, sports (25, 27, 28, 29)
2011	Sanya Declaration	youth, public health, science and technology and innovation (24, 28)
2012	Delhi Declaration	public health, science and technology, youth, education, culture, tourism, sports (42, 43, 48)
2013	Durban Declaration	Internet, health, think tank (34, 41, 42)
2014	Fortaleza Declaration	education, think tank, technological innovation (56, 59, 66, 67)
2015	Ufa Declaration	tourism, health, science and technology innovation, education, think tanks and academics, youth (56, 60, 62, 63, 64, 73, 74)
2016	Goa Declaration	think tank, health, education, youth, science and technology, youth, travel, film, sports (45, 71, 72, 73, 74, 77, 78, 79, 80, 94, 95, 99, 103)
2017	Xiamen Declaration	education, science and technology, sports, health, media institutions, libraries, museums, art galleries, drama, think tanks, youth, civil society organizations (6, 60, 61, 62, 63, 64, 65, 66)
2018	Johannesburg Declaration	sports, youth, film, culture, education and tourism, health, think tanks and academic, social organizations (5, 86, 87, 90, 91, 92, 93, 94, 95, 96, 97, 98)

Table 2: Statistics on Ministerial Conferences Involving BRICS People-to-people Exchanges

conference	date	location	major result
Meeting of BRICS Minister of Culture	2015	Moscow, Russia	Consultation on the BRICS Cultural Cooperation Agreement
	2017	Tianjing, China	The Action Plan for the Implementation of the Agreement on BRICS Intercultural Cooperation (2017-2021) was signed.
Meeting of BRICS Minister of Education	2013	Paris France	The BRICS-UNESCO Working Group was set up. It was proposed to establish a long-term cooperation mechanism among the five countries; To promote mutual recognition of academic qualifications, share educational information, strengthen educational exchanges at all levels, and focus on strengthening cooperation in higher education and vocational education; To extend bilateral pragmatic cooperation to five countries; To establish a five-country and UNESCO-based cooperation mechanism to jointly promote the global education agenda and develop educational quality standards and evaluation tools.
	2014	Brasilia, Brazil	
	2015	Moscow, Russia	The Moscow Declaration of the 3rd Meeting of BRICS Ministers of Education and the Memorandum of Understanding on the Establishment of the BRICS Network University were signed.
	2016	New Delhi, India	The New Delhi Education Declaration was published.
	2017	Beijing, China	The theme of the meeting was "BRICS Education Cooperation: Promote Excellence and Equity"; The result document such as the Beijing Education Declaration of the Fifth Meeting of BRICS Ministers of Education was adopted.

Continued Table

conference	date	location	major result
Meeting of BRICS Ministers of Health	2011	Beijing China	The Beijing Declaration of the 1st Meeting of BRICS Ministers of Health was published.
	January 2013	New Delhi, India	The Delhi Communique was published.
	November 2013	Cape Town, South Africa	The Cape TownCommunique was published.
	2014	Brasilia, Brazil	The Joint Communique was published.
	2015	Moscow, Russia	The Russian Declaration was published.
	2016	New Delhi, India	The Delhi Declaration was published.
	2017	Tianjin, China	The Tianjin Communique was published.
BRICS Science and Technology Innovation (STI) Ministerial Meeting	2014	Cape Town, South Africa	Theme of themeeting: Promote Equitable Growth and Sustainable Development through Strategic Partnerships in the Field of Technological Innovation; The Durban Declaration was published.
	March 2015	Brasilia, Brazil	The Brasilia Declaration was published. The Memorandum of Understanding on BRICS Intergovernmental Science and Technology Innovation Cooperation was signed.
	October 2015	Moscow, Russia	Main topics: to formulate BRICS research and innovation initiatives and BRICS science and technology innovation work plans; The Moscow Declaration was published. The BRICS 2015-2018 Work Plan was adopted.
	2016	Jaipur, India	The Jaipur Declaration was published.
	2017	Hangzhou, China	Theme of themeeting: Innovation Leads to Deepening Cooperation; Hangzhou Declaration, BRICS Innovation Cooperation Action Plan and BRICS 2017-2018 Science and Technology Innovation Work Plan were published,
Meeting of BRICS Ministers of Tourism	2016	Khajuraho, India	

In addition to discussing and identifying content and plans for people-to-people exchanges atsummits and ministerial meetings, it is even more important to fully implement these meeting decisions and plans. Therefore, the activities and practices bounded up with the mass and benefiting the well-being of people, such as BRICS Film Festival, the National Cultural Festival, the National Youth Forum, the National Trade Union Forum, the Young Scientists Forum, the Youth Forum, the Young Diplomat Forum, the National Exhibition Organization Symposium, the Political Party Think Tank and the Civil Society Organization "Three in One" Forum, The National Sports Games, Library Alliance, Museum Alliance, Art Gallery Alliance, Youth and Children's Theatre Alliance and University Alliance, have benefited the people's livelihood, truly exposed the people of the BRICS to the BRICS people-to-people exchanges results and have further narrowed the gap between countries.

II. Characteristics and Experience of BRICS People-to-people Exchanges

While the BRICS people-to-people exchanges have achieved fruitful results, they have also formed their own characteristics which can be summarized into the following three aspects:[①]

First, basic value identification is the basis of people-to-people exchanges.

---

① 原文化部对外联络局局长谢金英在2017年金砖国家厦门峰会期间的新闻发布会上概括了金砖国家人文交流的特点：其一，金砖国家有基本价值认同。开放、包容、平等、合作、共赢、尊重文化多样性是金砖国家展现的文化和价值共识，这种内在联系为金砖国家携手谋求经济增长，完善全球治理提供了精神动力。其二，金砖国家一致认同文化对社会可持续发展有重要意义，认为文化交流合作将成为经济和社会发展的新动力，为彼此创造一个更加繁荣安全的社会，在全球范围树立一个平等而富有创造性的伙伴关系。这也正契合厦门会晤"深化金砖伙伴关系，开辟更加光明未来"的主题。其三，在五国领导人高度重视和各界积极推动下，金砖国家文化交流与合作不断取得实质性进展，为增进金砖国家人民之间相互理解和友谊，夯实民意基础发挥了重要作用。《谢金英：人文交流作为金砖国家合作三大支柱之一》，http://news.china.com/internationalgd/10000166/20170903/31269856.html，2018年5月5日最后访问。

The BRICS involves Asia, South America, Europe and Africa. All countries have their own historical and cultural traditions and there are differences between them: "the main characteristic of China is that China is developing along the almost clear path of collectivism like other East Asian countries. The characteristic of Indian and Russian civilizations is that they adhere to the middle road - extensive development path, which is far from pure collectivism or individualism tendencies. So if the path of India is quite clear, then the development path of Russia is characterized by twists and turns. Especially in the 20th century: Soviet Union had tried to take the path of collectivism after the October Revolution, and after the collapse of the Soviet Union, Russia began to take the individualism path."①

However, the BRICS recognize each other and respect the cultural characteristics and historical traditions of their respective countries, and on this basis, the basic values have been recognized by BRICS, namely the spirit of "openness, inclusiveness, cooperation and mutual benefit". These basic values not only come from the cultural and historical traditions of the five countries, but also the values and norms that need to be followed and recognized in international cooperation in the contemporary world. It is the recognition of these basic values hat has enabled the BRICS to continue their in-depth cooperation and exchanges. In addition, the BRICS also use these basic values as a guideline for advancing international and regional issues. For example, in the declaration documents after the summits, they have repeatedly reaffirmed respect and support for the UN and the UN Charter, upholding multilateralism, efforts for sustainable development, and promotion of a more equitable, fair, and equitable international order.

Second, the coverage field of people-to-people exchanges is becoming wider and wider. As can be seen from Table 1 above, after nearly 10 years of

---

① [俄] 谢·卢涅夫, 刘锟译:《金砖国家的合作潜力与文化文明因素》,《俄罗斯文艺》2014 年第 4 期, 第 138 页。

development, the BRICS people-to-people exchanges havecovered more and more extensive fields: from the initial fields of science and technology, education, health, etc., to tourism, think tanks, social organizations, youth, the Internet, sports, media, film and television, etc., and the integration and exchanges between various fields are becoming more and more deep, such as exchange forums for young scientists, political parties, think tanks, and civil society organizations "three in one" forum.

The first reason why the BRICS people-to-people exchanges cover more and more fields is related to the purpose of people-to-people exchanges. As stated in the Johannesburg Declaration of 2018: "We emphasize that BRICS should place the people at the center of work". The purpose of people-to-people exchange is to promote understanding between the BRICS people, attract more people to participate in the BRICS cooperation, channel a strong impetus into the cooperation of the BRICS. The gradual increase in the field of people-to-people exchanges is both the result of its own continuous development and the need to meet the diverse needs of the people. In the process of global integration, people are eager to understand the "outside world". The exchange mechanism between the countries and the governments provides an effective carrier and a good foundation for people to participate in the process of global integration. For most Chinese, countries such as India, Brazil, and South Africa are still relatively unfamiliar because of language, geography, and culture. The "going out" and "bringing in" exchanges between the BRICS countries will enable more people to understand these countries, and intuitively feel the customs and cultural traditions of these countries.

The second reason is related to the broad characteristics of people-to-people exchanges. Compared with the other two pillars of political security and economic finance, "people-to-people" is a concept with a large extension and even some uncertainty. Therefore, it can cover a wide range. In addition to art, music, film and television, language, etc., education, youth, health, sports, tourism, think tanks, folk customs etc., are also included in the "people-to-people" category. It can be said that "people-to-people exchanges" has become the "bottom clause" of the BRICS exchanges. Any exchanges that does not belong to the political security and economic and financial fields can be classified into the category of "people-to-people exchanges", which also will make the country exchanges and cooperation not be restricted by the constraints of conceptual or written expression, but provide space and potential for the future expansion of the BRICS cooperation and exchanges.

The third reason is that the people-to-people exchange is closely related to the people. It is precisely because of the wide range of "people-to-people" that it has a closer relationship with the general public. The requirement of ordinary people in various countries for exchanges and cooperation in the humanities field has been becoming huger and more obvious, and they also directly and conveniently feel the exchange and cooperation results in the people-to-people field. Among them, tourism is the most direct way to enhance understanding. The trips of BRICS citizens to each other's countries have also become a new highlight in people-to-people exchange and cooperation: the global homestay booking platform Airbnbhas released BRICS report on August 31, 2017, which shows that since 2008, 4.1 million BRICS visitors have traveled to other BRICS countries through the platform, with destinations including more than 400 BRICS cities. Cape Town, St. Petersburg, Moscow, Rio de Janeiro, Johannesburg, Shanghai and Beijing are the most popular destinations for BRICS tourists.[1] According to the data of the former National Tourism Administration, the comprehensive contribution of China's tourism industry to GDP in 2017 was 9.13 trillion yuan, accounting for 11.04% of the total GDP.[2] The increasing demand for tourism has also affected the tourism policies of various countries. For example, South Africa is already considering relaxing a visa restriction on

---

[1] 《民宿共享平台报告: 金砖国家旅客互访增长134%》, http: //travel. people. com. cn/nl/2017/0831/c41570-29507980. html, 2018 年 5 月 27 日最后访问。

[2] 《2017 年全国旅游业对 GDP 的综合贡献为 9.13 万亿元》, http: //www. ce. cn/xwzx/gnsz/gdxw/201802/06/t20180206_28087540. shtml, 2018 年 8 月 5 日最后访问。

tourists from China. Education exchanges and cooperation approaches are also increasingly rich: receiving students from other BRICS countries, establishing BRICS university alliances, mutually recognizing academic qualifications, and setting up branch campuses in other BRICS countries. For China, the establishment of a Confucius Institute in the BRICS is not only an exchange of education, but also an important carrier for enhancing the exchanges of Chinese culture: "There are 6.6 of every 100 Confucius Institutes in the world in the BRICS. Among them, Brazil is the Latin American country with the largest number of Confucius Institutes and Confucius Classrooms. The 10 Confucius Institutes and 4 Confucius Classrooms cover 20,000 students. Many local primary and secondary schools have also begun to include Chinese in formal courses."① In terms of function, the Confucius Institute is no longer limited to the teaching of Chinese, and has developed into a "comprehensive platform for Chinese and foreign cultural exchanges". For example, the Confucius Institute at Durban University of Technology in South Africa not only provides Chinese language teaching classes for students in school and students fond of China outside the school, but also actively carries out various cultural exchange activities, with more than 50,000 person-times participating in these exchange activities, and creatively incorporate Chinese culture into the local cultural and artistic heritage month. In the 2017 BRICS Cultural Festival held in Xiamen, more than 30 performances by top domestic and foreign artists were freely available to the public, providing the Chinese people with the opportunity to experience the rich culture of other countries. In addition, the BRICS cooperation in the film is becoming more and more mature. The first film *Where Time Goes* was released in 2017 and the second film *Half the Sky* has also been filmed. In 2017, Indian film *Dangal* won nearly 1.3 billion box office and high reputation. President Xi Jinping also expressed his love for this film to

---

① 《[数字金砖] 人文大交流 民相亲心相通》, http://news.sina.com.cn/o/2017-08-31/doc-ifykpzey3274922.shtml, 2018 年 5 月 5 日最后访问。

Indian Prime Minister Modi at the SCO Astana Summit.

Third, the way of people-to-people exchanges has gradually been institutionalized. After 10 years of development, the BRICS cooperation mechanism is undergoing an important transformation. It is transforming from a "dialogue forum" focusing on economic governance and discussing principles to "full-fledged mechanism" paying equal attention to political and economic governance, and combining concrete issues with discussing principles.[1] In other words, the BRICS cooperation and exchanges are increasingly focusing on the "landing" and "implementation" of cooperation, with an aim to bring real benefits and feelings to countries and people. Influenced by the transformation of the cooperation mechanism, many people-to-people exchanges activities bounded up with the mass and benefiting the well-being of people have been gradually fixed from scratch to "prescribed actions" in the field of people-to-people exchanges. It is on the basis of institutionalization that the parties can continue to further deepen people-to-people exchanges activities, so that more BRICS stories can be circulated along with these fixed people-to-people exchanges activities to fully play the role of people-to-people exchanges. At present, there are other institutionalized people-to-people exchanges activitiesin addition to the ministerial conferences in different fields summarized in Table 2, such as: the BRICS Film Festival which was established in 2016 and has been held in India, China and South Africa for three consecutive sessions; the BRICS Games, which was founded in 2017 and has been held twice in Guangzhou, China and Johannesburg, South Africa; the BRICS Young Scientists Forum has been successfully held for three times; the BRICS Academic Forum has also been held ten times, etc.

In addition, the BRICS have also formed a people-to-people exchanges mechanism in the form of "National Year (Month)". For example, China and the other four countries have held various bilateral cultural exchanges in the

---

[1] 朱杰进:《金砖国家合作机制的转型》,《国际观察》2014年第7期,第59页。

above-mentioned form: China and Russia have jointly organized the theme activities of "2006 China 'Russia Year'" and "2007 Russia 'China Year'", achieving effective exchanges between the two countries in the fields of culture, politics, economy and military and enhancing mutual trust between China and Russia through mutually holding "thematic year activities". China and India jointly identified 2014 as the "China-India Year of Friendship", during which various activities were held to promote deeper exchanges between the two countries in the cultural field. In 2013, China and Brazil also hosted the "Cultural Month" event. The music, dance and literature of Brazil were fully displayed during the "Brazil Culture Month" in China, which exposed the Chinese people to the enthusiasm of the Samba country. In the "Chinese Culture Month" event in Brazil, Chinese folk music, acrobatics, dance and other oriental cultures were fully displayed and spread in Brazil, and they were sought after by local people. The consensus on the "Year of the Country" between China and South Africa was also implemented in 2014 and 2015 respectively, and good results have been achieved.

Of course, the BRICS people-to-people exchanges still need to be further improved.

Firstly, the participation of BRICS members is still uneven, which is actually related to the focus areas of national concerns in people-to-people exchanges. At present, some people-to-people exchange activities are held along with the annual summit. Therefore, the host countries of the summits have invested heavily in the content setting, participation level, and publicity of people-to-people exchange activities, while other participating countries may not be interested in the topics and content of people-to-people exchange specifically set by the host countries, so there will be differences in the input. For example, "India organized the BRICS Women's Parliamentarians' Forum for the first time during the 2016 presidency, and only 2 of the 42 female parliamentarians attending the conference were from

China and 3 were from Russia."① Therefore, how to balance the different focuses of countries in the humanities key fields and form the five countries' consensus on people-to-people exchanges, and achieve common ground while reserving differences is a very important issue.

Secondly, the influence of people-to-people exchanges on the BRICS still needs to be further strengthened. As mentioned above, BRICS ordinary people enjoy the results of the people-to-people exchanges the most directly, also raise the most direct demand for this field. Although they have achieved remarkable results under the joint efforts of the five countries, when compared with other countries such as American culture, the influence of BRICS people-to-people exchanges is still lacking. In the first place, the influence of people-to-people exchanges has a greater relationship with economic strength. The countries' constantly increasing economic strength can provide guarantee and support for their own culture "going out" on the one hand; on the other hand, it can also enhance the influence of national culture. Among the BRICS, China is also stronger in cultural influence than other countries based on its current economic volume and economic strength. Therefore, the three pillars of the BRICS exchanges are mutually influenced. "Economic finance" is in a basic position, and thus must be continuously consolidated through cooperation. In the second place, we must pay special attention to the BRICS folk people-to-people exchanges. What should be seen is that many of the BRICS people-to-people exchange activities have obvious government or official colors. This is very important at the beginning of people-to-people exchanges and can enable people-to-people exchanges to have a certain impact in a relatively short period and get more support based on the cooperation between governments or with the support of governments. However, the exchange in the humanities field is a process of "nourishing all without a sound". With the continuous deepening of

---

① 蒲公英:《金砖国家人文交流合作机制分析》,《俄罗斯东欧中亚研究》2017 年第 4 期,第 54 页。

exchanges, it is not enough to rely solely on government-led activities. Therefore, it is necessary to give full play to the strength of the BRICS folk organizations, so that the BRICS exchange activities can get more abundant and diverse and form a benign interactive relationship with the government-led exchange activities, which together constitute a mechanism for BRICS people-to-people exchanges.

III. Suggestions on Improving the BRICS People-to-people Exchanges Mechanism

The BRICS people-to-people exchange mechanism needs to be further improved from the following aspects:

First, the BRICS should attach great importance to and continuously enhance the role of people-to-people exchanges in the BRICS cooperation. The reason why people-to-people exchanges can play such an important role in the BRICS cooperation and exchanges is that it covers a wide range of areas and can expand more new areas of cooperation and exchange; it has the closest relationship with ordinary people and can attract different classes and groups of people to involve themselves in the tide of BRICS cooperation. Especially, it is important to give more support to the non-governmental forces in the BRICS cooperation and increase the frequency of exchanges between the five countries in the humanities field. Second, it is flexible and more easily accepted by the people of the five countries and gain their consensus. In the field of political security and economic finance, there are still many political and economic differencesin addition to the political values and economic laws followed by the five countries. These differences are not easy to dissipate in the short term. And it is easier for BRICS to achieve consistency in the humanities field, such as pursuing artistic "beauty", high-quality education, and deeper academic exchanges. For the differences in cultures of different countries, it is easier to "seek common ground while reserving differences" or even "narrow the difference with appropriate approaches" than to dissipate differences in the political and economic fields. More consistency in people-to-people exchanges can also promote and achieve greater respect and acceptance in the political and economic fields. Differences exist objectively and the cooperation between countries is to transform differences into complementary forces through mechanisms and systems. This is especially true for the BRICS mechanism. The five countries from four continents "have disputes and games around identity, goal orientation, topic setting, building institutional cooperation framework, and how to deal with other multilateral mechanisms. In this regard, the cooperation mechanism of balancing the interests of BRICS and seeking common ground while narrowing differences should be set up. For different interest appeals, the habitual thinking of avoiding conflicts in the past and passively shelving disputes or 'reserving differences' must be replaced by actively 'narrowing differences' and seeking common ground. BRICS should strengthen exchanges and coordination, understand each other's demands, take care of each other's concerns, and work hard to find a benefit integration point, an appropriate way to settle disputes and resolve differences."[1]

Second, the BRICS should pay attention to brand building and formal innovation in BRICS people-to-people exchanges. Building a brand of BRICS people-to-people exchanges is a higher requirement for the institutionalized BRICS people-to-people exchange activity. The process of brand building is a process of testing people-to-people exchange activities. It is necessary to screen the activities that reflect the characteristics of BRICS people-to-people exchanges, that are well received by the market and the people of the five countries, and that can have an impact on the world. To test the gains and losses of the activities can help to further improve the activities to form a brand. The

---

[1] 王友明：《金砖机制建设的角色定位于利益融合》，《国际问题研究》2015 年第 5 期，第 126 页

process of brand building is a process that highlights the key points of people-to-people exchange activities. At present, the key areas of BRICS people-to-people exchange are not prominent. This is related to the late launch of the people-to-people exchange field. Some institutionalized BRICS people-to-people exchange activities have only been held or established in the last two or three years and are limited in maturity and influence. Therefore, on the basis of enhancing the influence of BRICS people-to-people exchange activities, the five countries should select a number of outstanding development fields as the key fields of BRICS people-to-people exchanges and then form a brand according to the trend of people-to-people exchange development and the common values of BRICS.

In addition, the forms of BRICS people-to-people exchanges should also keep up with the latest development trends, and the role of the Internet should be given full play to build more online platforms, explore the establishment of a unified web portal and mobile clients, and provide multiple language options for people from different countries to browse and use conveniently. The network platform integrates the functions of releasing people-to-people exchange activities, displaying people-to-people exchanges, introducing historical and cultural traditions of various countries, applying for participation or the organization of people-to-people exchange activities to enhance the convenience of people-to-people exchanges.

Third, the BRICS should vigorously consolidate the foundation and guarantee of BRICS people-to-people exchanges. It is necessary to improve the foundation and guarantee of people-to-people exchanges so that the BRICS people-to-people exchanges are able to play a greater role. Language is the basis of humanistic exchanges, and also an obstacle in the current people-to-people exchanges in various countries. "Art is borderless". However, the effect of people-to-people exchanges will be compromised without the understanding and exchanges through language. For China, as mentioned above, the Confucius Institutes established in other BRICS countries have become an important channel for teaching and promoting Chinese. It is also an effective way to attract more international students from other BRICS countries. In addition to the promotion and popularization of Chinese, it is also very important to learn the language of other BRICS countries: the geographical conditions and historical origins between China and Russia make Russian have certain advantages in China; the languages of India and South Africa are quite complex for communication, but the influence of English on these two countries can facilitate exchanges between the two countries; the official language of Brazil is Portuguese, which is relatively unfamiliar to the Chinese people, also, Brazil is far from China. Thus, all these require more effort to improve. In addition to language, the basic national conditions of each country are also an important basis for people-to-people exchanges. Compared with consolidating the language foundation, the Internet provides great convenience for understanding each other's conditions.

In terms of theguarantee of people-to-people exchanges, the institutional guarantee is particularly important. The BRICS have formed a cooperation mechanism of "Summit - Ministerial Conference + Professional Forum". The specific systems involved in the field of people-to-people exchanges include the Conference of the Ministers of Science and Technology, the Conference of Ministers of Education, the Conference of Ministers of Health, the Conference of Ministers of Culture, and the Forum of Think Tanks, etc. These systems play an important role in the field of human exchanges. However, the need for brand building, the system and mechanism construction method based on the fields should be broken with the increasing importance of BRICS people-to-people exchanges in the BRICS cooperation and exchanges, the continuous expansion and deepening of the people-to-people exchange field. It is necessary to establish a people-to-people exchange guarantee system covering a wide range of fields and highlighting key fields and brands, and comprehensively consider and plan the BRICS people-to-people exchange from a higher level, so that the various fields can penetrate and integrate each other to enhance the effect of people-to-people exchanges.

The Establishment of a Quality Assurance System for BRICS People-to-people Exchanges

Sun Yixue[*]

Abstract: The promotion of establishing a quality assurance system of people-to-people exchanges is an important step to ensure the quality and effectiveness of BRICS people-to-people exchanges. The quality assurance system of BRICS people-to-people exchanges should be based on the principle of culture coexisting harmoniously, and institutionalized operating by negotiating to establish coordination management structure with a unified people-to-people mechanism, improving the people-to-people risk assessment system, and establishing a tracking and monitoring mechanism, to form "BRICS culture" and "BRICS wisdom" with world influence.

Keywords: BRICS; People-to-people Exchanges; Quality Assurance System

That the BRICS have developed from a concept to the present new model of international cooperation with potential and leading role depends on the BRICS having rationally constructed a scientific cooperation model and jointly

---

[*] Sun Yixue, Vice Dean, Professor and Doctoral Supervisor, the International School of Tongji University.

promoted the mutual benefit and mutual assistance. On this basis, the BRICS cooperation fields have expanded from the economy to politics, people-to-people, science and technology, diplomacy, security, and stability, and have been developing steadily like a butterfly transforming from pupa, and pottery from earth, and have become a veritable "BRICS mechanism". It means that the world's emerging economies can lead the world's new economic cooperation direction, develop themselves into a model of cooperation and win-win situation for different polities in the world, and can effectively improve the world political and cultural structure in the process of changing the world economy structure, so that the world's community of shared future will be always healthy and sound, smooth and steady, and is full of vitality.

On July 26, 2018, President Xi Jinping pointed out at the large-scale meeting of the BRICS Summit in Johannesburg: "The BRICS have fostered their splendid civilizations and complemented each other, so people-to-people exchanges and cooperation are promising." In the "Golden Decade" of BRICS cooperation, the people of the BRICS with similar dreams will make "the amity of people" into a big article. The subsections of this article center on issues of governing the country, movies, media, think tanks, youth, parliament, education, sports and tourism…and will be limitless and open, and always on the road, so that the cooperation between the BRICS can focus on the future of the BRICS, make the BRICS jointly advance toward the forefront of global development, but also serve the future of the world and play a more active and leading role in the international arena.

Facts have proved that the BRICS should further unite and cooperate, deepen their strategic partnerships, and achieve stability and harmony. It is necessary to achieve harmonious communication between the BRICS. people-to-people exchange is the starting point and the ultimate goal. As an important support for BRICS cooperation, the role of people-to-people exchange has been widely recognized by BRICS. In recent years, the BRICS Culture Ministers Meetings have been held around the people-to-people cooperation and exchanges. A series of documents, such as *the BRICS Intergovernmental Cultural Cooperation Agreement, the Implementation of the BRICS Intergovernmental Cultural Cooperation Agreement Action Plan*（2017-2021）（Annual）, *BRIC Action Plan of Strengthening Media Cooperation, BRICS Film Talent Exchange Training Program* have been issued to continuously expand the BRICS people-to-people cooperation field and platform, and make politics, economy, people-to-people commonly constitute the "three drives" pushing the BRICS cooperation, which has promoted the extensive participation of the societies of the five countries and kept the BRICS concept taking deep root in the hearts of the five countries.

An Irresistible Trend of Constructing Quality Assurance System for people-to-people Exchange.

In fact, with the diversification and maturity of BRICS people-to-people cooperation, the "BRIC model" has also exposed many problems, such as strong randomness, weak effectiveness, lack of unified coordination mechanism, and insufficient popularization. At the same time, the BRICS model has also been questioned frequently. The "BRICS Fading Theory", "BRICS Differentiation Theory" and "Honeymoon Ending Theory" have become the main themes of Western media.

In order to ensure the effect of BRICS people-to-people exchanges, based on the overall planning and goals of the human community of shared future and the overall understanding of the cultural ecosystems of the world, the BRICS must scientifically determine the connotation of people-to-people exchanges, sort out the integration path, and innovate communication methods to achieve accurate communication, sincere communication, collaborative communication, seek common ground while reserving differences, and have a definite object in view, finally construct a multi-operational mechanism for BRICS people-to-people exchanges with solving real problems as the reason, harmonious coexistence of cultures among nations as the goal, and mutual understanding and respect as the principle.

"Bronze bricks and silver bricksare made of bricks first, and the government must focus on their people." The "brick" that builds the public opinion foundation of the BRICS cooperation is humanity. The "brick" of humanity is the cause of the multi-cooperation of all countries and also is the "golden brick" that will be formed in the future. In order to make this "golden brick" universal and applicable to different soils of the five countries, a unified standard for the color, size and thickness of "golden brick" must be formed. Of course, the standard cannot be unitary, but different standards need to form according to the architectural characteristics and aesthetic culture in different cultural and geographical environments of the five countries. However, all these standards must pursue the principle of quality first, and be jointly agreed, supervised and implemented by the BRICS. The BRICS need to establish a unified quality standard system when the time is ripe, and negotiate to establish a unified people-to-people exchange quality assurance system that can be institutionalized and promoted, thus ensuring the quality and effectiveness of people-to-people exchange.

The Quality Assurance System Should be Based on the Principle of Culture Coexisting Harmoniously

Culture is blood. It needs to constantly extract external nutrition and accept new hematopoietic elements for an individual or a nation to maintain vitality, keep the blood full of fresh elements and provide continuous vitality for the body.

Cultural exchange is like blood transfusion between two independent bodies. The blooddonor must have a clear target and blood type matching. The receptor must provide appropriate channels for the donor, and ensure that they can recreate blood after receiving the appropriate amount of blood transfusion to continue life with the new blood needed. In other words, if any culture is to survive and develop in a foreign cultural environment, it must first obtain the soil for survival and the space for development in the foreign countries and rely on the resources of the local political, humanistic and social life in the host country to "transfuse" the blood of national culture and "borrow" the foreign body to recreate the blood containing the elements of the national culture, and when the time is ripe, it will promote new blood back, feed the national culture, make the matrix life become the life carrier of the world, and then feeds back the world with the new world blood, thus realizing the cycle of blood transfusion→hematopoiesis→re-transfusion between the national culture and other national culture. This is also the cycle of cultural creative transformation and creative development in all countries of the world. It is the highest stage and highest level of cultural exchange between China and foreign countries. It is also the foundation for the world values and eternal values of various national cultures in exchanges. Only by realizing this cycle can the national culture truly coexist with the worldview of other countries and the multi-cultures of the whole world.

The BRICS people-to-people exchange mechanism involves many countries and multi-cultures diversity. Therefore, the BRICS should jointly investigate the culture composition of different countries, analyze the status quo of different countries' national conditions, and establish a clear and targeted exchange strategy and path to promote effective integration and harmonious coexistence of national cultures to ensure that the five countries of BRICS can not only share the dividend of economic development with each other, but also mutually trust and cooperate with each other, deeply integrate with each other, share peace, common development and harmonious development based on the principle of mutual benefit and symbiosis, so as to ensure the smooth development of the BRICS people-to-people exchange mechanism in various countries and achieves sustainable development.

"Proper preparations should be made in advance." To ensure the quality of BRICS people-to-people exchanges, the most basic and most critical task is to establish effective policy support and "logistics support" for the harmonious progress of people-to-people exchange in all countries, and establish a comprehensive quality assurance system in line with reality. The quality assurance system should be based on the most targeted and most effective macro decision-making for the BRICS to respond to the complex forms of the national cultures with the rich connotations of different cultures, deal with the diversity of national cultural structures with a variety of communication methods, cope with ever-increasing new demands of all countries with continuously innovated new technology, win the sincere respect of all countries with sincere respect, respond to the ever-changing trend with good intentions, accommodate all kinds of dissidents with introspective minds, and respond to negative doubts with positive actions... At the same time, based on the principle of mutual trust and mutual recognition, the BRICS should coordinate the relevant forces to carry out systematic and holistic research, and concentrate on planning from the aspects of content, methods and objectives to ensure that the people-to-people exchange practice of the five countries serves the unified discourse system, unified development path, unified implementation goals, and unified evaluation criteria and eventually forms a people-to-people exchange discourse system with the BRICS characteristics, promotes the BRICS people-to-people exchanges and cooperation with the principle of multi-cultures coexisting harmoniously as the foundation, advances the optimization of their respective living spaces, achieves more rational resource allocation, and impels the mutual benefits and coexistence between different cultures in the world.

The Key to the Institutionalized Operation of the Quality Assurance System

The BRICS people-to-people exchanges should promote the harmonious coexistence of different cultures. First, it is necessary for each country to realize from the heart that "harmony in diversity" and "seeking common ground while reserving differences" are prerequisites for frank cooperation and common sustainable development among the five countries. In order to ensure the health and continuity of this symbiotic ecology, several key foundations should be firstly improved for the people-to-people exchange quality assurance system.

(1) Negotiating to Establish Coordination Management Structure with a Unified People-to-people Exchange Mechanism

At present, the BRICS have their own official institutions that publicize and disseminate their own culture and private institutions with official backgrounds for the inheritance and international dissemination of their own cultures. Based on their own needs, the institutions adopt more profitable communication policies to enable people-to-people exchange to serve the diplomatic needs and political needs of the country, and make the people-to-people exchanges with a strong utilitarian color.

The BRICS cooperation has great potential and may recreate the new future of the five countries. As a big country with the world's responsibility, China has the responsibility to recreate a world through the BRICS cooperation and become a veritableleading country. At present, the attitudes of the BRICS to foreign cultures are different; the legislation is not perfect, and it is difficult to coordinate them. However, the BRICS can uphold the principle of cultural equality and establish a unified and coordinated management structure that promotes equal exchanges between cultures through equal consultations based on international people-to-people exchanges, so as to achieve cultural equality and provide peaceful exchange services. This institution, in accordance with the principle of voluntary participation, equal rights, and mutual benefit, coordinates and balances the conflicts between different cultures, jointly determines the content and methods of international cultural communication among countries, and guides countries to undertake the cultural inheritance and dissemination arranged by the institution, and undertakes the responsibility of parallel supervision.

(2) Improving the People-to-people Exchange Risk Assessment System

Although the people-to-people exchanges among the members of BRICS adhere to the principle of equal cooperation and mutual benefit, it is impossible to achieve absolute balance. On the one hand, people-to-people exchange means that there must be contact between cultures, and then contacts may collide, and even conflict. The most important thing is that a country's culture must rely on a foreign social environment to survive and develop. There is no absolute balance of interests between communicators and disseminators; on the other hand, from the motive of both parties, the communicator is generally more active, so generally the benefits are greater, and the target of the communication is generally passive, more static and defensive, and gains less benefit. In the process of people-to-people exchange, the balance is temporary, and the conflict is eternal. This is the natural state of people-to-people exchange. Without this process, the communication behavior cannot be completed, and the purpose of communication will not be realized.

Each culture has a survival instinct to expand, and it is hoped to occupy more and more living space and acquire more and more resources to realize their further development. Communicators and disseminators must have a clear understanding of this. The BRICS must first recognize that this imbalance in people-to-people exchange is a normal phenomenon, and can scientifically understand and objectively identify the formation process of such a people-to-people exchange mechanism. This is of decisive significance for the construction of the coexistence mechanism of the people-to-people exchanges between the five countries.

At present, countries around the world generally adopt defensive strategies for dealing with foreign cultures. Official or private risk assessments on the dissemination of foreign cultures in their own countries are generally carried out to ensure the safety of their own culture and even the level of national security. This is the norm and common sense. The BRICS should not only evade or oppose, but also actively cooperate or directly participate in the people-to-people exchange risk assessment in the host country. The two parties or multi-parties should jointly develop the sequence and steps of people-to-people exchange and jointly coordinate the dissemination. The culture after risk assessment will be introduced by the host country and fully respected by the host country, and the quality of communication will be more assured.

The people-to-people exchange risk assessment of the BRICS is a scientific and perfect system. Based on specific issues, cultural differences, the principle of mutual benefit and reciprocity, evaluation criteria will be designed, then scientific conclusions will be drawn and the evaluation level will be determined. This risk assessment system can protect the value ecosystem of the host country from the strong attack of the communicator, and can also avoid the introduction of some values that harm the ecosystem of the host country.

(3) **Establishing a Tracking and Monitoring Mechanism to Ensure the Effectiveness of People-to-people Exchange**

people-to-people exchange is a dynamic and continuous process. It is always in the midst of development and change. Without tracking and monitoring, it is impossible to grasp the changes and causes, or make timely adjustments to ensure the rhythm and quality of exchange.

Establishing a people-to-people exchange tracking and monitoring system will not only make the people-to-people exchangesamong the members of the BRICS more scientific, reasonable, orderly and effective, but also promote mutual recognition that the communication of other countries' cultures in their own countries is within the control of both sides and will not pose a threat to the cultural and ecological security and national security, and thus the countries will more actively cooperate with the exchange and dissemination of foreign cultures in their country.

(4) Scientifically Setting People-to-people Exchange Risk Assessment Indicators

To ensure the accuracy and scientificity of the people-to-people exchange risk assessment, a corresponding risk assessment indicator system should be established. The establishment of risk assessment indicators should be based on a comprehensive grasp of the "physiological mechanisms", reproductive and communication capabilities, kinship and other information of the host country, and all relevant departments should play a positive role to make use of the "ubiquity" of indicators and institution to respond to the ubiquitous "ubiquity" of people-to-people exchange, and determine the balance state of the cooperation and exchange between the BRICS cultures and values and what kind of balance state the cooperation and exchange should be, so as to ensure the people-to-people exchanges between countries to be orderly, evidence-based, effective, and coexist harmoniously.

The effects of people-to-people exchange are uncertain, diffuse, comprehensive and mixed. The evaluation criteria are difficult to quantify, and it is difficult to form a unified evaluation standard with broad recognition. However, the effect of people-to-people exchange has both negative and dominant features. Based on the dominant features of people-to-people exchange effects, the breadth and depth of people-to-people exchange effects can be basically judged, and the integration degree and resolution degree of the symbiotic relationship between the communicator and the host can be measured so as to determine the angle and depth of people-to-people exchange. This is the realistic basis for assessment standards or indicators of people-to-people exchange effectiveness. Specific indicators can include:

The number of people-to-people exchange institutions: based on this, the degree and quantity of mutual needs of two or more cultures can be estimated to help to understand the ecological structure of their respective human environments.

The number of international students: the number of foreign students accepted by the host country, the number and type of people studying foreign culture in the host country and the ratio of the number of returned students to the number of people who remain in the host country.

The number and grade of schools and departments that offer other language and culture courses within the national education system of the host country.

The popularity of language tests: the number and type of language test institutions and the annual times of the test for foreigners.

Translation volume and circulation of foreign language publications: the number and type of publications translated and distributed for the host country, as well as the proportion of translators at home and abroad.

The number of overseasraces and the number of national language schools and media: overseas ethnic groups are not only the target of dissemination of their own culture, but also the communicators; overseas language schools and media are the main platforms for overseas cultural communication, which can break through the barriers to people-to-people and cultivate a cultural and ecological environment in which diverse cultures coexist harmoniously and create a more convenient communication channel and living environment for BRICS people-to-people exchanges.

The number of overseas companies and social institutions: with analyzing the quantity and output value of local enterprises in other countries and the degree of localization, the viability and survival status of our own culture in the host country can be judged.

The BRICS have large differences in political ecology and economic levels, geopolitical complexities and changes, and different social and cultural mechanisms. They should further standardize multilateral cooperation mechanisms, jointly face risks, share opportunities, and explore and improve scientific people-to-people exchange risk assessment system based on specific issues, cultural differences and the principle of mutual benefit and reciprocity, design assessment criteria, draw scientific conclusions, and determine the assessment levels. This kind of risk assessment system can not only protect the humanistic ecosystem of each country from the invasion of foreign culture, but also form a unified BRICS people-to-people exchange risk avoidance and mobility system to a certain extent. Based on this, the BRICS can jointly formulate the sequence and steps of mutual people-to-people exchange, and coordinate the rhythm of exchange, which also ensures mutual respect and makes people-to-people exchange full of human feelings.

Conclusion

Under the trend that the current world pattern is increasingly centeredon the optimization of a community with shared future for mankind, the BRICS mechanism will play an increasingly active leading role, and the function of people-to-people cooperation will be more and more valued. However, people-to-people exchange involves all aspects of human life, with heavy tasks, complicated threads and many obstacles. As a model of people-to-people cooperation and exchanges in the world, the BRICS should establish a cultural communication discourse system, operational mechanism and quality assurance system with the characteristics of BRICS and in accordance with world values on the basis of mutual understanding, so as to better serve the new requirements of the new world, jointly promote their splendid cultures to enrich and benefit the world, lead the development of the world's advanced culture, and form "BRICS Culture" and "BRICS Wisdom" with world influence in the process of advancing the integration of cultures of all countries in the world to jointly build a prosperous and developing community with shared future for mankind.

Analysis into Problems and Prospects of BRICS Higher Education Cooperation[*]

Pu Gongying[**]

Abstract: As the populous countries and the large regional countries in the world, five members of BRICS have more advantages and characteristics in the field of higher education. In the context of the irreversible globalization, with the gradual end of the extensive high-growth economic stage in the BRICS and emerging economies, the stage of economic development driven by human capital is bound to come, and the necessity and the importance of BRICS higher education cooperation become more and more prominent. In order to fully develop and utilize the resources of higher education, the member countries of the BRICS have begun to try to build relevant cooperation mechanisms, but whether the BRICS can break through the prejudice in their respective

---

[*] This article is research results of the Chongqing Municipal Social Science Planning Doctoral Development Project "Mirror and Inspiration: Russian Soft Power Diplomacy Research" (Project Approval Number: 2016BS062), Sichuan Foreign Studies University Annual Research Project Youth Project "Russian Soft Power Policy and Its Enlightenment on China (project approval number: sisu201621).

[**] Pu Gongying, Associate professor of Department of Russian, Sichuan International Studies University, Researcher of Institute of BRICS Studies.

educational concepts and realize mutual recognition of the higher education system are key issues in deepening cooperation of higher education under the BRICS framework. At the same time, the BRICS differences in the priority direction of education internationalization, the current trend of project cooperation and the financial problems faced are important factors hindering the development of higher education cooperation mechanism. According to this, under the BRICS framework, China can actively promote the development of BRICS higher education cooperation, give full play to the BRICS organizational advantages and resource endowments, strive to build a new type of international education cooperation, fully integrate China's market advantage and the scholarship system, and attract the outstanding talents of the BRICS to involve in the cooperation of higher education. At the same time, efforts should be made to activate the communication channels of educational authorities and educational researchers at all levels in BRICS and actively innovate BRICS cooperation projects so as to establish a good foundation for institutional cooperation of higher education.

Keywords: BRICS; Higher Education; Institutional Cooperation

In the present era with the knowledge economy rising and the globalization deepening, the competitiveness of higher education is an important indicator of a country's overall national strength. In the new economic era, the level of higher education can determine the country's capability forinnovation, industrial upgrading and the distribution of high-tech strength. Many countries regard it as an important factor directly linked to national competitiveness. At present, the BRICS have gradually evolved from the original concept to a global emerging country community that cannot be ignored by the world. The effectiveness of cooperation is gradually being highlighted in many fields such as economy, finance, politics and diplomacy. As the "locomotive" of emerging economies, BRICS outstanding performance in the development of the world economy has attracted people's attention, and cooperation in the humanities field has also caught up. In October 2016, President Xi Jinping highlighted the importance of people-to-people exchanges for the BRICS to jointly build an open world and deepen the partnership at the 8th BRICS Summit—"BRICS should strengthen people-to-people exchanges, promote amity between people and consolidate the foundation for the public opinion of the BRICS cooperation. As the populous countries and the large regional countries, BRICS members have a large educational group, a developed system and abundant resources in the field of higher education. How to actively and effectively promote BRICS higher education cooperation will be an inevitable selected topic for the community in deepening people-to-people exchanges and cooperation".

I. Development Status and Characteristics of BRICS Higher Education Cooperation

In recent years, BRICS higher education cooperation has gradually gained attention, and the BRICS have also begun toadvance the establishment of corresponding mechanisms. The BRICS have abundant resources for higher education. As the populous countries, the total population of the BRICS accounts for 42% of the world's total population. As a fast-growing new economy, the BRICS total amount of GDP in 2017 accounted for 27% of the world GDP.[1] A large population and a vibrant economy are good prerequisites for the development of BRICS higher education. In terms of quantity, the enrollment of BRICS higher education has an absolute advantage compared with that of other countries in the world. Among them, China's higher education enrollment ranks first in the world and India's higher education enrollment ranks second. The amount of China's higher education institutions ranks second in the world and that of India's higher education institutions ranks first. The gross

---

[1] 李胜利、解德渤:《金砖国家高等教育质量比较——基于2009—2015年〈全球竞争力报告〉的分析》,《高等教育研究》2016年第10期。

enrollment rate of Russian higher education is 76.1%, ranking the 18th in the world, while the other four countries still have a lot of room for improvement in gross enrollment.

Table1: The duration of compulsory education and the number of undergraduate graduates in 2018 in the BRICS countries

	number of undergraduate graduates in 2018 (in ten thousands)	duration of compulsory education (years)
China	820	9
Russia	71.6	11
Brazil	85	14
India	650	8
South Africa	70	9

Source: the author sorted out the data from public information.

Generally speaking, the countries of BRICS have their own advantages in the higher education: Russia provides a relatively complete classification education, and colleges and universities have large-scale and system-based advantages in terms of science and engineering experimental equipment and innovative infrastructure. India relies on the good traditions of higher education in the Commonwealth countries to implement a flexible model of teaching and facilitating classes in English, and its information engineering and management graduates are favored by the international market. China ranks among the top in the world in terms of the scale of higher education and investment in higher education. The attraction of high-level talents is constantly increasing, and the professionalization of talent training is getting better. While relying on the educational resources of the Commonwealth, South Africa uses its relatively free market economy environment and has unique advantages in cultivating business talents. Brazil has a unique diversity in higher education, and makes use of its special links with Europe and North America to have an advantage in nurturing elite talents.①

In order to make full use of the higher education resources, the BRICS member states have begun to try to build relevant cooperation mechanisms. In November 2013, the BRICS began the first meeting of ministers of education. At the intergovernmental level, the BRICS only took higher education cooperation as part of human cooperation before 2014 from the joint declaration issued by the BRICS Summits. The 2014 Fortaleza Summit and the forthcoming Fortaleza Action Plan included cooperation between the education sectors as a long-term mechanism for the first time. In the 7th BRICS Summit in 2015, the Ufa Declaration first proposed higher education as one of the directions for cooperation among member states, and clarified the specific implementation direction of higher education cooperation: "efforts should be channeled into strengthening exchanges in recognizing university diplomas and degrees; BRICS relevant departments are required to cooperate on degree identification and mutual recognition, and BRICS network universities and university alliances are supported to establish."②

Under the impetus of government leaders, active higher education cooperationin the following tracks has also been carried out on the diplomatic level: in 2011, Russian President Dmitry Medvedev promoted the establishment of the BRICS Inter-country Research Committee on BRICS issues, and the Russian Academy of Sciences and The Russian Ministry of Foreign Affairs have been specifically responsible for implementing the BRICS cooperation of research institutes.③ In 2012, under the promotion of Russia, the BRICS Summit decided to establish BRICS Inter-faculties Coordination Committee

---

① 唐晓玲:《"金砖国家"高等教育竞争力研究——基于巴西、俄罗斯、印度、中国的数据比较》,《现代教育管理》2018年第9期。

② 2016年之前金砖国家领导人峰会的历次联合宣言可见金砖国家联合体信息门户网站: http://infobrics.org/。

③ М. С. Липоватая, Вопросы Сотрудничества Стран Брикс в сферевысшегообразования, вестн. моск. ун_та. сер. 27. глобалистика и геополитика. 2017. № 4.

based on the School of Public Administration of the Moscow University of Russia, which is responsible for promoting BRICS cooperation among faculties of colleges and universities. In October 2015, China promoted the establishment of the "Beijing Consensus" among the presidents of the BRICS, and established the BRICS University Alliance based on Beijing Normal University. In 2015, Russia led the establishment of the BRICS Network University in Moscow. These two mechanisms were evaluated by the BRICS Joint Declaration as "promoting BRICS cooperation and partnership in higher education". In December 2016, the Russian National University of Management hosted an international forum on Artificial Intelligence and Digital Economy among BRICS universities in Moscow, and signed agreements on the development of digital society. Joint research will be carried out among BRICS universities and a joint laboratory and research center will be built.

II. The Significance of BRICS Higher Education Cooperation

2.1 Accumulating Future-oriented Human Capital

Unlike other fields, BRICS higher education cooperation has a typical "development investment" nature. According to the *Human Capital Report* released by the World Economic Forum, countries in the world face severe challenges in the development of human capital, especially the BRICS with a large population. Among the most important "Human Capital Index" data listed in the report, Russia is the highest, ranking the 26th; China ranks the 64th; Brazil ranks the 78th; South Africa and India are already out of the 90th.[1] Obviously, the huge population base of the BRICS has not been transformed into the dominant human capital that adapts to the development of the global economy. The structural vacancy between the human resources and the population supply

---

[1] Human Capital Report 2015: Employment, Skills and Human Capital, Global Challenge Insight Report, World Economic Forum.

will constitute the main development challenges for the BRICS in the upcoming years.

For the BRICS countries, with the gradual end of the extensive high-growth economic stage, any country will enter a stage of human capital-driven economic development. At this stage, the country needs to carry out difficult industrial restructuring and upgrading, and human capital is the most important resource to support industrial restructuring.[1] Different from other economic factors, the input and output of human capital must be realized through higher education. Relevant research shows that China's increased investment in education and training will bring a potential growth rate of 0.1 percentage point to the Chinese economy in the middle and low-speed stage.[2] International research also points out that low level human capital cannot have a significant impact on economic growth. Only higher education for improving the education level and skills accumulation of workers can significantly improve the economic development status. Therefore, higher education development in the future needs to be strengthened for the emerging economies represented by the BRICS.

2.2 Rebuilding the Cornerstone of Globalization

At present, because the problems of economic structure and income distribution cannot be solved for a long time, the anti-globalization consciousness such as anti-globalization and populism is continuously projected into the political situation of developed countries, which in turn affects relevant foreign decision-making in countries such as Europe and the United States, and poses a formidable challenge to economic globalization. Unlike previous

---

[1] Aoki, M. (2012) Five Phases of Economic Development and Institutional Evolution in China, Japan and Korea, Part I, in Aoki, M., T. Kuran and G. R. Roland, eds, Institutions and Comparative Economic Development, Basingstoke: Palgrave Macmillan.

[2] Lu, Y. and F. Cai (2014) China's Shift from the Demographic Dividend to the Reform Dividend, in L. Song, R. Garnaut and F. Cai (eds), Deepening Reform for China's Long Term Growth and Development, ANU E Press, Canberra, pp. 27-50.

questions about specific policies and mechanisms, the biggest challenge to the current economic globalization is employment, and many people question that it cannot give participants a clear sense of professionalism. Relying on economic policies to solve the employment problem is a very complicated internal and external policy game. The Trump administration's actions on this issue show that it is difficult for the country to properly solve the employment problem through economic policies, and education is an effective solution to the employment problem. Brad Enzimand, Minister of Education of the South African believes that education and training can bring more opportunities for young people to better address unemployment and inequality. It is a "strategic area" for BRICS cooperation.[1]

The improvement of higher education depends on the input and accumulation of physical capital on the one hand, and the deepening of education internationalization on the other. After the reform and opening up, the education internationalization pace of China is basically consistent with the speed of national economic development. The United States clearly listed China as a major strategic competitor in several strategic security reports in 2018. Moreover, the United States and European countries have begun to strengthen the review of Chinese students studying abroad and visiting students on the grounds of preventing the theft of high technology. However, as the state finances have not been able to solve the debt problem smoothly after the 2008 financial crisis, the major partners of China's education internationalization-the United States, the United Kingdom, Canada, New Zealand and Australia-have significantly increased the tuition fees of our overseas studentsin recent years. The education internationalization situation of China needs to be reconstructed. This phenomenon not only appears in China, but also deeply affects other members of BRICS. As the education internationalization shrinks, the youth groups around the world begin to gradually change from supporting globalization

---

[1] 余燕:《金砖国家教育部长：加强教育培训与合作》,《世界教育信息》2016 年第 3 期。

to disgusting globalization. For example, American college students began to have negative views on China because of the high tuition fees and the burden of student loans. Therefore, strengthening BRICS higher education cooperation will help consolidate the youth groups in the countries concerned and build the cornerstone of globalization.

III. Problems and Challenges Faced by BRICS Higher Education Cooperation

Despite the bright prospects, the BRICS higher education cooperation faces more complicated problems and challenges.

3.1 The BRICS consensus onhigher education has yet to be established.

The author believes that it is necessary to pay attention to the national educational philosophy in the field of education. If the educational concepts between the two countries cannot be bridged, bilateral education cooperation is difficult to last and deepen. Although the BRICS cooperation mechanism has effectively promoted the development of diplomatic relations between the five countries, it is difficult for BRICS to deepen cooperation in higher education because of different educational concepts.

China's higher education concept is based onmass education. Since the founding of New China, it has built the world's largest education system. China regards higher education as the main way to cultivate talents and an important means of building social civilization. In recent years, China's higher education has placed more emphasis on professional education, but the concept of higher education serving to the public has not changed. Russia and China's educational concepts are relatively close, with popular higher education as the mainstay. However, with the reform of education marketization in recent years, part of the higher education has moved toward elite education, especially the institutions of higher learning that participate in the education internationalization focusing on jointly cultivating elites with Europe and the United States.

India and South Africa adhere to the British concept of "elite education", which has created a polarization of talent cultivation in the actual higher education system: high-end talents are at the highest international level, butits number is insufficient and far from meeting the needs of national development. The middle and low-level talents needed for the industrial economy are obviously insufficiently supplied, and a large number of low-end laborers are unemployed in the domestic employment market. Brazil learns more about the concept of "educational autonomy" in the United States. The government is only responsible for relevant policy guidance in the education system, and transfers specific school-running power and school-running supervision to private professionals and professional organizations through the democratically elected system, which is also the main reason for its high tuition fees.

In terms of promoting the BRICS higher education cooperation in the future, how to bridge the differences in educational concepts may become the biggest challenge. Considering that education has the dual function of shaping economic development and ideology for each member state, whether BRICS can break through the prejudice in their respective educational concepts and realize mutual recognition and understanding of each other's higher education system is the key issue of deepening higher education cooperation under the BRICS framework.

3.2 It is difficult to move from "projectized" cooperation to "institutionalized" cooperation in the short term

The higheststate of cooperation in higher education is "institutionalized" cooperation. The main representatives in this regard are the European Union-sponsored Sorbonne Declaration and the Bologna Process. In order to promote the cooperation of higher education mechanisms within the EU, in May 1998, the Ministers of Education of France, Germany, Italy and the United Kingdom took the lead in gathering at the Sorbonne University in France to study how to accelerate the promotion of the mobility and qualifications of higher education personnel. During the meeting, they jointly signed an agreement to promote the coordination of the four countries' higher education system, the "Sorbonne Declaration". The main contents of the "Sorbonne Declaration" are: to promote the establishment of the overall framework of European higher education degree and academic system in a step-by-step manner, establish a common academic system and academic qualifications, strengthen and promote the flow of teachers and students, remove barriers to the flow of academic staff and promote the recognition of academic qualifications and deal with the unemployment problem caused by the shortage of labor structure and intelligence. The Bologna Process is a European higher education reform plan proposed by 29 European countries in Bologna, Italy in 1999. The goal of the plan was to integrate the EU's higher education resources and open up the education system. The sponsors and participating countries of the Bologna Process hoped that by 2010, the diplomas and achievements of university graduates from any of the countries in the "Bologna Process" in Europe would be recognized by other signatory countries, and the university graduates can apply for a master's degree course or find employment opportunities in other European countries without any obstacles, so as to realize European higher education and technology integration, build a European higher education zone, and contribute to the European integration process.

In the long run, the BRICS higher education cooperation should reach the level of the Bologna Process, and truly achieve institutionalized cooperation. However, there are still many conditions for restricting the BRICS to achieve institutionalized cooperation:

First, the education system brought about by different educational concepts is very different. It takes a long time for the BRICS education authorities and educational executives to familiarize themselves with each other's mechanisms. For example, the postgraduate education system in Russia is significantly different fromthose of other BRICS countries. In order to achieve mutual recognition and exchange of credits, it is first necessary to reach a consensus among the BRICS around the Russian teaching system. The undergraduate education in India and South Africa is quite different from the undergraduate education in China. The highly autonomous education system in Brazil has caused many countries to have a lot of confusion about the Brazilian education system.

Second, countries have different priorities for the education internationalization. China hopes to give priority to higher education cooperation in high-tech fields. Russia hopes that other BRIC can make more use of Russia's more surplus higher education resources, while India is worried about that the involvement in BRICS higher education cooperation may result in the alienation of the core educational resources of the United Kingdom and the United States. The domestic education community in South Africa is deeply estranged in the education system and the fair selection mechanism of the Sino-Russian higher education system, fearing that black students of their own may encounter racial discrimination.

Third, in terms of the current diplomatic attitude, the BRICS governments should encourage "projectized" cooperation. Since the higher education system is deeply embedded in the ideology and elite grouping of a country, governments are also more jealous of the institutionalized cooperation among the fully liberalized higher education. In the joint statement of the BRICS and leaders, we can see that the top leaders of the BRICS have encouraged "projectized" cooperation. The Chinese government encourages joint degree training and the establishment of Chinese-foreign joint universities. The Russian government encourages joint research projects, while the South African and Indian governments focus on cooperation in general education and skills education. For the BRICS governments, the policy resistance and domestic suspicion of "projectized" cooperation are less, and due to the limited number of participants and clear division of labor, they can achieve results in a short period of time, and give confidence to more collaborators.

Fourth, a principled opinionhas not yet been reached on the issue of funding for higher education. If higher education wants to deepen international cooperation, the BRICS need to form a principled opinion on the issue of funding. At present, since cooperation among BRICS is mainly based on the "projectized" cooperation, the funding problem can be solved through bilateral channels. If multilateral international cooperation among BRICS is to be achieved in the future, member states need to reach a principled opinion on funding issues within the framework of the BRICS. Considering that some of the current member states are burdened with heavy government debt, it will be a big challenge to find the right funding source for multilateral cooperation.

IV. Prospects for Higher Education Cooperation between China and the Other Members of BRICS

China has made remarkable achievements in the field of higher education in recent years. The overall level of competitiveness is at the forefront of the "BRICS", but the pattern that China's higher education is "big in size but not strong in strength" will continue for many years. Under the background of the increasingly competitive situation between China and the United States, the road to internationalization of China's higher education, which mainly relies on cooperation between Europe and the United States, faces enormous challenges. China needs to rely on the multilateral mechanisms of non-European and American countries such as the BRICS to promote the education internationalization in another direction to achieve the strategic goal of the country to enhance the competitiveness of education. Looking ahead, China can take the initiative in the following areas to promote the development of BRICS higher education cooperation.

The first is to give full play to BRICS organizational advantages and resource endowments, and strive to build a new type of education internationalization and cooperation. The BRICS have the characteristics of different resource endowments and decentralized organizational forms in the higher education cooperation. Against the background of the increasingly fierce geopolitical competition in the world, China should make use of BRICS comparative advantages to promote a new round of education internationalization development.

The second is to fully integrate China's market advantage and scholarship system, and try to absorb the outstanding talents of other members of BRICS to participate in higher education cooperation. China's economic strength is in the leading position among the BRICS, and the domestically developed consumer market also attracts investors and laborers from all over the world. At present, China has provided a number of scholarships for students from other countries of BRICS. However, the related scholarship system cannot be linked with the employment system of foreigners in China, which reduces the willingness of relevant students to study and develop in China. China can consider the combination of domestic talent demand and scholarship system from the perspective of top-level design, promote a new system of visiting and studying in China for higher education talents within countries of BRICS, and fully take advantage of the dividends brought by the development of BRICS higher education.

The third is to fully communicate with the BRICS education authorities and educational researchers at all levels. Under the guidance of the concept of "a community of shared destiny for mankind", China should fully communicate and discuss on trying to find common intersections among countries in education concepts, and promote the BRICS to issue a joint declaration in the field of education as soon as possible. China and other countries of BRICS can try to develop common principles that are suitable for the BRICS in terms of social governance, economic development and human rights protection related to higher education.

The fourth is to actively innovate in cooperation projects. China can launch corresponding cooperation projects according to the specific conditions of each BRICS countries. Also, China can expand the proportion of international students and international teachers in all BRICS countries, and encourage qualified colleges to recruit a large number of students with different backgrounds and cultures from other countries of BRICS, international teachers not only may teach in China, but also may conduct global research projects, empirical research and joint experiments within the BRICS. China can also cooperate with more distinctive education systems of India, South Africa and Brazil to add regional specialties into the specialized courses of colleges and universities, guide students to observe and discover the differences in understanding different knowledge among BRICS, and encourage more international exchange programs with Russia and India. Considering that the international travel expenses and living expenses of these two countries are not high, more Chinese university students should be promoted to exchange in the universities of Russia and India. Relying on the resources of colleges and universities, the BRICS can organize short-term visiting groups and organize relevant students, teachers and practitioners in related industries to study and visit and exchange in the BRICS. According to the characteristic that industrial and commercial cooperation is more active under the BRICS framework, China can also organize relevant universities to carry out international internship cooperation, conduct internships in outstanding enterprises in the BRICS, enhance mutual understanding, and help students to obtain better international experience. China can also consider jointly establishing a research center with other countries of BRICS and establishing overseas campuses in relevant countries. The research center mainly helps university researchers and students to better understand the latest academic progress and help them establish relationships with academic institutions, alumni and industrialists in the local countries. The establishment of overseas campuses will benefit China and the host country in bilateral relationships and provide a reliable infrastructure for students and academics wishing to study, exchange and visit in these countries.

Higher education is an importantfield for the BRICS future sustainable cooperation and an important talent guarantee for the BRICS to jointly promote global governance. While promoting the focus of education in our country, transferring from "knowing" to "going" and achieving the strategic goal of strengthening the country with talents, we can also consider continuously integrating and condensing the higher education resources of developing countries in the world from a global perspective so as to provide a more solid talent foundation for the construction of a community with shared destiny for mankind.

China and BRICS People-to-people Exchanges[*]

Zhu Tianxiang[**] Zhang Mingyao[***]

Abstract: China is a promoter and leader of BRICS people-to-people exchanges and has played an active and important role in advancing people-to-people exchanges to be a pillar of BRICS cooperation. China holds that the BRICS people-to-people exchanges are both possible and feasible. BRICS should uphold the principles of equality, openness and inclusiveness, impel cooperation in the fields of culture, education, health, sports, tourism and locality, pay more attention to the mass participation than to government guidance, and continue their cooperation perseveringly so as to achieve the goal of providing convenience for all-round cooperation of the BRICS on the basis of achieving the goal of people-to-people exchanges. To this end, China has

---

[*] 本文是2018年度重庆市社科规划培育项目"中国特色大国外交的'一对多'整体合作模式研究"的阶段性成果,项目编号2018PY06。

[**] Zhu Tianxiang, Director of Center for External Relations Studies, Institute of BRICS Studies, Sichuan International Studies University.

[***] Zhang Mingyao, Master of Comparative Institutional Studies, School of International relations, Sichuan International Studies University.

continuously contributed the Chinese approach and China's strength to the field of BRICS people-to-people exchanges, especially through establishing bilateral high-level exchanges with Russia, South Africa and India to consolidate the foundation of BRICS people-to-people exchanges. In this context, the China-Brazil advanced people-to-people exchanges mechanism is established to fully cover the mechanisms of China and other members of BRICS, which is also an important contribution of China to the BRICS people-to-people exchanges.

Keywords: BRICS; People-to-people Exchange; China; Position; Practice

President Xi Jinping has pointed out: "China is a staunch supporter and participant in the BRICS mechanism and holds BRICS cooperation as an important direction of China's diplomacy."① To this end, China has actively contributed to the Chinese approach at the beginning of the BRICS cooperation.② In these two BRICS summits that have been hosted so far, many important ideas and pragmatic measures with Chinese characteristics, world vision and BRICS Views have been put forward. Especially during the Xiamen Summit in 2017, President Xi has proposed three important proposals: BRICS should "treat each other with equality and seek common ground while reserving differences", "deal with concrete matters and make innovation, cooperate to seek win-win", "cherish the world in mind, make others succeed first and then one can succeed", which pointed out the direction for future BRICS cooperation. Among them, it is particularly worth mentioning that "people-to-people exchanges as a rising star has become a highlight of the BRICS China Year" and has developed into a "new pillar

---

① 习近平:《坚定信心 共谋发展——在金砖国家领导人第八次会晤大范围会议上的讲话》, 2016 年 10 月 16 日, https://www. fmprc. gov. cn/web/gjhdq_676201/gjhdqzz_681964/jzgj_682158/zyjh_682168/t1406096. shtml。

② 2009 年 6 月 16 日, 时任国家主席胡锦涛在首届"金砖四国"领导人会晤时就曾建议, 金砖国家可以从"增强政治互信""深化经济合作""推进人文交流""提倡经验互鉴"四个方面开展合作。参见胡锦涛:《在"金砖四国"领导人会晤时的讲话》, 2009 年 6 月 16 日, https://www. fmprc. gov. cn/web/gjhdq_676201/gjhdqzz_681964/jzgj_682158/zyjh_682168/t568042. shtml。

of BRICS cooperation" under the influence of China.[①] It can be said that China has paid special attention to the people-to-people exchanges in the BRICS. In this context, it is of great practical significance to explore China's position on BRICS people-to-people exchanges, sort out China's practice in the field of BRICS people-to-people exchanges, and summarize the characteristics of China's participation in BRICS people-to-people exchanges.

Ⅰ. China's Position on BRICS People-to-people Exchanges

Although the Chinese government has not issued a special document to declare its position on the people-to-people exchanges of the BRICS, the speeches of Chinese national leaders at the previous BRICS summits can still serve as an important channel for understanding official policies. On June 16, 2009, the former President Hu Jintao pointed out that the BRICS should actively develop exchange and cooperation in the fields of culture, education, health, tourism and sports, promote mutual understanding of the people, promote all circles to become good friends and good partners, and lay a solid social foundation for deepening all-round cooperation in view of the long history and culture, the deep cultural heritage and people's long-standing friendship of the BRICS.[②] On April 15, 2010, the then President Hu once again proposed that one of the reasons for the BRICS with different political systems, development methods, religious beliefs, and cultural tradition to become good friends and good partners lies in their mutual learning of civilizations and the mutual

---

① 参见《杨洁篪就金砖国家领导人第九次会晤和新兴市场国家与发展中国家对话会接受媒体采访》，2017年9月6日，https://www.brics2017.org/dtxw/201709/t20170906_2010.html。

② 参见胡锦涛：《在"金砖四国"领导人会晤时的讲话》，2009年6月16日，https://www.fmprc.gov.cn/web/gjhdq_676201/gjhdqzz_681964/jzgj_682158/zyjh_682168/t568042.shtml。

exchange of different cultures and traditions.① On April 14, 2011, when President Hu advocated maintaining world peace and stability, he stressed that the BRICS should "respect the diversity of civilizations, complement each other through learning from each other's strengths and make progress together."② On March 29, 2012, President Hu appeal to the BRICS once again to "try to make cooperation in various fields, play their due role and consolidate the economic, social and public opinion foundation of BRICS cooperation."

On March 27, 2013, President Xi Jinping proposed that "BRICS should link closely with the partnership" and work hard to promote cooperation in the field of personnel exchanges and move toward the goal of "cultural exchanges".③ On July 15, 2014, President Xi described the "different cultural civilizations" as one of the important connotations of the spirit of inclusiveness when interpreting the unique spirit of cooperative partners among the BRICS.④ On July 9, 2015, President Xi proposed "building, developing and expanding a partnership for multiculturalism" as an important aspect of strengthening the BRICS partnership. He pointed out that "the success of BRICS cooperation has proved that countries with different social systems can be mutually inclusive; countries with different development models can cooperate with each other; countries with different value and cultures can communicate with each other. We must persist in open and inclusive, learn from each other in exchanges and

---

① 参见胡锦涛:《合作 开放 互利 共赢——在"金砖四国"领导人会晤时的讲话》,2010 年 4 月 15 日, https://www.fmprc.gov.cn/web/gjhdq_676201/gjhdqzz_681964/jzgj_682158/zyjh_682168/t682096.shtml。

② 参见胡锦涛:《展望未来 共享繁荣——在金砖国家领导人第三次会晤时的讲话》,2011 年 4 月 14 日, https://www.fmprc.gov.cn/web/gjhdq_676201/gjhdqzz_681964/jzgj_682158/zyjh_682168/t815150.shtml。

③ 参见习近平:《携手合作 共同发展——在金砖国家领导人第五次会晤时的主旨讲话》,2013 年 3 月 27 日, https://www.fmprc.gov.cn/web/gjhdq_676201/gjhdqzz_681964/jzgj_682158/zyjh_682168/t1025978.shtml。

④ 参见习近平:《新起点 新愿景 新动力——在金砖国家领导人第六次会晤上的讲话》,2014 年 7 月 15 日, https://www.fmprc.gov.cn/web/gjhdq_676201/gjhdqzz_681964/jzgj_682158/zyjh_682168/t1174958.shtml。

mutual learning, seek common ground and move forward together while reserving differences."① On October 16, 2016, President Xi once again stressed that the BRICS should "enhance the exchange of humanities, advance the communication of the people, and consolidate the public opinion foundation of cooperation among the BRICS", so as to achieve the goal of "jointly deepening partnership".②

On September 4, 2017, President Xi further appealed that the BRICS should "be devoted to promoting humanities and people-to-people exchanges" with an aim to comprehensively deepen the BRICS partnership and open the second "Golden Decade" of the BRICS cooperation. He emphasized that "The amity between people holds the key to sound relations between states and only deep cultivation can make friendship and cooperation flourishing. It is a work worthy of long-term investment to strengthen the cultural exchanges between the five countries and let the partnership concept take root in the hearts of the people, which if well-done, will enable the BRICS cooperation to last forever and maintain vitality. He also hopes that the existing people-to-people exchanges and cooperation activities "can be regularized, institutionalized, and strive to penetrate the grassroots level and face the masses of the people to make exchanges and cooperation like a hundred flowers in bloom under the common concern and promotion of the leaders of the five BRICS.③ On July 26, 2018, President Xi continued to advocate the BRICS to "deeply expand people-to-people exchanges and cooperation" under the principle of consolidating the

---

① 参见习近平:《共建伙伴关系 共创美好未来——在金砖国家领导人第七次会晤上的讲话》, 2015 年 7 月 9 日, https://www.fmprc.gov.cn/web/gjhdq_676201/gjhdqzz_681964/jzgj_682158/zyjh_682168/t1280127.shtml。

② 参见习近平:《坚定信心 共谋发展——在金砖国家领导人第八次会晤大范围会议上的讲话》, 2016 年 10 月 16 日, https://www.fmprc.gov.cn/web/gjhdq_676201/gjhdqzz_681964/jzgj_682158/zyjh_682168/t1406096.shtml。

③ 参见习近平:《深化金砖伙伴关系 开辟更加光明未来——在金砖国家领导人厦门会晤大范围会议上的讲话》, 2017 年 9 月 4 日, https://www.brics2017.org/dtxw/201709/t20170904_1892.html。

cooperation framework driven by cooperation in economy and trade, finance, political security and people-to-people exchanges. In his view, the BRICS have nurtured their own splendid civilizations and complemented each other, which has attested that people-to-people exchanges and cooperation are promising. The BRICS should "continue to use amity between people as their purpose to extensively carry out cultural exchanges in various fields such as culture, education, health, sports, tourism, etc., and build a solid foundation for the public opinion of BRICS." To this end, China has also put forward proposals of "holding a joint exhibition of BRICS museums, art galleries and library alliances", "strengthening cooperation in cultural and creative industries, tourism, local cities and other fields", "telling more exciting and touching stories" and other specific recommendations.[①]

In general, China's position on the people-to-people exchanges of the BRICS can be roughly divided into two periods. The first period was from 2009 to 2012. At this time, the Chinese government has put more emphasis on the "why" issue of people-to-people exchange, which is to mobilize the BRICS to increase investment in people-to-people exchanges and cooperation by explaining the benefits of people-to-people exchanges. The second period is from 2013 to the present. Relatively speaking, in addition to continuing to pay attention to the "why" issue at this stage, the Chinese government has increasingly focused on the "how" issue of people-to-people exchanges, which is to propose operational policy measures to attract BRICS to expand their participation in people-to-people exchanges and cooperation. Moreover, the position of the Chinese government has a distingwishing feature since 2013. The feature is that people-to-people exchanges are placed under the framework of the BRICS partnership, and efforts are made to promote it as an important embodiment of the BRICS partner spirit, an important pillar of the BRICS

[①] 参见习近平:《让美好愿景变为现实——在金砖国家领导人约翰内斯堡晤大范围会议上的讲话》, 2018 年 7 月 26 日, http://cpc.people.com.cn/nl/2018/0727/c64094-30173944.html。

partnership and an important guarantee for the overall deepening of the BRICS partnership. In addition, the comparison before and after has shown that China's position gradually presents a general trend that is more systematic in the top-level design and more specialized in the specific implementation.

Specifically, China's position on BRICS people-to-people exchanges can be summarized as follows:

First, the possibility and feasibility of people-to-people exchanges; The Chinese government believes that the BRICS are the main representatives of their specific civilizations, and most of these civilizations have a long history and profound foundation, and have great potential for mutual attraction. At the same time, the civilizations and cultures represented by the BRICS are not only geographically distinct, but also have different characteristics in the pedigree, so the BRICS have good prospects of learning from each other.

Second, the goals and objectives of people-to-people exchanges; The Chinese government holds that the direct goal of BRICS people-to-people exchanges is to promote a comprehensive, multi-disciplinary, three-dimensional cultural exchange, and to create a BRICS partnership based on multiple civilizations. Its fundamental purpose is to lay a solid foundation for social and public opinion for the cooperation of the BRICS, enhance mutual political trust through the amity of the people, and facilitate economic and trade cooperation.

Third, the basic principles of people-to-people exchanges; The Chinese government deems that the people-to-people exchanges in the BRICS should first be an equal exchange. There is no distinction between states, peoples, civilizations and cultures. Each has the right to be fully respected by other parties; then, the people-to-people exchanges should be open. The BRICS should have the courage of cultural self-confidence, and also facilitate the exchanges between the people through tangible policy measures; At last, the cultural exchanges should be inclusive. The BRICS should not be culturally proud or culturally inferior, but should have the same mentality of seeking common ground while reserving differences.

Fourth, the main content of people-to-people exchanges; The Chinese government stands that the main fields of people-to-people exchanges in the BRICS can include culture, education, health, sports, tourism, and localities. Among them, more cooperation issues can also be refined from each field. For example, cooperation in the field of culture can involve cultural and creative industries as well as joint exhibitions of museums, art galleries, and library alliance.

Fifth, the ways and means of people-to-people exchanges; The Chinese government believes that on the one hand, BRICS governments should actively impel the people-to-people exchange mechanism of the BRICS to be deepened and practical, and build platforms, formulate policies, remove obstacles, create an atmosphere, and play an active role in guiding people's exchanges; on the other hand, the BRICS should pay special attention to the people-to-people exchange activities on primary level, and find ways to make more and better people-to-people exchanges reach the grassroots level and benefit common people.

Sixth, matters concerning the people-to-people exchanges; The Chinese government considers that compared with the BRICS cooperation in the political and economic fields, people-to-people exchanges are more invested and slower to take effect, but once they form a good effect, they will play an active role. Therefore, the BRICS must have patience, confidence and perseverance in dealing with people-to-people exchanges, and use strategic vision and systematic thinking to exclude short-term interests and local interests, so that the cultural exchanges in the BRICS can run smoothly and achieve the great goal, give good responses and exert positive impacts.

II. China's Practice in the Field of BRICS People-to-people Exchanges

On September 3, 2017, President Xi Jinping pointed out that the opening ceremony of the BRICS Business Forum: "but an action team uniting knowing and doing. Aiming at achieving trade and investment markets, monetary and financial circulation, infrastructure connectivity and people-to-people exchanges, our five countries will promote pragmatic cooperation in various fields. At present, the cooperation has covered dozens of fields such as economy, trade, finance, science, education, culture and health, and vividly interpreted the new international relations of cooperation and win-win." [1] Among them, in terms of boosting BRICS people-to-people exchanges, China has also hosted or undertaken a series of distinctive people-to-people exchange activities and has sincerely contributed Chinese approach and Chinese power to the BRICS in addition to actively participating in various activities organized by other members of BRICS.

List of BRICS People-to-people Exchange Activities Hosted or Undertaken by China (as of June 2019)

Time	Location	Event Name	Main Content
Dce. 2-3, 2011	Sanya	1st BRICS Friendship City and Local Government Cooperation Forum	The forum focused on the theme of "looking forward, sharing prosperity, developing friendly cities, and promoting cooperation". The forum has explored how BRICS friendly cities and local governments respond to the problems and challenges in the development process, mainly involving issues of food security, financial crisis, and urban development, low-carbon environmental protection, energy strategy, and cultural integration.

---

① 参见习近平：《共同开创金砖合作第二个"金色十年"——在金砖国家工商论坛开幕上的讲话》，2017 年 9 月 3 日，https: //www. brics2017. org/dtxw/201709/t20170903_1878. html。

Continued Table

Time	Location	Event Name	Main Content
Sep. 26-27, 2012	Chongqing	2012 BRICS Think Tank Forum	Forum topics included: "Adjustment of the BRICS Development Model in the Context of the International Financial Crisis", "The Feasibility of Creating a BRICS Development Bank", and "Promoting the Economic and BRICS Trade Cooperation".
Sep. 11, 2013	Shanghai	BRICS Information Sharing and Communication Platform	The platform was formally established and opened for operation. Through the joint construction and operation of the China Council of the BRICS Business Council and the BRICS National Research Center of Fudan University, it has been continuously improved and provided high-quality information service for promoting the BRICS cooperation in global governance.
Nov. 6, 2014	Beijing	1st BRICS Economic Think Tank Forum	The forum aimed to explore how the BRICS can work together to meet the challenges and seek to reform the international financial system.
Oct. 18, 2015	Beijing	BRICS University Alliance	More than 50 prestigious university presidents from Russia, Brazil, India, South Africa and China announced the establishment of the Alliance and reached the "Beijing Consensus" at Beijing Normal University.

Continued Table

Time	Location	Event Name	Main Content
Dec. 1, 2015	Beijing	1st BRICS Media Summit	The summit aimed to establish a high-end dialogue and exchange platform for BRICS mainstream media, and promote the innovative development of the media industry in the five countries, enhance the understanding of the world's people on the BRICS, and the friendship between the BRICS people.
Mar. 22, 2017	Beijing	"Strengthening Financial Cooperation and Promoting BRICS Development 2017 BRICS Think Tank Symposium"	The topics of the symposium included: "Global Economic Governance and the Role of the BRICS", "BRICS Financial Cooperation: Process Assessment and Future Prospects", and "BRICS Financial Cooperation and China".
Mar. 30-Jun. 3, 2017	Beijing	The 3rd BRICS Young Diplomat Forum	With the theme of "Deepening the BRICS Partnership and Opening a Brighter Future", the forum included "Emerging Markets and Developing Countries and Countries to Develop Together", "BRIC Economic and Trade Cooperation" and "BRIC Interconnection". In the meantime, around the theme of "BRICS Cultural Exchange", the BRICS young diplomats also had a discussion with representatives of teachers and students of Beijing Normal University.

Continued Table

Time	Location	Event Name	Main Content
Jun. 7-8, 2017	Beijing	BRICS Media Forum	The forum was based on the theme of "Deepening BRICS Media Cooperation and Promoting Fairness and Justice in International Public Opinion", including "All-media Innovation and Media Development" and "Media Obligations and Social Responsibility". After the forum, the "BRIC Strengthening Media Cooperation Action Plan" was published.
Jun. 10-12, 2017	Fuzhou	BRICS Political Parties, Think-Tanks and Civil Society Organizations Forum	The BRICS political party dialogue was based on the issue of "playing the role of political parties and leading the direction of cooperation". The BRICS academic forum centered on the theme of "collecting ideas and wisdom, innovating cooperation thinking", and the BRICS Civil Society Organizations Forum moved around "promoting the amity of people and consolidating the foundation for cooperation". The forum has passed the "Fuzhou Initiative" and reached an agreement on "the proposal of the 9th BRICS Academic Forum for the meeting of BRICS leaders in Xiamen."

Continued Table

Time	Location	Event Name	Main Content
Jun. 17-21, 2017	Guangzhou	First BRICS Games	Therewere 3 major events and 10 small events in the Games, including martial arts projects with distinctive Chinese characteristics, as well as competitive and ornamental basketball and volleyball programs with high popularity and great influence.
Jun. 23-27, 2017	Chengdu	2017 China Chengdu BRICS Film Festival	The film forum focused on the "BRICS Film Cooperation Path" and mainly explored the BRICS cooperative methodological mode in shooting. The National Film Day event was based on the theme of "different cultures with same wonderfulness" and had exhibited the films of every country with the manner of "screening one country and one kind of film culture every day" to highlight the film culture of BRICS in all aspects and give more audiences the opportunity to experience the cultural charm of different countries. In addition, the film *Where Time Goes*, which was completed by the master directors from the BRICS, was also premiered during the festival.

Continued Table

Time	Location	Event Name	Main Content
Jul. 1-3, 2017	Zhengzhou	2017 BRICS Network University AnnualConference	The annual conferencewas based on the theme of "international education and pragmatic cooperation". After the conference, the parties had signed a series of heavyweight documents such as the "Constitution of the International Management Board of the BRICS Network University", "2017-2018 BRICS Network Action Plan", "2017 BRICS Network University Annual Conference Zhengzhou Consensus" and a series of multilateral documents and bilateral cooperation agreement.
Jul. 5, 2017	Beijing	5th BRICS Ministers of Education Meeting	With the theme of "BRICS Education Cooperation: Promoting Excellence and Equity", themeeting passed the outcome document such as the "Beijing Education Declaration of 5th BRICS Ministers of Education Meeting" and reached a series of consensus on the future cooperation of BRICS education.
Jul. 6, 2017	Tianjin	The 7th BRICS Health Ministers Meeting and High Level Meeting on Traditional Medicine	The meeting adopted the "Tianjin Bulletin", which aimed to strengthen the role of BRICS in global health governance, and actively share useful experiences in improving health systems and promoting the quality of health services, and achieving health-related sustainable development goals.

Continued Table

Time	Location	Event Name	Main Content
Jul. 6, 2017	Tianjin	Second Meeting of BRICS Ministers of Culture	The representatives of the five countries signed the Action Plan for the Implementation of the BRICS Inter-Governmental Cultural Agreement (2017-2021), and witnessed the BRICS Library Alliance, the Museum Alliance, the Gallery Alliance and the Youth and Children's Theatre Alliance signing outcome documents.
Jul. 12, 2017	Chengdu	2017 BRICS Friendship City and Local Government Cooperation Forum	The forum was based on the theme of "Interactive Development, Co-creating and Sharing", including high-end interviews with provincial and municipal heads, as well as theme forums such as urban internationalization and educational exchanges, and the *Chengdu Initiative* was launched to promote the institutionalization of local exchanges and cooperation among BRICS countries.
Jul. 12-14, 2017	Hangzhou	The 2nd BRICS Young Scientists Forum	The theme of the forum was "to jointly build the science and technology innovative leadership of young scientists", and set up three sub-forums of energy, materials and biomedicine, and an interdisciplinary sub-forum.

Continued Table

Time	Location	Event Name	Main Content
Jul. 18, 2017	Hangzhou	The 5th BRICS Science, Technology & Innovation (STI) Ministerial Meeting	The meeting reached a number of important achievements in the exchange of scientific and technological innovation policies, cooperation in thematic areas, joint funding of multilateral research and development projects, youth innovation and entrepreneurship, exchanges of young scientists, and cooperation in science parks. After the meeting, the *Hangzhou Declaration*, *BRICS Innovative Cooperation Action Plan* and *BRICS 2017-2018 Science and Technology Innovation Work Plan* were published.
Jul. 24-25, 2017	Beijing	The 6th BRICS Trade Unions Forum	The theme of the forum was "sustainable development and the role of trade unions", including "sustainable development: opportunities and challenges facing the world of work", "advancing the 2030 agenda: the historical mission of trade unions", and "opening a new golden decade: strengthening the exchanges and cooperation of the BRICS labor world. The forum passed the documents such as the *BRICS Trade Union Forum Declaration*, the *Joint Statement of the BRICS Trade Union to the BRICS Ministers of Labor Employment*, and the *Interim Rules of the BRICS Trade Union Forum*.

Continued Table

Time	Location	Event Name	Main Content
Jul. 25-27, 2017	Beijing	2017 BRICS Youth Forum	Participant scentered on topics of "the focal points and characteristics of youth policies in the new era" and "the BRICS youth innovation and entrepreneurship" and finally the 2017 BRICS Youth Forum Action Plan was formed.
Aug. 15-22, 2017	Putian	2017 BRICS Junior Football Invitational Tournament	More than 600 athletes from 24 teams from the BRICS participated in the competition.
Aug. 22-26, 2017	Hangzhou	BRICS Skills Development and Technology Innovation Competition- 3D Printing and Intelligent Manufacturing Skills Competition	3D Printing Modeling Technology Competition + Intelligent Manufacturing Production Line Operation and Maintenance Competition.
Sep. 15-22, 2017	Xiamen	BRICS Cultural Festival	The theme of the festival was "making civilizations compatible and connecting peoples". More than 210 artists from the BRICS countries were invited to hold more than 30 related events such as theater performances, outdoor performances, art master classes, theme exhibitions and BRICS film screenings.
Sep. 21, 2017	Beijing	A Survey of the BRICS Youth's Understanding on Chinese Culture	Thesurvey was aimed to understand BRICS youth's perceptions and preferences of Chinese cultural symbols, their willingness and channels of contacting Chinese culture, and their preferences of Chinese cultural products and cultural activities. The research group of the Institute of Cultural Innovation and Communication of Beijing Normal University conducted the survey on young people from four countries of Russia, India, Brazil, and South Africa.

Continued Table

Time	Location	Event Name	Main Content
May. 6-7, 2018	Beijing	"Deepen the BRICS Partnership and Promote New International Development Cooperation" - BRICS International Think Tank International Symposium and the 17th "Wanshou Forum"	Forum topics included: "Human Destiny Community and New International Development View", "New Mechanism and New Path of BRICS Cooperation", "BRICS Cooperation and Realization of International Sustainable Development", "International Development and Cooperation: from BRICS Best experience".
Jun. 9, 2018	Chongqing	"BRICS people-to-people Exchange: Government's Leading Role and people-to-people Interaction" - 2018 BRICS International Think Tank International Symposium and 21st Wanshou Forum	Forum topics included: "Thoughts and Measures for Innovation and Synergic Development of the BRICS people-to-people Exchange Mechanism" and "Paths and Ways for BRICS People-to-people Exchange to Promote the Amity of the Five Nationalities".
Jul. 10-13, 2018	Hangzhou	2018 Belt & Road and BRICS Skills Development and Technology Innovation Competition - The First Mould Digital Design and Intelligent Manufacturing Skills Competition	It was aimed to promote BRICS skills development and technical exchanges, implement the memorandum on talent development cooperation signed by the BRICS, and build international talents cooperation platform for the Belt & Road and BRICS vocational skills development, engineering capacity development and intelligent technology innovation.
Jul. 20-Aug. 22, 2018	Beijing	BRICS Drama Alliance for Children and Youth Series Activities	The activities covered the "BRICS children's drama show and BRICS Children and Youth Drama Alliance meeting."

Continued Table

Time	Location	Event Name	Main Content
Oct. 25, 2018	Beijing	The 1st BRICS Alliance of Museums Conference	Representatives from the Brazilian Museum of Natural History, the Royal Museum of Brazil, the Russian National History Museum, the National Museum of India, the National Museum of China, and the Dixon Museum of South Africa jointly witnessed the establishment of the BRICS Alliance of Museums and jointly negotiated a win-win situation for the BRICS museums.
Nov. 1, 2018	Beijing	2018 BRICS International Think Tank International Symposium 25th Wanshou Forum and the 1st Ward Forum	With the theme of "promoting the cooperation of BRICS traditional medicines and building a community of human health", the forum set up issues of the "Global Health Situation and Traditional Medicine Development Strategy", "The Fourth Industrial Revolution and the Development of Traditional Medicine Innovation", "Healthy Urban Construction and Traditional Medical Development", etc.
May. 10, 2019	Beijing	Premiere of the Film *Half the Sky*	The second BRICS cooperation film *Half the Sky* which was produced by Chinese director Jia Zhangke, was released on May 10. The film is co-operated by the female directors of the five countries. With the theme of "Contemporary Women's Emotions and Society", the film voices female suggestion from the perspective of women, understand women, listen to women, and pay attention to the realization of women's self-worth.

Continued Table

Time	Location	Event Name	Main Content
May. 26, 2019	Shanghai	The 1st Plenary Session of the BRICS Alliance of Universities in 2019	The conference focused on BRICS pragmatic cooperation in education and hoped to effectively promote cooperation and exchanges among member universities and discuss the sustainable development strategy of the BRICS Alliance of Universities.
Jul. 29, 2019	Beijing	2019 BRICS International Think Tank International Symposium	The symposium centered on the topic of "Global Governance and Multilateralism", and included issues: "how BRICS defend multilateralism under the trend of unilateralism" and "the responsibility and role of the BRICS in global development governance", "how the BRICS lead the reshaping of the rules of the global economic and trade system" and "the role of the BRICS in the global governance of the new territories in the context of the new industrial revolution".

Source: The information derives from the public information on the Internet, and the form is self-made by the author.

Although the above information does not cover all the practices of China in the field of BRICS people-to-people exchanges over the past decade, from these representative activities we can still find that the actual investment of China in people-to-people exchange is quite limited in the long period after the opening of the BRICS summits. Of course, this is closely related to the development and evolution of the BRICS cooperation mechanism itself. In the context of emphasizing the politically and economically driven cooperation of the BRICS, it was somewhat out of place to intervene in the people-to-people exchanges. In the same way, when the BRICS increasingly discover the potential value and significant impact of people-to-people exchanges and formally determine them as the third pillar of the BRICS cooperation, the attention and investment of the BRICS to people-to-people exchange would naturally be different. Not to mention the fact that China has host the 9th BRICS Summit. Therefore, the people-to-people exchange activities held by China in 2017 were extremely rich, including not only the inheritance of the previous institutionalized activities, but also some innovations full of Chinese wisdom. Although most of the activities of people-to-people exchange were undertaken by the host country of the summit, China has been also maintaining more positive attitude towards the BRICS people-to-people exchanges during the non-hosting period.

III. China's Bilateral Model for Promoting BRICS People-to-People Exchanges

The BRICS countries are the basis for BRICS cooperation. Dealing with bilateral relations with other four countries is the responsibility and obligation of every BRICS member. It is also an important prerequisite for promoting and guaranteeing the smooth development of BRICS cooperation. In this sense, establishing people-to-people exchange mechanisms with Russia, South Africa, India and Brazil is also an important way for China to promote BRICS people-to-people exchanges. So far, in addition to Brazil, China has established advanced high-level language exchange mechanisms with Russia, South Africa and India. Among them, the earliest established bilateral people-to-people exchange mechanism is the Sino-Russian Humanities Cooperation Committee. On July 18, 2000, the previous President Jiang Zemin and Russian President Vladimir Putin signed the Beijing Declaration of the People's Republic of China and the Russian Federation in Beijing. The declaration stated that "cooperation in the fields of science, technology, education, culture and sports should be strengthened and expanded" and stressed that "the friendship between the two peoples for generations is the common aspiration of the Chinese people and the Russian people. It also requires the broad participation and unremitting efforts of the two peoples and the two governments to achieve this goal. To this end, the work of the China-Russia Friendship, Peace and Development Committee has been actively supported and other forms of non-governmental exchanges between the two countries have been encouraged". [1] In this context, the Sino-Russian Cooperation Committee on Education, Culture and Sports was formally established in November of the same year.

On July 16, 2001, China and Russia formally signed the "Sino-Russian Treaty of Good-Neighborliness, Friendship and Cooperation" in Moscow. Article 16 of the Treaty stipulates: "The contracting parties will vigorously promote the development of exchanges and cooperation in the fields of culture, education, health, information, tourism, sports and the legal system." Subsequently, the people-to-people exchanges between China and Russia have been increased substantially, and the fields of communication and cooperation far exceed the scope of education, culture, health and sports. Therefore, on July 13, 2007, the two sides officially renamed the Committee on Education, Culture, Sports and Health to the China-Russia Humanities Cooperation Committee, which consists of seven sub-committees including education, culture, health, sports, tourism, media and film, and the archives cooperation working group. [2] As of October 2018, the China-Russia Humanities Cooperation Committee has held 19 meetings, and the people-to-people exchange activities such as youth

---

[1] 参见《中华人民共和国和俄罗斯联邦宣言》, 2000 年 7 月 18 日, https://www.fmprc.gov.cn/web/gjhdq_676201/gj_676203/oz_678770/1206_679110/1207_679122/t6787.shtml。

[2] 参见李亚男:《论中俄关系发展进程中的人文交流与合作》,《东北亚论坛》2011 年第 6 期, 第 115 页。

exchanges, media forums, cultural festivals, youth games, film festivals, traditional medicine cooperation, and tourism years carried out by the two countries under this framework have also had an important impact on the planning and design of BRICS people-to-people exchanges, and have been reflected in the specific implementation process of BRICS people-to-people exchange activities. At the same time, with the increasingly strong people-to-people exchange atmosphere in the BRICS, the successful practice of the Sino-Russian bilateral people-to-people exchange mechanism has also provided important reference for China to advance the establishment of corresponding mechanisms with other countries of BRICS.

On December 4, 2015, President Xi Jinping said at the opening ceremony of the Johannesburg Summit of the China-Africa Cooperation Forum, "strengthening and consolidating the 'five pillars' is to promote the new strategic partnership between China and Africa to be a comprehensive strategic partnership". Among them, the third pillar is to "adhere to the exchange and mutual understanding in civilization." President Xi hoped to "strengthen the exchanges between the two major civilizations of China and Africa and focus on strengthening exchanges between young people, women, think tanks, the media, universities and other people from all works of life, promote cultural harmony, policy integration, people-to-people communication, advance common progress, and make the Chinese and African people friendly for generations."[①] Under the direct promotion of the two heads of countries, the China-South Africa senior exchange mechanism was officially established on April 24, 2017. This mechanism is the first high-level exchange mechanism between China and African countries. One of its purposes is to create new opportunities for the development and enrichment of existing bilateral and multilateral cooperation

---

① 参见习近平:《开启中非合作共赢共同发展的新时代——在中非合作论坛约翰内斯堡峰会开幕式上的致辞》,2015 年 12 月 4 日, http://www.xinhuanet.com/world/2015-12/04/c_1117363197.htm。

and exchange mechanisms and projects.① As President Xi said in his congratulatory letter to the first meeting of the mechanism, "the launch of the mechanism will consolidate the public opinion foundation of China-South Africa relations and effectively promote people-to-people exchanges between the two countries". "China and South Africa are both big developing countries and members of the BRICS" and the people-to-people exchanges between China and South Africa will certainly help to further expand and deepen the BRICS people-to-people exchanges. In a certain sense, the establishment of a high-level Chinese-South African exchange mechanism is also intended to better support China, the host of Xiamen Summit to push people-to-people exchanges as the new pillar of the BRICS cooperation.

On June 18, 2017, Indian border guards crossed the border to block China's construction of roads in the Donglang area on the Sino-Indian border, which triggered a confrontation between the two sides for more than two months. At this time, China was hosting the 9th BRICS summit and it was also questioned whether Prime Minister Modi would normally attend the Xiamen Summit. Although the Indian army withdrew all cross-border personnel and equipment to the Indian side of the border on August 28, the Indian government announced at the last minute that Modi would attend the BRICS summit as scheduled, but the incident showed that China and India Territorial disputes and sovereignty disputes in the border areas had actually affected the normal development of the BRICS cooperation. However, in the absence of a clear timetable for the complete resolution of the border issue, military co-management and political mutual respect will become the norm. In fact, in addition to this, communication and exchanges in the humanities are also a good medicine to slow down the vicious effects of competition and conflict.

To this end, during the Wuhan meeting with Prime Minister Modi in April

---

① 参见《中南高级别人文交流机制》, http://www.moe.gov.cn/s78/A20/s3117/moe_854/201707/t20170731_310399.html。

2018, President Xi Jinping particularly emphasized that promoting more extensive people-to-people exchanges should be one of the important contents of the next phase of comprehensive cooperation planning between the two countries. It was also during this meeting that the leaders of the two countries unanimously agreed to establish a high-level exchange mechanism for the two countries. What is particularly interesting is that one of the reasons why China chose to meet India in Wuhan is based on Wuhan's own profound historical heritage and its historical origins with India since the Spring and Autumn Period.[①] On December 21, 2018, the China-India senior exchange mechanism was officially established. Both China and India agreed that they should actively participate in the people-to-people exchanges of various multilateral mechanisms, including the BRICS countries, so as to make positive contributions to promoting regional and world peace and development.[②]

So far, among the BRICS countries, China has not yet established a high-level exchange mechanism with Brazil. However, this does not mean that there has been no people-to-people exchanges and cooperation between China and Brazil. In fact, when it comes to the people-to-people exchange between China and Brazil, more than 300 Chinese tea farmers have been invited by the Portuguese Prince Regent John VI to cultivate tea trees in Rio de Janeiro in 1812, which has always been the source of people-to-people exchanges between China and Brazil.[③] Since then, the people-to-people exchanges between China and Brazil have marched on step by step and have made good progress in various fields. On July 17, 2014, the joint statement issued by China and Brazil on further deepening China-Brazil comprehensive strategic partnership emphasized

---

① 参见《外交部副部长孔铉佑就中印领导人非正式会晤举行媒体吹风会》，2018 年 4 月 24 日，http://www.xinhuanet.com/world/2018-04/24/c_1122736469.htm。
② 参见《中印高级别人文交流机制首次会议达成一系列共识》，2018 年 12 月 22 日，http://world.people.com.cn/nl/2018/1222/c1002-30482144.html。
③ 参见《中国—拉美人文交流应深耕细作》，2015 年 5 月 26 日，http://www.gov.cn/xinwen/2015-05/26/content_2868913.htm。

that "the exchanges between the two governments, legislative bodies, political parties, social organizations and localities should be further strengthened."① On May 19, 2015, during an official visit to Brazil, Premier Li Keqiang and the then Brazilian President Rousseff issued a joint statement stating that the two sides would deepen mutual understanding by expanding cooperation in education, research and think tanks.② In September 2017, then Brazilian President Temer visited China. During his talks with President Temer, President Xi Jinping pointed out that China and Brazil should expand exchanges and cooperation in the fields of culture, journalism, tourism and sports. In this regard, President Temer also expressed his willingness to expand the above exchanges and enhance mutual understanding and friendship between the two peoples.③ The Brazilian ambassador to China even stressed that "compared with the past presidential visit to Brazil, President Temer's visit to China has been added with considerable proportion of people-to-people exchanges and cooperation……people-to-people exchanges and cooperation have injected fresh blood into China-Brazil relations and have expanded the connotation of the relationship between the two countries."④

In October 2019, Brazilian President Bossonaro will visit China and intend to strengthen bilateral cooperation with China in the economic and trade field. Although the relevant content of people-to-people exchange has not been seen in the known access agenda, Brazilian scholars have pointed out that people-to-

---

① 参见《中国和巴西关于进一步深化中巴全面战略伙伴关系的联合声明》，2014 年 7 月 18 日，https: //www. fmprc. gov. cn/web/gjhdq_676201/gj_676203/nmz_680924/1206_680974/1207_680986/t1175756. shtml。

② 参见《中华人民共和国政府和巴西联邦共和国政府联合声明》，2015 年 5 月 20 日，https: //www. fmprc. gov. cn/web/gjhdq_676201/gj_676203/nmz_680924/1206_680974/1207_680986/t1265272. shtml。

③ 参见《习近平同巴西总统特梅尔举行会谈》，2017 年 9 月 1 日，http: //www. xinhuanet. com/politics/2017-09/01/c_1121588439. htm。

④ 参见中共中央办公厅、国务院办公厅印发：《关于加强和改进中外人文交流工作的若干意见》，2017 年 12 月 21 日，http: //www. gov. cn/zhengce/2017 - 12/21/content_5249241. htm。

people exchanges will benefit China and Brazil in further cooperation in the economic and trade field.[①] In fact, as early as the beginning of 2019, the Brazilian Minister of Citizenship and Social Action Tracy had made it clear that "China is an important partner of Brazil, and Brazil hopes to increase people-to-people exchanges with China through cooperation in culture, sports, art, youth, society and other fields, so as to push the sustained development of bilateral relations."[②] There are indications that the conditions for establishing a high-level foreign exchange mechanism between China and Brazil are ripe, and China should make full use of President Bossanoro's visit to China to push the success of the mechanism, so as to create a more people-to-people exchanges atmosphere for the 11th BRICS summit in Brasilia in November 2019.

Conclusion

In July 2017, the Central Leading Group for Comprehensively Continuing Reform reviewed and approved the "Several Opinions on Strengthening and Improving Chinese and Foreign People-to-people Exchanges". The opinion clearly points out that "Chinese and foreign people-to-people exchanges are an important part of the work of the party and the country in the field of external relations, an important way to consolidate the social public opinion foundation of Sino-foreign relations and improve the level of China's opening up to the outside world", and propose "incorporating people-to-people exchanges and cooperation concepts into each field of foreign exchanges".[③] From the time node, this is closely related to the BRICS summit highlighting the people-to-

---

① 参见《巴西学者：人文交流将促进中巴经贸往来》，2019年4月28日，http://news.cctv.com/2019/04/28/ARTIPPMxYQ76sdYPlGp5AWmh190428.shtml。

② 参见《巴西希望加大与中国的人文交流》，2019年1月29日，http://world.people.com.cn/nl/2019/0129/c1002-30597536.html。

③ 参见中共中央办公厅、国务院办公厅印发：《关于加强和改进中外人文交流工作的若干意见》，2017年12月21日，http://www.gov.cn/zhengce/2017-12/21/content_5249241.htm。

people exchanges and promoting people-to-people exchanges to become the pillar in September of the same year. It can be said that China's pioneering efforts and practical actions to promote BRICS people-to-people exchanges are an important manifestation of China's further implementation of Sino-foreign people-to-people exchanges. On July 26, 2019, State Councilor and Minister of Foreign Affairs Wang Yi said at the formal meeting of the BRICS foreign ministers that the BRICS should "fully balance and promote the three drives of economic and trade finance, political security and people-to-people exchanges, continuously channel a strong impetus into BRICS cooperation, and take a new path for the mutual understanding and harmonious symbiosis among different civilizations".[1] It is foreseeable that China will continue to support the BRICS people-to-people exchanges and play a leading role in the BRICS people-to-people exchanges to ensure the steady advancement of all-round BRICS cooperation through people-to-people exchanges.

---

[1] 参见《王毅出席金砖国家外长正式会晤》，2019 年 7 月 27 日，https://www.fmprc.gov.cn/web/wjbzhd/t1683857.shtml。

Book Review

The Book Review of BRICS: Construir a educação para o futuro-prioridades para o desenvolvimento nacional e a cooperação internacional

Liu Mengru[*]

Abstract: Same to the developing countries, it is still the primary task of BRICS to develop economy. With the advent of the "knowledge economy" era, the contribution of education to the economic and social development of a country has become increasingly prominent. In recent years, the BRICS have paid more and more attention to education development and cooperation, but there are still many shortcomings and some aspects to be improved. In the field of elementary education, the BRICS strive to popularize preschool education and high school education, but the situation of preschool education is significantly different among countries; in the field of higher education, the BRICS attach importance to their development, actively develop relevant plans and cooperate with each other, but lack common normative policy guidelines, and differences in social environment and economic development result in the inequality of

---

[*] Liu Mengru, Lecturer, Department of Spanish and Portuguese Languages, Sichuan International Studies University; PhD student in Linguistics, Sichuan International Studies University.

education popularization; in the field of vocational education, the current socio-economic development does not meet the demand of the BRICS labor market. In addition, issues such as educational equity and educational quality have become the shackles of BRICS education development, and the educational cooperation and the formulation of common standards have become an important measure to get rid of the current constraints. Although the BRICS have different priorities in the fields of education and skills development, the formulation of policies and the problems they face are interoperable. Therefore, strengthening BRICS education cooperation should adhere to "seeking common ground while reserving differences", deepening BRICS education cooperation, enhancing BRICS people-to-people exchanges and cooperation and promoting the sound development of the BRICS economy and society.

Keywords: BRICS; Elementary Education; Higher Education; Vocational Education

I. Introduction to the Content

Education is the foundation of the country and is the support of social and economic development. The official establishment of the Meeting of BRICS Ministers of Education mechanism has not only provided more opportunities for BRICS cooperation in the future education, but also contributed to the sustainable development of the global economy. In this context, UNESCO has published a report on the BRICS future education in 2014- *BRICS: Construir a educação para o futuro-Prioridades para o desenvolvimento nacional ea cooperação internacional.*[1]

This report introduces and analyzes the BRICSeducational mechanisms and policies, policies for skills development and vocational education, and cooperation in the field of education and skills development. It provides some suggestions for future cooperation and provides BRICS with a platform for mutual learning and experience exchange. Particular emphasis is placed on the trend of quality and equality in education development, and the development of professional skills, especially vocational education and skills training, is a key factor in achieving sustainable development and inclusive growth.

This report analyzes the status quothrough collecting existing data, and proposes that the education needs of BRICS should focus on the prevalence and development of preschool education and higher education. For vocational education and skills development, it is necessary to focus on improving professional skills, setting standards, strengthening links with the labor market, eliminating inequality, providing training for vulnerable groups and improving their employability. The education system, education strategy and skill development plan formulated by BRIC based on their respective national conditions have reference and representativeness, and can provide valuable experience and valuable data information for the future development and cooperation of countries in the world in the field of education, and lay a new path for the future development of education.

The report is divided into four chapters, covering the BRICS education

---

[1] 《BRICS: Construir a educação para o futuro- propriedades para o desenvolvimento nacional e a cooperação internacional》是 2014 年由联合国教科文组织出版的《BRICS-Building education for the future: priorities for national development and international cooperation》的葡语版，由玛利亚·岳吉利卡·贝阿尔维斯达席尔瓦（Maria Angélica B. Alves da Silva）翻译。原版主要作者为弗郎索瓦·勒克莱克（François Leclercq）。凯特琳娜·亚纳尼亚多（Katerina Ananiadou）和伯尼恩·卡克伦（Borhene Chakroun）提供第三章中涉及的数据信息。阿尔伯特·默提瓦斯（Albert Motivans）和帕特里克·蒙组里德斯（Patrick Montjouridès）提供有关工作的数据信息。铁奥帕帕尼亚·查瓦特齐亚（Theophania Chavatzia）提供协助。娄德鲁·乔维斯（Andrew Johnston）编辑报告。卡拉·戴维斯（Cara Davis）在迪艾拉·麦克马洪（Tierra McMahon）的帮助下管理报告制作。

mechanisms, BRICS vocational education and skills development and policies, BRICS international cooperation in the field of education and skills development, and future cooperation proposals.

II. A Sketch of the Main Viewpoints

The book points out that data in recent years show that the preschool education in India and South Africa has spread, and the number of people receiving higher education in various countries has shown varying degrees of growth. The BRICS are paying attention to how to improve the quality of education and enable students to make achievements in their lives and work, thus contributing to economic development.

In fact, despite the rapid development of education, the acceptance rate of higher education is still low, and the teaching quality of formal vocational education and training institutions is not satisfactory. This also makes a large part of adolescents and adults lack of professional skills, resulting in a weak employability, hindering social development and progress. Based on this, the book proposes that the quality of elementary education should be improved, and literacy plans and vocational skills development plans for vulnerable groups should be formulated.

In order to achieve fair economic growth and sustainable development, the book also proposes that must take action on the field of elementary education, higher education and skills development. 1) Elementary education: Brazil, China, India and South Africa should achieve primary and secondary schools education popularization and focus on quality education and preschool education; 2) Higher education: BRICS should expand the coverage of higher education and establish a world-class teaching and research center; 3) Skills development: BRICS should create comprehensive skills development mechanism to diversify its economic base, set and implement national qualification framework standards and qualification judgment on skills, expand secondary and advanced vocational technology roads, encourage companies to train employees and expand training programs for disadvantaged youth and adults.[1]

III. Brief Introduction to the Main Contents of the Chapters:

(1) Analysis and Policy Suggestions of the BRICS Education System

The book points out that in terms of elementary education, the BRICS have different problems because of their different national conditions. In particular, in addition to expanding the coverage of elementary education, India needs to increase investment to improve the infrastructure of schools in rural areas. Comparing BRICS situation of elementary education and policy measures adopted, it can be seen that the five countries are striving to popularize preschool education and high school education, but preschool education is quite different among the five countries. Among them, Russia's preschool education lasts three to four years, while South Africa's is less than one year. The main reason is that India and South Africa face enormous challenges in protecting children's health and nutrition.[2]

The BRICS have guaranteed children's right to receive education in all countries through the Constitution. The children must accept nine years of elementary and junior high school education (eight years in India).[3] Most of

---

[1] François Leclercq, et al., Maria Angélica B. Alves da Silva (tradutora da versão em português), BRICS-Construir a educação para o futuro: Propriedades para o desenvolvimento nacional e a cooperação internacional, Escritório da UNESCO em Brasília, 2014, p. 3.

[2] François Leclercq, et al., Maria Angélica B. Alves da Silva (tradutora da versão em português), BRICS-Construir a educação para o futuro: Propriedades para o desenvolvimento nacional e a cooperação internacional, Escritório da UNESCO em Brasília, 2014, p. 6.

[3] François Leclercq, et al., Maria Angélica B. Alves da Silva (tradutora da versão em português), BRICS-Construir a educação para o futuro: Propriedades para o desenvolvimento nacional e a cooperação internacional, Escritório da UNESCO em Brasília, 2014, p. 12.

the elementary education institutions are state public institutions, and there are relatively few private institutions, and the government must intervene to ensure that they meet the requirements. In China and Brazil, private institutions for preschool education are more common than private institutions in elementary education.

In addition, the BRICS have also formulated national plans that are in line with the current state of education in various countries, pointed out the current education problems and proposed solutions. These programs are aimed at popularizing preschool education, higher education, improving academic performance, expanding skills and higher education development programs to meet the needs of the knowledge-based economy.[①]

According to relevant data and information, for the prevalence of preschool education, the BRICS have formulated the following policies concerning the preschool education according to their different national conditions: Brazil has planned to achieve the popularization of two-years preschool education by 2016; China has planned to achieve the popularization of one to three-years preschool education by 2020, establish new classrooms and teaching buildings in rural areas to provide opportunities for rural left-behind children to go to school; India has set a goal to provide all children with at least one year of preschool education funding; Russia has restored the infrastructure of preschool institutions and provided compensation for families attending private kindergarten; South Africa has regarded the education of preschool children as a top priority and taken a series of measures to address health, nutrition and education issues.

Moreover, the five countries will also promote the development of higher education as a top priority. Brazil plans to develop 60, 000 masters and 25,

---

[①] François Leclercq, et al., Maria Angélica B. Alves da Silva (tradutora da versão em português), *BRICS-Construir a educação para o futuro: Propriedades para o desenvolvimento nacional e a cooperação internacional*, Escritório da UNESCO em Brasília, 2014, p. 19-20.

000 doctors per year by 2020; China focuses on developing the universities into world-class higher education institutions, improving their global competitiveness, encouraging students to participate in research, strengthening the cooperation between universities and businesses, reorganizing courses and disciplines, and channeling efforts into eliminating inequalities between regions; India plans to popularize the higher education and guarantee its fairness and quality through new institutions, expansion of existing institutions, improvement of infrastructure, and establishment of a national higher education commission; Russia establishes a federal university to optimize the resources available in various regions and strengthen the links between universities and the economy and society; South Africa plans to provide free higher education to the poor and strengthen the research and innovation capabilities of the universities.[1]

The BRICS have also made significant contributions to student exchanges. The Brazilian government launched the "Borderless Science" project in 2011 to provide 100, 000 scholarships[2] to Brazilian scholars studying science, engineering and mathematics at universities abroad by 2015. At the same time, the BRICS have become increasingly attractive destinations for studying abroad. However, the student exchanges between the BRICS countries are not ideal.

The book points out that the main challenge facing the BRICS is the formulation of public policies. Only by formulating appropriate policy guidelines can the higher education system continue to meet the needs and provide high-quality education for different student groups. With the continuous development and deepening of globalization, it is necessary to establish international higher education standards to regulate higher education. In this

---

[1] François Leclercq, et al., Maria Angélica B. Alves da Silva (tradutora da versão em português), *BRICS-Construir a educação para o futuro: Propriedades para o desenvolvimento nacional e a cooperação internacional*, Escritório da UNESCO em Brasília, 2014, pp. 20-21.

[2] François Leclercq, et al., Maria Angélica B. Alves da Silva (tradutora da versão em português), *BRICS-Construir a educação para o futuro: Propriedades para o desenvolvimento nacional e a cooperação internacional*, Escritório da UNESCO em Brasília, 2014, p. 21.

regard, UNESCO actively advocates the ratification and implementation of the Regional Convention[1] for the recognition of higher education qualifications.

It is also mentioned that in the process of achieving education popularization, the difference between social environment and economic development leads to the inequality of education. Specifically, the educational level and educational facilities in rural and economically underdeveloped areas are poor, while the educational level and educational facilities in urban and economically developed areas are superior. This difference, in turn, increases the difference in economic development, making inequality more significant and thus posing a serious threat to social cohesion. In this regard, the BRICS are making plans and policies to improve the fairness of education. At the same time, the BRICS are also improving their education assessment system and setting clear educational goals based on their own educational development.

In general, the different education systems of the BRICS provide opportunities for mutual learning and cooperation. The five countries are more concerned about improving the quality and fairness of compulsory education, popularizing preschool education and higher education, and achieving effective management and funding of education in different environments.[2]

In summary, the book proposes the following policy recommendations: improving education management and funding to ensure the quality and equity of education in public schools, developing and implementing general standards for national education examinations, promoting student mobility in higher education,

---

[1] François Leclercq, et al., Maria Angélica B. Alves da Silva (tradutora da versão em português), BRICS-Construir a educação para o futuro: Propriedades para o desenvolvimento nacional e a cooperação internacional, Escritório da UNESCO em Brasília, 2014, p. 21.

[2] François Leclercq, et al., Maria Angélica B. Alves da Silva (tradutora da versão em português) , BRICS-Construir a educação para o futuro: Propriedades para o desenvolvimento nacional e a cooperação internacional, Escritório da UNESCO em Brasília, 2014, p. 25.

in particular promoting stndent exchange between BRICS higher education institutions. ①

(2) Development and Policy Suggestions of BRICS Vocational Education

In order torise in the economy and become high-income countries, the BRICS are striving to achieve diversification of the economic base, reduce dependence on raw material exports, produce higher value-added products, promote the creation of new economic activities, encourage innovation, and provide support for realizing the steady growth of economy. Nowadays, the challenge for BRICS governments is mainly how to provide qualified technical talent for the labor market. In this regard, the book points out that vocational education and training can solve the problem of youth unemployment and enhance the working ability of employees to improve productivity and competitiveness.

Despite the rapid economic growth of the BRICS, it is undeniable that they are also facing the increasing gap between the rich and the poor, which will pose challenges to the stability of the BRICS society and policies. And all BRICS governments are aware that strengthening vocational education and cultivating technical talents are crucial to balancing economic development and maintaining social stability.

The report states that the BRICS economic development does not meet the demand in the job market. The uneven proportion of men and women in work and the formality of employment are issues that also need to be resolved urgently. According to the data collected, the adult unemployment rate in China and Russia is not much different from the world average; although most of Russia's employment is formal, the youth unemployment rate is still high; many

---

① François Leclercq, et al., Maria Angélica B. Alves da Silva (tradutora da versão em português), *BRICS-Construir a educação para o futuro: Propriedades para o desenvolvimento nacional e a cooperação internacional*, Escritório da UNESCO em Brasília, 2014, p. 25.

young people in Brazil are unemployed, and more than one-third of non-agricultural jobs are informal; in South Africa, both the unemployment rate of youth and that of adults is high; in addition to the reality that almost two-thirds of women have no jobs, more than 80% of non-agricultural jobs in India are informal.[1]

In the face of growing population, increasing aging and urbanization, in order to maintain economic development and social stability, the BRICS are developing plans and strategies to provide talents for the labor market. On the one hand, the elementary technical training, vocational education, higher education, continuing education, training and other means are taken advantage of to enhance the skill level of talents; on the other hand, the qualification framework is set up to make demands on the skills of employees to better serve the labor market.

The book points out that how to solve the unfairness between different regions, such as urban and rural areas, first-tier cities and second-tier cities, and the imbalance of resource allocation between the central and western regions, is also the challenge that the BRICS countries are facing. In this regard, the BRICS need to increase funding, optimize funding programs, and encourage and strengthen links with the private sector.

In order to strengthen the BRICS cooperation in promoting vocational education, solving employment problems and realizing economic transformation, the following policy recommendations are proposed: developing a labor market information system to analyze skills, establishing a national qualification framework and qualification standards, strengthening the link between vocational education companies and institutions to encourage further study, meeting the training needs of women and vulnerable groups and encouraging them to

---

[1] François Leclercq, et al., Maria Angélica B. Alves da Silva (tradutora da versão em português), BRICS-Construir a educação para o futuro: Propriedades para o desenvolvimento nacional e a cooperação internacional, Escritório da UNESCO em Brasília, 2014, p. 32.

participate in the labor market.[1]

(3) BRICS Cooperation in the Field of Education and Skills Development

Although the BRICS have different priorities in the field of education and skills development, they have the following in common: focusing on equal and mutually beneficial relations with other developing countries, emphasizing that cooperation is driven by the needs and common goals of partners, advocating non-interference in the affairs of other countries, not attaching political conditions to aid, mainly providing technical assistance, not distinguishing cooperation in development, trade and investment, paying attention to countries with historical or strategic partnerships and taking UN Development and Cooperation Forum as a platform for discussing cooperation.[2]

The book summarizes the different cooperation ways of BRICS in the field of education and skills development.[3]

1) Brazil cooperates on "South-South cooperation" as a platform and encourages education bureaus, higher education institutions, private enterprises and social organizations to participate in educational development cooperation. In terms of education development, Brazil prioritizes education quality, teacher training, technological innovation, vocational education and education system management.

2) China has always been committed to developing cooperation with other countries and providing assistance for other developing countries under the

---

[1] François Leclercq, et al., Maria Angélica B. Alves da Silva (tradutora da versão em português), *BRICS-Construir a educação para o futuro: Propriedades para o desenvolvimento nacional e a cooperação internacional*, Escritório da UNESCO em Brasília, 2014, p. 49.

[2] François Leclercq, et al., Maria Angélica B. Alves da Silva (tradutora da versão em português), *BRICS-Construir a educação para o futuro: Propriedades para o desenvolvimento nacional e a cooperação internacional*, Escritório da UNESCO em Brasília, 2014, pp. 53-54.

[3] François Leclercq, et al., Maria Angélica B. Alves da Silva (tradutora da versão em português), *BRICS-Construir a educação para o futuro: Propriedades para o desenvolvimento nacional e a cooperação internacional*, Escritório da UNESCO em Brasília, 2014, pp. 55-65.

management of the Ministry of Commerce. In terms of foreign aid, China has focused its assistance on teacher-student exchanges with partner countries.

3) India, as the main recipient of education assistance, plays an important role in "South-South cooperation". India's focus is not on project funding, but on sharing skills and expertise. India takes the education and training as the core of developing cooperation, draws up technical and economic cooperation programmes, in order to provide multi-disciplinary training for partner countries and carry out project cooperation with partner countries.

4) Russia cooperates with neighboring countries to strengthen its international reputation and plans to set up a special development agency. In addition, scholarships, education funds, and bilateral project cooperation are provided for international students.

5) South Africa plays an important role in African international relations, and supports a time-sensitive agenda for aid and South-South cooperation. Both public institutions and state-owned enterprises of South Africa participate in international cooperation, but there lacks effective cooperation mechanisms. In this regard, South Africa is planning to establish a South African Development Partner Institution to reform development and cooperation, work out triangular cooperation projects in higher education and training, and develop strategies to guide future cooperation in education and skills development.

From the above all, although the BRICS vary in development and cooperation policies and practices, they all emphasize technical assistance, support Africa's development, improve the quality of BRICS development assistance, and combine these commonly concerned areas with the priorities of national development to establish a foundation for future cooperation.

(4) **Proposals for Future Cooperation**

Based on the status of cooperation and development of the BRICS in the field of education, the book puts forward the following suggestions: BRICS can help each other in improving education mechanisms, upgrading higher education levels and promoting skills development: sharing the experience in realizing equality of public schools education, promoting school education quality, developing and implementing national student test standards; promoting the popularization of higher education, promoting the flow of students and teaching staff among BRICS; developing a labor market information system to analyze and forecast the labor market; establishing and implementing national education examinations; strengthening linkages between business and vocational education and training institutions, encouraging practitioners to pursue further education; developing policies to encourage women and vulnerable groups to participate in work, and meeting the training needs of women and vulnerable groups.[1]

In order to achieve the goal of cooperation between BRICS countries to promote the development and progress of global education, the book also proposes the following suggestions: supporting the education development of developing countries, establishing an information and data sharing center concerning education development cooperation, developing a joint program for supporting African education or establishing a joint fund and being committed to jointly support education development. In addition, BRICS can also establish cooperation platforms based on existing experience and current status to achieve cooperation in more fields.[2]

IV. Inspiration from the Book

The improvement of comprehensive national strength and international competitiveness require the impetus of knowledge level, and the knowledge level

---

[1] François Leclercq, et al., Maria Angélica B. Alves da Silva (tradutora da versão em português), *BRICS-Construir a educação para o futuro: Propriedades para o desenvolvimento nacional e a cooperação internacional*, Escritório da UNESCO em Brasília, 2014, pp. 68-70.

[2] François Leclercq, et al., Maria Angélica B. Alves da Silva (tradutora da versão em português), *BRICS-Construir a educação para o futuro: Propriedades para o desenvolvimento nacional e a cooperação internacional*, Escritório da UNESCO em Brasília, 2014, p. 71.

mainly depends on the development of education. In other words, education is the cornerstone of national development, and it plays a decisive role in both economic development and social progress. How to develop education in the context of globalization, how to improve the quality of education, and how to make education drive economic development and social progress are issues that need to be considered at the moment.

This written report provides an objective and comprehensive introduction and analysis of the BRICS education mechanism and policies, skills development plan and the vocational education policy, and the cooperationstatus in the field of education and skills development. It provides a high reference value for both the academic staff in the BRICS and researchers in the field of national policies. The book, with the content based on convincing data information, summarizes the phenomena and problems reflected by the data, and provides recommendations. In the book, the emphasis on strengthening international student exchanges and personnel training exchanges is of great significance to social development. Communication can enrich knowledge, expand horizons, and contribute to the national culture's entering the international stage. It can not only strengthen the exchanges between countries in the academic and technical fields, but also deepen mutual understanding between countries and promote common development and lay the foundation for realizing the amity of people.

Inspired by this report, we can see thatdespite the various national conditions, the policies adopted by BRICS are interoperable and the problems they face have commonalities. These interoperability and commonalities have built a bridge for BRICS people-to-people exchange. Strengthening "people-to-people exchanges" is a necessary means to enhance the national soft power, and education cooperation is an important way to promote "people-to-people exchanges". Both strengthening the exchange of teachers and students abroad and the joint cooperation in the field of skills development can provide assistance for tightening the humanities ties and contribute to the improvement of the national comprehensive competitiveness.